T0214192

Lecture Notes in Computer Science 12286

More information about this series at http://www.springer.com/series/7407

Hector Zenil (Ed.)

Cellular Automata and Discrete Complex Systems

26th IFIP WG 1.5 International Workshop, AUTOMATA 2020
Stockholm, Sweden, August 10–12, 2020
Proceedings

 Springer

Editor
Hector Zenil 🄳
Oxford Immune Algorithmics
Reading, UK

ISSN 0302-9743   ISSN 1611-3349   (electronic)
Lecture Notes in Computer Science
ISBN 978-3-030-61587-1   ISBN 978-3-030-61588-8   (eBook)
https://doi.org/10.1007/978-3-030-61588-8

LNCS Sublibrary: SL1 – Theoretical Computer Science and General Issues

This Springer imprint is published by the registered company Springer Nature Switzerland AG
The registered company address is: Gewerbestrasse 11, 6330 Cham, Switzerland

Preface

This volume contains the papers accepted and presented at the 26th International Workshop on Cellular Automata (CA) and Discrete Complex Systems (DCS), AUTOMATA 2020, held during August 10–12,2020, hosted online by the Algorithmic Dynamics Lab, Karolinska Institute, Stockholm, Sweden; and Oxford Immune Algorithmics, Reading, UK. The conference is the official annual event of the International Federation for Information Processing (IFIP), Working Group 5, on CA and DCS, of the Technical Committee 1, on Foundations of Computer Science.

AUTOMATA 2020 is part of an annual series established in 1995 as a collaboration forum between researchers in CA and DCS. Current topics of the conference include, but are not limited to, dynamical, topological, ergodic and algebraic aspects of CA and DCS, algorithmic and complexity issues, emergent properties, formal languages, symbolic dynamics, tilings, models of parallelism and distributed systems, timing schemes, synchronous versus asynchronous models, phenomenological descriptions, scientific modeling, and practical applications.

While AUTOMATA 2020 was innovating on several aspects, including remote attendance because of concerns around carbon footprint, due to the pandemic this is the first time AUTOMATA took place fully online.

AUTOMATA 2020 hosted seven invited speakers, including, Alyssa Adams, Genaro Martínez, Chiara Marletto, Samira El Yacoubi, Rodrigo Torres-Aviles, Andrew Wuensche, and Stephen Wolfram; we sincerely thank them for accepting the invitation. The abstracts of the invited talks are included in this volume.

The conference received 21 submissions and each submission was reviewed by at least three members of the Program or Steering Committees. Based on these reviews and an open discussion, 11 papers were accepted to be presented at the conference and to be included in the proceedings. We thank all authors for their contributions and hard work that made this event possible. The conference program also involved short presentations from exploratory papers not included in these proceedings, and we wish to extend our thanks to the authors of the exploratory submissions.

This year, AUTOMATA also included a special session on Algorithmic Information Dynamics, an exciting new area of research.

We are indebted to the Steering Committee, Program Committee, and additional reviewers for their valuable help during the last months. We acknowledge the generous support and funding provided by IFIP, Oxford Immune Algorithmics, and the FQXi by way of the Silicon Valley Community Foundation.

We are also very grateful for the support of the Local Organizing Committee, in particular Martin Lind, Narsis A. Kiani, and Mariana González Castellón; and to the

Lecture Notes in Computer Science team from Springer for their support in producing this volume.

August 2020   Hector Zenil

Organization

Steering Committee

Jan Baetens — Ghent University, Belgium
Alonso Castillo-Ramírez — University of Guadalajara, Mexico
Alberto Dennunzio — Università degli Studi di Milano, Italy
Jarkko Kari — University of Turku, Finland
Pedro de Oliveira — Mackenzie Presbyterian University, Brazil

Program Committee

Hector Zenil (Chair) — Oxford Immune Algorithmics, UK, Karolinska Institute, Sweden, and Algorithmic Nature Group, France
Gilles Dowek — ENS Paris-Saclay, France
Alonso Castillo-Ramirez — University of Guadalajara, Mexico
Nazim Fatès — Inria Nancy, France
Paola Flocchini — University of Ottawa, Canada
Enrico Formenti — Université Nice Sophia Antipolis, France
Anahí Gajardo — University of Concepción, Chile
Eric Goles — Adolfo Ibáñez University, Chile
Jarkko Kari — University of Turku, Finland
Martin Kutrib — Universität Gießen, Germany
Andreas Malcher — Universität Gießen, Germany
David A. Rosenblueth — Universidad Nacional Autónoma de México, Mexico
Genaro Martínez — Instituto Politécnico Nacional, Mexico, and University of the West of England, UK
Hiroshi Umeo — Osaka Electro-Communication University, Japan
Kenichi Morita — Hiroshima University, Japan
Pedro de Oliveira — Mackenzie Presbyterian University, Brazil
Nicolas Ollinger — Université d'Orléans, France
Narsis A. Kiani — Karolinska Institute, Sweden, and Algorithmic Nature Group, France
Ivan Rapaport — Universidad de Chile, Chile
Hiroshi Umeo — University of Osaka Electro-Communication, Japan
Jürgen Riedel — Algorithmic Nature Group, LABORES, France, and Oxford Immune Algorithmics, UK
Andrew Adamatzky — University of the West of England, UK
Francisco Hernández-Quiroz — Universidad Nacional Autónoma de México, Mexico

Jan Baetens   Ghent University, Belgium
Fernando Soler-Toscano   University of Seville, Spain, and Algorithmic Nature
                              Group, LABORES, France

Organizing Committee

Hector Zenil (Chair)   Oxford Immune Algorithmics, UK, Karolinska
                              Institute, Sweden, and Algorithmic Nature Group,
                              France
Narsis A. Kiani   Karolinska Institute, Sweden, and Algorithmic Nature
                              Group, France
Jürgen Riedel   LABORES, France, and Oxford Immune Algorithmics,
                              UK
Jesper Tegnér   Karolinska Institute, Sweden, and King Abdullah
                              University of Science and Technology, Saudi Arabia
Martin Lind   Automacoin Foundation, UK
M. T. I. Mariana   Oxford Immune Algorithmics, UK
  G. Castellón

Abstracts of Invited Talks

Constructor Theory of Life and Its Applications

Chiara Marletto

University of Oxford, UK

Current explanations for the emergence of life rely crucially on the possibility of certain physical processes: mainly, gene replication and natural selection. What is required of the laws of physics for those processes to be allowed? I will use constructor theory's new mode of explanation to answer this question and to explore the implications for von Neumann's original theory of self-reproducing automata. Under no-design laws, an accurate replicator requires the existence of a 'vehicle' constituting, together with the replicator, a self-reproducer.

The Role of Emergence in Open-Ended Systems

Alyssa Adams

University of Wisconsin-Madison, USA

Biological systems are notorious for their complex behavior within short timescales (e.g., metabolic activity) and longer time scales (e.g., evolutionary selection), along with their complex spatial organization. Because of their complexity and their ability to innovate with respect to their environment, living systems are considered to be open-ended. Historically, it has been difficult to model open-ended evolution and innovation. As a result, our understanding of the exact mechanisms that distinguish open-ended living systems from non-living ones is limited. One of the biggest barriers is understanding how multiple, complex parts within a single system interact and contribute to the complex, emergent behavior of the system as a whole. In biology, this is essential for understanding systems such as the human gut, which contain multiple microbial communities that contribute to the overall health of a person. How do interactions between parts of a system lead to more complex behavior of the system as a whole? What types of interactions contribute to open-ended behavior? In this talk, two interacting cellular automata (CA) are used as an abstract model to address the effects of complex interactions between two individual entities embedded within a larger system. Unlike elementary CA, these CA are state-dependent because they change their update rules as a function of the system's state as a whole. The resulting behavior of the two-CA system suggests that complex interaction rules between the two CA have little to no effect on the complexity of each component CA. However, having an interaction rule that is random results in open-ended evolution regardless of the specific type of state-dependency. This suggests that randomness does indeed contribute to open-ended evolution, but not by random perturbations of the states as previously speculated.

Collision-Based Computing with Cellular Automata

Genaro J. Martínez[1,2]

[1] Escuela Superior de Cómputo, Instituto Politécnico Nacional, Mexico
[2] Unconventional Computing Lab, University of the West of England,
Bristol, UK

Unconventional and natural computing has the capacity to handle information at an atomic and molecular level. Examples of these developments can be found in collision-based computers, reaction-diffusion computers, Physarum computers, quantum computers, molecular computing, and DNA computers. In this way, the cellular automata theory conceived by John von Neumann as a tool of super computation which work with indivisible elements and they are inherently and massively parallel. The second essential element and problem on these abstract machines is controller and design reliable components from unreliable organisms. Indeed, this issue is the nature of any unconventional computing architecture.

In theoretical computer science there are several models of unconventional computing, which are based on processes in spatially extended non-linear media with different physics and non-classical logics. In this talk, we will discuss how a collision-based computer employs mobile compact finite patterns represented as mobile self-localized excitations (as particles, gliders, waves, signals) to represent quanta of information in an active non-linear medium. Information values are given by either absence or presence of the particles or other parameters of the localizations. The particles travel in space and when they collide the occuring result can be interpreted as a computation. In this way, any part of the medium space can be used as a wire, particles can collide anywhere within a space sample, there are no fixed positions at which specific operations occur, nor location specified gates with fixed operations. The particles undergo transformations and form bound states, annihilate, or fuse when they interact with other particles. Information values of particles are transformed as a result of the collision.

Particles in complex one-dimensional cellular automata are compact sets of non-quiescent patterns translating along evolution space. These non-trivial patterns can be coded as binary strings or symbols traveling along a one-dimensional ring, interacting with each other and changing their states, or symbolic values, as a result of interactions and computation.

Typically, we can find all types of localizations manifested in cellular automata particles, including positive, negative, and with neutral displacements. This phenomenon can be found in an ample number of complex cellular automata rules.[1] The

---

[1] Complex cellular automata repository. http://www.comunidad.escom.ipn.mx/genaro/Complex_CA_repository.html.

number of collisions between particles in complex cellular automata is determined by the their periods (phases) and a number of contact points. A lot of synchronized particles, packages of them or particles with capacity of extensions, are introduced to universes with an infinity of collisions.

A cellular automaton collider is a finite state machine built of rings of one-dimensional cellular automata. We will discuss how a computation can be performed on the collider by exploiting interactions between these particles. In 2002, Tommaso Toffoli introduced the basis of symbol super collider which synthesize the collision-based computing dynamics. In this way, we fuse this framework with the universality of the elementary cellular automaton rule 110 to show how a cellular automata collider works.

References

1. Adamatzky, A. (ed.).: Collision-Based Computing. Springer, Heidelberg (2012). https://doi.org/10.1007/978-1-4471-0129-1
2. Adamatzky, A. (ed.): Advances in Unconventional Computing: Volume 1: Theory, vol. 22. Springer, Heidelberg (2012). https://doi.org/10.1007/978-3-319-33924-5
3. Cook, M.: Universality in elementary cellular automata. Complex Syst. **15**(1), 1–40 (2004)
4. Hey, A.J.G. (ed.): Feynman and Computation: Exploring the Limits of Computers. Perseus Books Publishing (1999)
5. McIntosh, H.V.: One dimensional Cellular Automata. Luniver Press (2009)
6. Margolus, N., Toffoli, T., Vichniac, G.: Cellular-automata supercomputers for fluid-dynamics modeling. Phys. Rev. Lett. **56**(16), 1694 (1986)
7. Martínez, G.J., Adamatzky, A., McIntosh, H.V.: Computing on rings. In: Zenil, H. (ed.) A Computable Universe: Understanding and Exploring Nature as Computation, pp. 257–276 (2013)
8. Martínez, G.J., Adamatzky, A., McIntosh, H.V.: Complete characterization of structure of rule 54. Complex Syst. **23**(3), 259–293 (2014)
9. Martínez, G.J., Adamatzky, A., McIntosh, H.V.: Computing with virtual cellular automata collider. In: 2015 Science and Information Conference (SAI), pp. 62–68. IEEE (2015)
10. Martínez G.J., Adamatzky A., McIntosh H.V.: A computation in a cellular automaton collider rule 110. In: Adamatzky, A. (eds.) Advances in Unconventional Computing. Emergence, Complexity and Computation, vol 22, pp. 391–428 (2017). Springer, Cham. https://doi.org/10.1007/978-3-319-33924-5_15
11. Martínez, G.J., Adamatzky, A., Stephens, C.R., Hoeflich, A.F.: Cellular automaton super-colliders. Int. J. Mod. Phys. C, **22**(4), 419–439 (2011)
12. Mills, J.W., Parker, M., Himebaugh, B., Shue, C., Kopecky, B., Weilemann, C.: Empty space computes: the evolution of an unconventional supercomputer. In: Proceedings of the 3rd Conference on Computing Frontiers, pp. 115–126. ACM (2006)
13. Moore, C., Mertens, S.: The Nature of Computation. OUP Oxford (2011)
14. Martínez, G.J., McIntosh, H.V., Seck-Tuoh-Mora, J.C., Chapa-Vergara, S.V.: Reproducing the cyclic tag system developed by Matthew cook with rule 110 using the phases $f_i - 1$. J. Cell. Autom. **6**(2–3), 121–161 (2011)
15. Martínez, G.J., Seck-Tuoh-Mora, J.C., Zenil, H.: Computation and universality: class iv versus class iii cellular automata. J. Cell. Autom. **7**(5–6), 393–430 (2013)

16. Ninagawa, S., Martínez, G.J.: 1/f Noise in the computation process by rule 110. J. Cell. Autom. **12**(1–2), 47–61 (2016)
17. Regev, A., Shapiro, E.: Cells as computation. Nature, **419**(6905) (2002)
18. Wolfram, S.: Computation theory of cellular automata. Commun. Math. Phys. **96**(1), 15–57 (1984). https://doi.org/10.1007/BF01217347
19. Wolfram, S.: A New Kind of Science. Wolfram Media, Champaign (2002)
20. Wuensche, A.: Exploring Discrete Dynamics. Luniver Press (2011)
21. von Neumann, J.: Theory of self-reproducing automata. University of Illinois Press, Urbana and London (1966). (Completed by A.W. Burks)
22. Toffoli, T.: Non-conventional computers. In: Webster, J. (ed.) Encyclopedia of Electrical and Electronics Engineering, vol. 14, pp. 455–471 (1998)
23. Toffoli T.: Symbol super colliders. In: Adamatzky A. (eds) Collision-Based Computing, pp. 1–23. Springer, London (2002). https://doi.org/10.1007/978-1-4471-0129-1_1

Some Control and Observation Issues
in Cellular Automata

Samira El Yacoubi[1,2], Sara Dridi[1,2], and Théo Plénet[1,2]

[1] IMAGES ESPACE-DEV, University of Perpignan Via Domitia, France
[2] ESPACE-DEV, University of Montpellier, IRD, Université des Antilles,
Université de Guyane, Université de La Réunion, France
{yacoubi,sara.dridi,theo.plenet}@univ-perp.fr

This talk is based on some recent work carried out in collaboration with my PhD students Sara Dridi and Théo Plenet and other colleagues: Franco Bagnoli, Laurent Lefèvre, and Clément Raïevsky. It focuses on studying problems of observability and controllability of cellular automata (CA) considered in the context of control theory, an important feature of which is the adoption of a state space model. This model traditionally uses a set of partial differential equations (PDEs) in the description of system input–output dynamics. While the controllability concerns the ability to steer controlled evolution processes, observability deals with the capability to reconstruct the initial state of the system, taking into account sufficient knowledge of the system dynamics through certain output measurements. These two major concepts have already been studied for continuous systems described by PDEs as reported in the literature [3, 7,16]. In the case of deterministic linear systems analysis, the so-called Kalman condition [11, 12] is essential and has been widely used to obtain the main characterization results according to the choice of actuator/sensor structures, locations, number, and types (mobile or fixed), see for example [7, 8] and the references therein.

Our work first consists of generalizing the obtained results to systems described by CA considered as the discrete counterpart of PDEs, and exploring other suitable approaches to prove controllability and observability. CA are widely used mathematical models for studying dynamical properties of discrete systems and constitute very promising tools for describing complex natural systems in terms of local interactions [2, 14, 15]. After having introduced the notion of control and observation in CA, in a similar way to the case of discrete-time distributed parameter systems [10], we started to investigate these key concepts of control theory in the case of complex systems modeled by CA.

The case of Boolean CA has been particularly examined to investigate the special case of boundary regional controllability [4]. It consists of considering objectives to be achieved only on a subregion of the whole domain through the application of controls exerted on the boundary of the target region. The problem has been apprehended using several tools: Kalman theorem, Markov Chains, and graph theory [5, 6]. The extension to non-linear CA has also been studied. For the problem of observability, we assume that the studied system is autonomous and we applied the tools mentioned above to prove observability. The first results for affine CA can be found in [13]. The non-linear case as well as the probabilistic case are currently under investigation.

Keywords: Controllability · Observability · Cellular Automata · Kalman condition

References

1. Bagnoli, F., El Yacoubi, S., Rechtman, R.: Toward a boundary regional control problem for Boolean cellular automata. Nat. Comput. **17**(3):479–486 (2018). https://doi.org/10.1007/s11047-017-9626-1
2. Chopard, B., Droz, M.: Cellular Automata Modeling of Physical Systems, Cambridge University Press (1998)
3. Curtain, R.F., Zwart, H.: An introduction to Infinite Dimensional Linear Systems Theory. Springer, Heidelberg (1995). https://doi.org/10.1007/978-1-4612-4224-6
4. Dridi, S., El Yacoubi, S., Bagnoli, F.: Boundary regional controllability of linear boolean cellular automata using Markov chain. In: Zerrik, E., Melliani, S., Castillo, O. (eds.) Recent Advances in Modeling, Analysis and Systems Control: Theoretical Aspects and Applications. Studies in Systems, Decision and Control, vol 243, 37–48. Springer, Cham (2020). https://doi.org/10.1007/978-3-030-26149-8_4
5. Dridi, S., Bagnoli, F., EL Yacoubi, S: Markov chains approach for regional controllability of deterministic cellular automata, via boundary actions. J. Cell. Autom. **14**(5/6), 479–498 (2019)
6. Dridi, S., EL Yacoubi, S., Bagnoli, F., Fontaine, A.: A graph theory approach for regional controllability of boolean cellular automata. Int. J. Parallel Emergent Distrib. Syst. 1–15 (2019). https://doi.org/10.1080/17445760.2019.1608442.
7. El Jai, A.: Distributed systems analysis via sensors and actuators. Sen. Actuators A: Phys. **29**(1), 1–11 (1991)
8. El Jai, A., El Yacoubi, S.: On the relations between actuator structures and final constraint minimum-energy problem. Sen. Actuators A: Phys. **33**(3), 175–182 (1992)
9. El Yacoubi, S., El Jai, A., Ammor, N.: Regional controllability with cellular automata models. Lecture Notes on Computer Sciences, **14**(3), 227–253 (2002)
10. El Yacoubi, S: A mathematical method for control problems on cellular automata models. Int. J. Syst. Sci **39**(5), 529–538 (2008)
11. Kalman, R.E.: On the general theory of control systems. In: Proceedings First International Conference on Automatic Control, Moscow, USSR (1960)
12. Kalman, R.E.: Mathematical description of linear dynamical systems. J. Soc. Ind. Appl. Math. Ser. Control **1**(2), 152–192 (1963)
13. Plénet, T., El Yacoubi, S., Raïevsky, C. and Lefévre, L.: Observability of Affine Cellular Automata through Mobile Sensors, accepted for publication in LNCS, ACRI 2020
14. Wolfram, S.: Cellular Automata and Complexity. Science Mathematics Computing. Addison-Wesley (1994)
15. Wuensche, A., Lesser, M.: The global dynamics of cellular automata. In: An Atlas of Basin of Attraction Fields of One-Dimensional Cellular Automata. Addison-Wesley (1992)
16. Zerrik E., Boutoulout A., El Jai A.: Actuators and regional boundary controllability for parabolic systems. Int. J. Syst. Sci. **31**, 73–82 (2000)

Topological Dynamical Properties in Turing Machines

Rodrigo Torres-Aviles

Universidad de Concepción, Chile

The goal of this talk is to review a non-exhaustive compilation of some of the work in topological properties in Turing machine Dynamical Systems. We follow two interesting lines, born in Kurka's seminal paper: Topological Entropy, where we talk about Jeandel's computability algorithm and undecidability of positivity; and Aperiodicity, where the existence of the property leads to the existence and undecidability of Topological Transitivity, Minimality, and Mixing, among others.

Isotropic Cellular Automata

Andrew Wuensche

Unconventional Computing Lab, University of the West of England, UK

To respect physics and nature, cellular automata (CA) models of self-organization, emergence, computation, and logical universality should be isotropic, having equivalent dynamics in all directions. I will present a novel paradigm, the iso-rule, a concise expression for isotropic CA by the output table for each isotropic neighborhood group, allowing an efficient method of navigating and exploring iso-rule-space. I will describe new functions and tools in DDLab to generate iso-groups and manipulate iso-rule tables, for multi-value as well as binary, in one, two, and three dimensions. These methods include editing, filing, filtering, searching, mutating, analyzing dynamics by input-frequency and entropy, and identifying the critical iso-groups for glider-gun/eater dynamics. I will illustrate these ideas and methods for two dimensional CA on square and hexagonal lattices, focusing on mutant families of logical universal rules found in iso-rule-space, as well as among the narrower iso-subsets of totalistic and survival/birth rules.

A New Kind of Automata, That May Be Our Universe

Stephen Wolfram

Wolfram Research, USA

A class of models intended to be as minimal and structureless as possible is introduced. Even in cases with simple rules, rich and complex behavior is found to emerge, and striking correspondences to some important core known features of fundamental physics are seen, suggesting the possibility that the models may provide a new approach to finding a fundamental theory of physics.

Quantum mechanics and general relativity–both introduced more than a century ago–have delivered many impressive successes in physics. But so far they have not allowed the formulation of a complete, fundamental theory of our universe, and at this point it seems worthwhile to try exploring other foundations from which space, time, general relativity, quantum mechanics, and all the other known features of physics could emerge.

The purpose here is to introduce a class of models that could be relevant. The models are set up to be as minimal and structureless as possible, but despite the simplicity of their construction, they can nevertheless exhibit great complexity and structure in their behavior. Even independent of their possible relevance to fundamental physics, the models appear to be of significant interest in their own right, not least as sources of examples amenable to rich analysis by modern methods in mathematics and mathematical physics.

But what is potentially significant for physics is that with exceptionally little input, the models already seem able to reproduce some important and sophisticated features of known fundamental physics–and give suggestive indications of being able to reproduce much more.

Our approach here is to carry out a fairly extensive empirical investigation of the models, then to use the results of this to make connections with known mathematical and other features of physics. We do not know a priori whether any model that we would recognize as simple can completely describe the operation of our universe–although the very existence of physical laws does seem to indicate some simplicity. But it is basically inevitable that if a simple model exists, then almost nothing about the universe as we normally perceive it–including notions like space and time–will fit recognizably into the model.

And given this, the approach we take is to consider models that are as minimal and structureless as possible, so that in effect there is the greatest opportunity for the phenomenon of emergence to operate. The models introduced here have their origins in network-based models studied in the 1990s, but the present models are more minimal and structureless. They can be thought of as abstracted versions of a surprisingly wide range of types of mathematical and computational systems, including combinatorial, functional, categorical, algebraic, and axiomatic ones.

Special Session: Algorithmic Information Dynamics

Algorithmic Information Dynamics (AID) [1] is an algorithmic probabilistic framework for causal discovery and causal analysis. It enables the solution of inverse problems on the basis of algorithmic probability, using computational tools drawn from algorithmic complexity theory. AID studies dynamical systems in software space where all possible computable models live and is able to explain discrete longitudinal data such as particle orbits in state and phase space, or to approximate continuous systems by discrete computable models. AID provides tools such as algorithmic perturbation analysis to guide the search and use of precomputed models to find relevant generative mechanisms representing causal first principles of a domain of interest, and is an alternative or complement to other approaches and methods of experimental inference, such as statistical machine learning and classical information theory.

AID is related to other areas such as computational mechanics and program synthesis. However, unlike methods such as Bayesian networks, AID does not rely on graphical models or the (often inaccessible) empirical estimation of mass probability distributions. AID encompasses the foundations and methods that make the area of algorithmic information and algorithmic complexity more relevant to scientific discovery and causal analysis. AID also connects with and across other parallel fields of active research such as logical inference, causal reasoning, and neuro-symbolic computation. AID studies how candidate discrete computable equations such as how generating mechanisms are affected by changes in observed phenomena over time as a result of a system evolving (e.g., under the influence of noise) or being externally perturbed (the location in time and space of such perturbations being hypothesized using algorithmic perturbation analysis).

Presenters in this session included Dr. Narsis Kiani, Dr. Felipe S. Abrahão, Dr. Santiago Hernández-Orozco, Dr. Jürgen Riedel, Dr. Victor Iapascurta, Cameron Sajedi, Martin Lind, and Dr. Hector Zenil who presented a number of introductions to the foundations, methods, and applications of AID, ranging from complex networks [2] to machine learning [3], cryptocurrency (Automacoin), and an application to epileptic seizure prediction [4].

In the context of the cryptocurrency project, the conference served as a platform to introduce Automacoin [5]. Automacoin was conceived to be the first cryptocurrency designed to be Turing-universal and also the most eco-friendly of all coins, as its computations are not only the most general-purpose and fundamental, but are stored and never lost or wasted, so they remain available which increases its value.

The Automacoin network behind the cryptocurrency computation is not only meaningful but it may, in a fundamental way, be considered to be the ultimate meaningful task that intelligent beings can perform to use all the energy available to answer all possible questions by mechanistic (computable) means.

References

1. Zenil, H., Kiani, N.A., Abrahão, F.S., Tegnér, J., Algorithmic Information Dynamics. Scholarpedia **15**(7), 53143 (2020)
2. Abrahão, F.S., Wehmuth, K., Ziviani, A.: Algorithmic networks: central time to trigger expected emergent open-endedness. Theor. Comput. Sci. **785**, 83–116 (2019)
3. Hernóndez-Orozco, S., Zenil, H., Riedel, J., Uccello A., Kiani N.A., Tegnér, J.: Algorithmic Probability-guided Machine Learning On Non-differentiable Spaces, Frontiers in AI (accepted) [cs.LG] (2020)
4. Iapascurta, V.: Detection of Movement toward randomness by applying the block decomposition method to a simple model of the circulatory system. Complex Syst. **28**(1), 59–76 (2019)
5. https://www.automacoin.com/foundations.html. Accessed 6 August 2020

Contents

Exploring Millions of 6-State FSSP Solutions: The Formal Notion of Local CA Simulation

Tien Thao Nguyen[(⊠)] and Luidnel Maignan[(⊠)]

LACL, Univ Paris Est Creteil, 94010 Creteil, France
ntienthao87@gmail.com, luidnel.maignan@u-pec.fr

Abstract. In this paper, we come back on the notion of local simulation allowing to transform a cellular automaton into a closely related one with different local encoding of information. This notion is used to explore solutions of the Firing Squad Synchronization Problem that are minimal both in time ($2n - 2$ for n cells) and, up to current knowledge, also in states (6 states). While only one such solution was proposed by Mazoyer since 1987, 718 new solutions have been generated by Clergue, Verel and Formenti in 2018 with a cluster of machines. We show here that, starting from existing solutions, it is possible to generate millions of such solutions using local simulations using a single common personal computer.

Keywords: Cellular automata · Automata minimization · Firing squad synchronization problem.

1 Introduction

1.1 Firing Squad Synchronization Problem and the Less-State Race

The Firing Squad Synchronization Problem (FSSP) was proposed by John Myhill in 1957. The goal is to find a single cellular automaton that synchronizes any one-dimensional horizontal array of an arbitrary number of cells. More precisely, one considers that at initial time, all cells are inactive (i.e. in the *quiescent state*) except for the leftmost cell which is the general (i.e. in the *general state*). One wants the evolution of the cellular automaton to lead all cells to transition to a special state (i.e. the *synchronization* or *firing state*) *for* the first time *at* the same time. This time t_s is called the synchronization time and it is known that its minimal possible value is $2n - 2$ where n is the number of cells.

For this problem, many minimum-time solutions were proposed using different approaches. As indicated in [12], the first one was proposed by Goto in 1962 [12] with many thousands of states, followed by Waksman in 1966 [14], Balzer in 1967 [1], Gerken in 1987 [4], and finally Mazoyer in 1987 [8] who presented respectively a 16-state, 8-state, 7-state and 6-state minimum-time solution, with no further improvements since 1987. Indeed, Balzer [1] already shows

H. Zenil (Ed.): AUTOMATA 2020, LNCS 12286, pp. 1–13, 2020.
https://doi.org/10.1007/978-3-030-61588-8_1

that there are no 4-state minimal-time solutions, latter confirmed by Sanders [11] through an exhaustive search and some corrections to Balzer's work. Whether there exists any 5-state minimumal-time solution or not is still an open question.

Note that all these solutions use a "divide and conquer" strategy. Goto's solution were pretty complex with two types of divisions. The following ones used a "mid-way" division but Mazoyer's 6-state solution uses for the first time a "two-third" type of division[1]. In 2018, Clergue, Verel and Formenti [2] generated 718 new 6-state solutions using an Iterated Local Search algorithm to explore the space of 6-state solutions on a cluster of heterogeneous machines: 717 of these solutions use a "mid-way" division, and only one use a "two-third" division.

1.2   Context of the Initial Motivations

In 2012, Maignan and Yunes proposed the methodology of *cellular fields* to described formally the high-level implementation of a CA, and also formally the generation of the "low-level" transition table. One of the expected benefits was to have an infinite CA cleanly modularized into many cellular fields with clear semantical proof of correctness together with a correctness-preserving reduction procedure into a finite state CA [5] using a particular kind of cellular field, "reductions". This is very similar to what happen in usual computer programming where one writes in a high-level language then transform the code into assembly using a semantic-preserving transformation, *i.e.* a compiler. In 2014, they made precise a particular reduction of the infinite CA into 21 states [6,7].

From theses works and concepts, two intertwined research directions emerge. One direction is to ask whether a reduction to fewer states is firstly possible, and secondly automatically generable, in the same spirit as compiler optimization, with the possible application of reducing further the 21 states. The second direction is to build a map of as many FSSP solutions as possible and study how they relate through the notion of "reduction" introduced, with application the discovery of techniques used in hand-made transition table and also the factorisation of correctness proofs. In 2018, Maignan and Nguyen [9] exhibited a few of these relations and in particular the fact the infinite Maignan-Yunes CA could be reduced to the 8-state solutions of Noguchi [10].

1.3   From the Initial Motivations to a Surprise

The initial motivations whose to complete the "map of reductions" by including the 718 solutions into the picture. In particular, a quick look at the 718 solutions gave to the authors the feeling that they could be grouped into equivalence classes using the notion of "reduction". Also, inspired by the idea of *local search* and exploration through small modifications used in [2] to generate the 718 solutions, the first author tried such search algorithms to generate "reductions" of existing solutions rather than transition tables directly. Although the idea of local search is to navigate randomly in a landscape with few actual

---

[1] See Fig. 1c for a mid-way division, and Fig. 1a for a two-third division.

solutions, the discovered landscape of reductions has so many solutions that a "best-effort-exhaustive" exploration have been tried, leading to *many millions* of 6-states solutions. Also, this space is much more easily explored because of its nice computational properties.

1.4   Organization of the Content

In Sect. 2, we define formally cellular automata, local simulations, FSSP solutions and related objects. In Sect. 3, we present nice properties relating these objects and allowing the search algorithm to save a huge amount of time. In Sect. 4, we describe the exploration algorithm and continue in Sect. 5 with some experimental results and a small analysis of the 718 solutions. We conclude in Sect. 6 with some formal and experimental future work.

2   Background

In this section, we define formally cellular automata, local mappings and FSSP solutions in a way suitable to the current study. The material here is a considerable re-organization of the material found in [9].

2.1   Cellular Automata

Definition 1. *A* cellular automaton α *consists of a finite set of* states Σ_α, *a set of* initial configurations $I_\alpha \subseteq \Sigma_\alpha^{\mathbb{Z}}$ *and a partial function* $\delta_\alpha : \Sigma_\alpha^3 \nrightarrow \Sigma_\alpha$ *called the* local transition function *or* local transition table. *The elements of* $\Sigma_\alpha^{\mathbb{Z}}$ *are called* (global) configurations *and those of* Σ_α^3 *are called* local configurations. *For any* $c \in I_\alpha$, *its* space-time diagram $D_\alpha(c) : \mathbb{N} \times \mathbb{Z} \to \Sigma_\alpha$ *is defined as:*

$$D_\alpha(c)(t, p) = \begin{cases} c(p) & \text{if } t = 0, \\ \delta_\alpha(l_{-1}, l_0, l_1) & \text{if } t > 0 \text{ with } l_i = D_\alpha(c)(t - 1, p + i). \end{cases}$$

The partial function δ_α *is required to be such that all space-time diagrams are totally defined. When* $D_\alpha(c)(t, p) = s$, *we say that, for the cellular automaton* α *and initial configuration* c, *the cell at position* p *has state* s *at time* t.

Definition 2. *A* family of space-time diagrams D *consists of a set of states* Σ_D *and an arbitrary set* $D \subseteq \Sigma_D^{\mathbb{N} \times \mathbb{Z}}$ *of space-time diagrams. The* local transition relation $\delta_D \subseteq \Sigma_D^3 \times \Sigma_D$ *of* D *is defined as:*

$$((l_{-1}^0, l_0^0, l_1^0), l_0^1) \in \delta_D :\Leftrightarrow \exists (d, t, p) \in D \times \mathbb{N} \times \mathbb{Z} \text{ s.t. } l_i^j = d(t + j, p + i).$$

We call D *a* deterministic family *if its local transition relation is functional.*

Definition 3. *Given a deterministic family* D, *its* associated cellular automaton Γ_D *is defined as having the set of states* $\Sigma_{\Gamma_D} = \Sigma_D$, *the set of initial configurations[2]* $I_{\Gamma_D} = \{d(0, -) \mid d \in D\}$, *and the local transition function* $\delta_{\Gamma_D} = \delta_D$.

---

[2] Here, $d(0, -)$ is the function from $\mathbb{Z}$ to Σ_D defined as $d(0, -)(p) = d(0, p)$.

Definition 4. *Given a cellular automaton α, its associated family of space-time diagrams (abusively denoted) D_α is defined as having the set of states $\Sigma_{D_\alpha} = \Sigma_\alpha$, and the set of space-time diagrams $D_\alpha := \{ D_\alpha(c) \mid c \in I_\alpha \}$ and is clearly deterministic.*

These inverse constructions show that deterministic families and cellular automata are two presentations of the same object. For practical purposes, it is also useful to note that, since δ_D has a finite domain, there are finite subsets of D that are enough to specify it completely.

2.2   Local Mappings and Local Simulations

These two concepts are more easily pictured with space-time diagrams. Given a space-time diagram $d \in S^{\mathbb{N} \times \mathbb{Z}}$, we build a new one d' where each state $d'(t,p)$ is computed through a function h on the little cone $\langle d(t - dt, p + dp) \mid dt \in \{0,1\}, dp \in [\![-dt, +dt]\!]\rangle$ in d. This cone is simply a state for $t = 0$, and when d is generated by a CA, this cone is entirely determined by $\langle d(t - 1, p + dp) \mid dp \in [\![-1, 1]\!]\rangle$ for $t \geq 1$. Since the set of all these triplets is exactly $\mathrm{dom}(\delta_\alpha)$, the following definitions suffice for the current study. We call this h a local mapping, because the new diagram $d' = h(d)$ is determined locally by the original one. When transforming a deterministic family, the result might not be deterministic, but if it is, we speak of a local simulation between two CA.

Definition 5. *A local mapping h from a CA α to a finite set S consists of two functions $h_z : \{d(0,x) \mid (d,x) \in D_\alpha \times \mathbb{Z}\} \to S$ and $h_s : \mathrm{dom}(\delta_\alpha) \to S$.*

Definition 6. *Given a local mapping h from a CA α to a finite set S, we define its associated family of diagrams $\Phi_h = \{h(d) \mid d \in D_\alpha\}$ where:*

$$h(d)(t,p) = \begin{cases} h_z(d(0,p)) & \text{if } t = 0, \\ h_s(l_{-1}, l_0, l_1) & \text{if } t > 0 \text{ with } l_i = d(t-1)(p+i). \end{cases}$$

Definition 7. *A local mapping h from a CA α to a finite set S whose associated family of diagrams Φ_h is deterministic is called a local simulation from α to Γ_{Φ_h}.*

Proposition 1. *Equivalently, a local simulation h from a CA α to a CA β is a local mapping from α to the set Σ_β such that $\{h_z(c) \mid c \in I_\alpha\} = I_\beta$ and for all $(c,t,p) \in I_\alpha \times \mathbb{N} \times \mathbb{Z}$, we have $h_s(l_{-1}, l_0, l_1) = l'_0$ with $l_i = D_\alpha(c)(t, p+i)$ and $l'_0 = D_\beta(h_z(c))(t+1, p)$. The details of these formula are more easily seen graphically.*

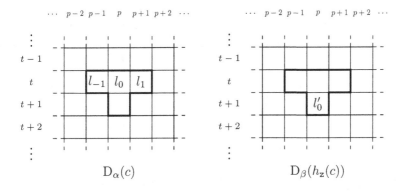

$$D_\alpha(c) \qquad\qquad D_\beta(h_z(c))$$

2.3   The Firing Squad Synchronization Problem

Definition 8. *A cellular automaton is* FSSP-candidate *if there are four special states* $\star_\alpha, G_\alpha, Q_\alpha, F_\alpha \in \Sigma_\alpha$, *if* $I_\alpha = \{\overline{n}_\alpha \mid n \geq 2\}$ *with* $\overline{n}_\alpha$ *being the* FSSP *initial configuration of size* n, *i.e.* $\overline{n}_\alpha(p) = \star_\alpha, G_\alpha, Q_\alpha, \star_\alpha$ *if* p *is respectively* $p \leq 0$, $p = 1$, $p \in [\![2, n]\!]$, *and* $p \geq n + 1$. *Moreover,* $\star_\alpha$ *must be the* outside *state, i.e. for any* $(l_{-1}, l_0, l_1) \in dom(\delta_\alpha)$, *we must have* $\delta(l_{-1}, l_0, l_1) = \star_\alpha$ *if and only if* $l_0 = \star_\alpha$. *Also,* Q_α *must be a* quiescent *state so* $\delta_\alpha(Q_\alpha, Q_\alpha, Q_\alpha) = \delta_\alpha(Q_\alpha, Q_\alpha, \star_\alpha) = Q_\alpha$.

The $\star_\alpha$ state is not really counted as a state since it represents cells that should be considered as non-existing. Therefore, an FSSP-candidate cellular automaton α will be said to have s states when $|\Sigma_\alpha \setminus \{\star_\alpha\}| = s$, and m transitions when $|dom(\delta_\alpha) \setminus \Sigma_\alpha \times \{\star_\alpha\} \times \Sigma_\alpha| = m$.

Definition 9. *A FSSP-candidate cellular automaton* α *is a* minimal-time FSSP solution *if for any size* n, $D_\alpha(\overline{n}_\alpha)(t, p) = F_\alpha$ *if and only if* $t \geq 2n - 2$ *and* $p \in [\![1, n]\!]$. *We are only concerned with minimal-time solutions but sometimes simply write* FSSP solution, *or* solution *for short.*

3   Some Useful Algorithmic Properties

Our global strategy to find new FSSP solutions is to build them from local simulations of already existing FSSP solution α. Taking literally the previous definitions could lead to the following procedure for a given local mapping h. First, generate sufficiently many space-time diagrams of D_α. Secondly, use h to transform each of these diagrams $d \in D_\alpha$ into a new one $h(d)$, thus producing a sub-family of Φ_h. At the same time, build δ_{Φ_h} by collecting all local transitions appearing in each $h(d)$ and check for determinism and correct synchronization. If everything goes fine, we have a new FSSP solution $\beta = \Gamma_{\Phi_h}$.

Such a procedure is time-consuming. We show here useful properties that reduces drastically this procedure to a few steps. In fact, the space-time diagrams of Φ_h never need to be computed, neither to build the local transition relation δ_{Φ_h} (Sect. 3.1), nor to check that Γ_{Φ_h} is an FSSP solution as showed in this section (Sect. 3.2).

3.1 Summarizing Families into Super Local Transition Tables

When trying to construct a CA β from a CA α and a local mapping h from the families of space-time diagrams as suggested by the formal definitions, there is huge amount of redundancy. All entries of the local transition relation δ_{Φ_h} appear many times in Φ_h, each of them being produced from the same recurring patterns in the space-time diagrams of α. In fact, it is more efficient to simply collect these recurring patterns that we may call *super local transitions*, and work from them without constructing Φ_h at all. It is specially useful because we consider a huge number of local mappings from a single CA α.

Definition 10. *For a given CA α, the* super local transition table Δ_α *consists of two sets* $(\Delta_\alpha)_z \subseteq \Sigma_\alpha{}^3$ *and* $(\Delta_\alpha)_s \subseteq \Sigma_\alpha{}^5 \times \Sigma_\alpha{}^3$ *defined as:*

$$(s_{-1}, s_0, s_1) \in (\Delta_\alpha)_z :\Leftrightarrow \exists (d, p) \in D_\alpha \times \mathbb{Z}$$
$$s.t. \ s_i = d(0, p + i),$$
$$((s^0_{-2}, s^0_{-1}, s^0_0, s^0_1, s^0_2), (s^1_{-1}, s^1_0, s^1_1)) \in (\Delta_\alpha)_s :\Leftrightarrow \exists (d, t, p) \in D_\alpha \times \mathbb{N} \times \mathbb{Z}$$
$$s.t. \ s^j_i = d(t + j, p + i)$$

Once all these patterns collected, it is possible to construct the local transition relation δ_{Φ_h} as specified in the following proposition.

Proposition 2. *Let h be a local mapping from a CA α to a set S. The local transition relation δ_{Φ_h} of the family of space-time diagram Φ_h generated by h and the super local transition function Δ_α of α obey:*

$$((l^0_{-1}, l^0_0, l^0_1), l^1_0) \in \delta_{\Phi_h} \Leftrightarrow \exists (s_{-1}, s_0, s_1) \in (\Delta_\alpha)_z$$
$$s.t. \ l^0_i = h_z(s_i) \ and \ l^1_0 = h_s(s_{-1}, s_0, s_1)$$
$$\vee \ \exists ((s^0_{-2}, s^0_{-1}, s^0_0, s^0_1, s^0_2), (s^1_{-1}, s^1_0, s^1_1)) \in (\Delta_\alpha)_s$$
$$s.t. \ l^j_i = h_s(s^j_{i-1}, s^j_i, s^j_{i+1})$$

We now have an efficient way to build the local transition relation δ_{Φ_h}. When it is functional, it determines a cellular automaton $\beta = \Gamma_{\Phi_h}$. For our purpose, we need to test or ensure in some way that β is an FSSP solution.

3.2 Local Mappings and FSSP

We first note that the constraints put by the FSSP on space-time diagrams induces constraints on local simulations between FSSP solutions. So we can restrict our attention to local mappings respecting these constraints as formalized by the following definition and proposition.

Definition 11. *A local mapping h from an FSSP solution α to the states Σ_β of an FSSP-candidate CA β is said to be* FSSP-compliant *if it is such that (0) $h_\mathbf{z}$ maps $\star_\alpha$, G_α, and Q_α respectively to $\star_\beta$, G_β, and Q_β, (1) $h_\mathbf{s}(l_{-1}, l_0, l_1) = \star_\beta$ if and only if $\delta_\alpha(l_{-1}, l_0, l_1) = \star_\alpha$ (meaning simply $l_0 = \star_\alpha$), (2) $h_\mathbf{s}(l_{-1}, l_0, l_1) = \mathsf{F}_\beta$ if and only if $\delta_\alpha(l_{-1}, l_0, l_1) = \mathsf{F}_\alpha$, and (3) $h_\mathbf{s}(\mathsf{Q}_\alpha, \mathsf{Q}_\alpha, \mathsf{Q}_\alpha) = h_\mathbf{s}(\mathsf{Q}_\alpha, \mathsf{Q}_\alpha, \star) = \mathsf{Q}_\beta$.*

Proposition 3. *Let α be an FSSP solution CA, β an FSSP-candidate CA and h a local simulation from α to β. If β is an FSSP solution, then h is FSSP-compliant.*

The following proposition is at the same time not difficult once noted, but extremely surprising and useful: the simple constraints above are also "totally characterizing" and the previous implication is in fact an equivalence. This means in particular that it is not necessary to generate space-time diagrams to check if a constructed CA is an FSSP solution, which saves lots of computations.

Proposition 4. *Let α be an FSSP solution, β an FSSP-candidate CA and h be local simulation from α to β. If h is FSSP-compliant, then β is an FSSP solution.*

To see this, consider a diagram $d \in \mathsf{D}_\alpha$ of the solution α. The special FSSP states appear at specific places and h ensures that these special states/places are conserved in $h(d) \in \mathsf{D}_\beta$. So all diagram of β are correct and β is a solution.

4 Exploring the Graph of Local Mappings

4.1 The Graph of FSSP-Compliant Local Mappings

In our actual algorithm, we take as input an existing FSSP solution α and fix a set of state S of size $|\Sigma_\alpha|$. The search space consists of all FSSP-compliant local mappings from α to S, the neighbors $N(h)$ of a local mapping h being all h' that differ from h on exactly one entry, *i.e.* $N(h) := \{h' \mid \exists!(l_{-1}, l_0, l_1) \in \mathrm{dom}(\delta_\alpha)$ s.t. $h_\mathbf{s}(l_{-1}, l_0, l_1) \neq h'_\mathbf{s}(l_{-1}, l_0, l_1)\}$. More precisely, the mappings are considered modulo bijections of S. Indeed, two mappings h and h' are considered equivalent if there is some bijection $r : S \to S$ such that $h_\mathbf{z} = r \circ h'_\mathbf{z}$ and $h_\mathbf{s} = r \circ h'_\mathbf{s}$. So the search space is, in a sense, made of equivalence classes, each class being represented by a particular element. This element is chosen to be the only mapping h in the class such that $h_\mathbf{s}$ is monotonic according to arbitrary total orders on $\mathrm{dom}(\delta_\alpha)$ and S fixed for the entire run of the algorithm.

Considering 6-states solutions, let us denote $\Sigma_\alpha = \{\star_\alpha, \mathsf{G}_\alpha, \mathsf{Q}_\alpha, \mathsf{F}_\alpha, \mathsf{A}_\alpha, \mathsf{B}_\alpha, \mathsf{C}_\alpha\}$ and $S = \{\star, \mathsf{G}, \mathsf{Q}, \mathsf{F}, \mathsf{A}, \mathsf{B}, \mathsf{C}\}^3$. In each of these sets, four of the states are the special FSSP solution states (Definitions 8 and 9). Only the three states A, B, C come with no constraints. We can thus evaluate the size of the search space by looking at the degrees of freedom of FSSP-compliant local mappings (Definition 11).

---

[3] Recall that we do not count the $\star$ states.

Indeed, all FSSP-compliant local mappings h from α to S have the same partial function h_z, and the same value $h_s(l_{-1}, l_0, l_1)$ for those entries $(l_{-1}, l_0, l_1) \in \text{dom}(\delta_\alpha)$ forced to $\star$, Q or F. For all other entries (l_{-1}, l_0, l_1), $h_s(l_{-1}, l_0, l_1)$ cannot take the values $\star$ nor F, leaving 5 values available. So given an initial solution α, the number of local mappings is 5^x where x is the size of $\text{dom}(\delta_\alpha)$ without those entries constrained in Definition 11. To give an idea, for the solution 668 of the 718 solutions, $x = 86$ to the size of the search has 61 digits, and for Mazoyer's solution, $x = 112$ leading to a number with 79 digits.

4.2   Preparation Before the Algorithm

As described in Sect. 3.1, the local mappings are evaluated from the super local transition table. To build this table, we generate, for each size n from 2 to 5000, the space-time diagram $D_\alpha(\bar{n})$ and collect all super local transitions occurring from time 0 to $2n-4$ and from position 1 to n. Note that for all known minimum-time 6-state solutions, no additional super local transitions appear after $n = 250$.

The starting point of the exploration is the local mapping h_α corresponding to the local transition function δ_α itself, *i.e.* $(h_\alpha)_z = \rho \upharpoonright \{\star_\alpha, G_\alpha, Q_\alpha\}$ and $(h_\alpha)_s = \rho \circ \delta_\alpha$ for the obvious bijection $\rho : \Sigma_\alpha \to S$. This local mapping is obviously FSSP-compliant since it is local simulation from α to α.

4.3   The Exploration Algorithm

Algorithm 1:

```
1  explore(Δα, hα, k)
2      H ← {hα}
3      Hcurrent ← {hα}
4      while |Hcurrent| > 0 do
5          Hnext ← {}
6          for h ∈ Hcurrent do
7              S, H ← pertN(Δα, H, h, k)
8              for h' ∈ (S \ H) do
9                  if isSimul(h', Δα) then
10                     Hnext ← Hnext ∪ {h'}
11                     H ← H ∪ {h'}
12                 end
13             end
14         end
15         Hcurrent ← Hnext
16     end
17     return H
```

Algorithm 2:

```
1  pertN(Δα, H, h, k)
2      S ← N(h)
3      h' ← perturbation(h, k)
4      if h' ∉ H then
5          S ← S ∪ N(h')
6          if isSimul(h', Δα) then
7              H ← H ∪ {h'}
8          end
9      end
10     return S, H
```

To explain the algorithm, let us first consider the last parameter k to be 0, so that line 7 of the `explore` algorithm can be considered to be simply $S \leftarrow N(h)$. In this case, the algorithm starts with h_α, and explores its neighbors to collect all local simulations. Then the neighbors of those local simulations are considered to collect more local simulations, and so on so forth. In other words, the connected component of the sub-graph consisting only of the local simulations is collected. More precisely, the variable H collects all local simulations, $H_{current}$ contains the simulation discovered in the previous round and whose neighbors should be examined in current round, and the newly discovered local simulations are put in H_{next} for the next round. The function `isSimul` uses the super local transition table to construct the local transition relation of Φ_h and check if it is functional, *i.e.* if it is a local transition function of a valid CA Γ_{Φ_h}. By our construction, a valid CA is necessarily an FSSP solution making this operation really cheap.

When $k > 0$, line 7 puts in S not only $N(h)$ but also $N(h')$ for some local *mapping* h' obtained by k random modifications of h. The hope is to jump to another connected component of the "local simulation sub-graph". Since h' could be a (new or already considered) local *simulation*, a quick check is necessary.

5   Analyzing the Results

5.1   Analyzing the 718 Solutions

As mentioned in the introduction, this study began by the desire to analyse the 718 solutions found in [2]. These solutions, numbered from 0 to 717, are freely available online. We tried to search local simulation relation between them as done in [9]. Firstly, we found a slight mistake since there are 12 pairs of equivalent solutions up to renaming of states: (105, 676), (127, 659), (243, 599), (562, 626), (588, 619), (601, 609), (603, 689), (611, 651), (629, 714), (663, 684), (590, 596) and (679, 707). This means that there are really 706 solutions, but we still refer to them as the 718 solutions with their original numbering.

Once local simulation relation established between the 718 solutions, we analyzed in the number of connected components and found 193 while expecting only a few. When there is a local simulation h from a CA α and a CA β, the number of differences between h_α and h varies a lot, but the median value is 3.

5.2   Analyzing the Local Simulations

To find more FSSP solutions, we implemented many algorithms, gradually simplifying them into the one presented in this paper. It has been run on an Ubuntu Marvin machine with 32 cores of 2.00 GHz speed and 126 Gb of memory. However, the implementation being sequential, only two cores was used by the program. The original plan was to generate as many solutions as possible but we had some problems with the management of quotas in the shared machine. So we only expose the some selected data to show the relevance of the approach.

When running the program with the solution 355 and $k = 0$, the program used 14 Gb of memory and stopped after 27.5 h and found 9,584,134 local simulations! A second run of the program for this solution with $k = 3$ found 11,506,263 local simulations after 80.5 h. This indicates that perturbations are useful but the second run find only 1,922,129 additional local simulations but its computing time is three times more than the first run. Testing whether a local simulation belongs to set H obviously takes more and more time as more local mappings are discovered but there might be some understanding to gain about the proper mapping landscape too in order to improve the situation.

The transition table for the original Mazoyer's solution can be found in [8], but also in [13] together with other minimal-time solution transition tables. When running the program of the original Mazoyer's solution with different values of k we obtained the following number of new solutions for different runs.

k	Number of solutions found by 10 different runs
0	**644**
1	20682, 17645, 20731, 16139, **20731**, 9538, 20626, 20682, 20054, 20490
2	9451, 9451, 20595, 8241, **37275**, 3817, 17421, 8241, 17317, 19895
3	644, 644, 644, 644, 644, 644, 644, 731, 8241, **8241**
4	644, 644, 644, 2908, 644, 644, 644, 644, 644, **8241**
5	644, 644, 644, 644, 644, 644, 644, 644, 644, 644

The behavior with $k = 1$ seems to be pretty robust, but the bigger number of results is obtained with $k = 2$. For $k \geq 3$, the perturbations seem to be too violent and do not generally lead to more solutions. Note that while the solutions do not have less states, the number of transitions do change. We show in Fig. 1a the solution 668 (the only Mazoyer-like solutions found among the 718 solutions), and one of its simulations having less transitions in Fig. 1b. For fun, we also show in Fig. 1d a local simulation of the solution 355 having alternating states at time $2n - 3$, illustrating how local simulation rearrange locally the information. The identical part is represented with lighter colors to highlight the differences.

Proposition 5. *There are at least 11,506,263 minimum-time 6-state FSSP solutions.*

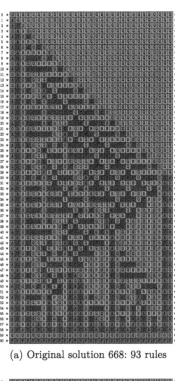

(a) Original solution 668: 93 rules

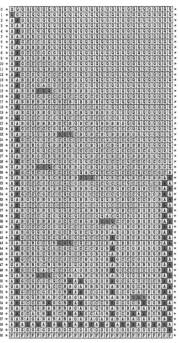

(b) A local simulation of 668: 90 rules

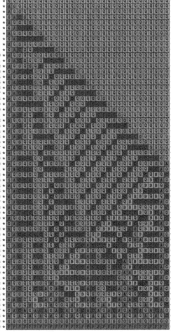

(c) Original solution 355: 101 rules

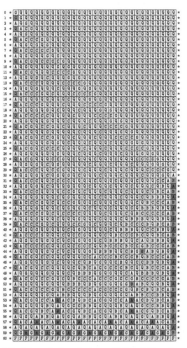

(d) A local simulation of 355: 102 rules

Fig. 1. Some FSSP space-time diagrams of size 31.

6   Conclusion

This paper presents only a small part of many ongoing experimentations. The notion of local simulation presented here is just a particular case of the notion of cellular field that can be used more broadly to investigate these questions. For example, we relate here only the small cones $\langle d(t - dt, p + dp) \mid dt \in \{0, 1\}, dp \in [\![-dt, +dt]\!]\rangle$ of any space-time diagram d in local mappings. If we increase the range of dt in this definition to be $[\![0, h]\!]$ for some $h > 1$, we allow CA to be transformed to a bigger extent. Another justification for this extension is that the composition of two local simulations is not a local simulation. In fact, composing an h-local simulation with an h'-local simulation produces an $(h+h')$-local simulation in general. A 0-local simulation is just a (possibly non-injective) renaming of the states. Note that since local mappings of local mappings are not local mappings, running the above algorithm on newly found solutions should a priori generate more solutions! Of course, a more exhaustive study is required.

Our guess is that, with a properly large notion of such simulations, it should be possible to classify the 718 solutions into only a few equivalence classes, more or less in two groups: the "mid-way division" solutions and the "two-third division" solutions. This results is also an important step in the understanding of automatic optimization of the number of states or transitions of CA.

Finally, the content of Sect. 3.2 about the preservation of correctness by FSSP-compliant local simulation is really interesting because of the simplicity of checking FSSP-compliance. It implies that a proof of correctness of a small FSSP solution can indeed be made on some huge, possibly infinite, simulating CA where everything is explicit as considered in [6,7]. This can be applied to ease the formal proof of correctness of Mazoyer's solution. Up to our knowledge, it is known to be long and hard but also to be the only proof to be precise enough to actually be implemented in the Coq Proof Assistant [3].

We would like to give special thanks to Jean-Baptiste Yunès who pointed us the 718 solutions paper. If we are right, he also partly inspired the work which led to the 718 solutions by a discussion during a conference.

References

1. Balzer, R.: An 8-state minimal time solution to the firing squad synchronization problem. Inf. Control **10**(1), 22–42 (1967)
2. Clergue, M., Vérel, S., Formenti, E.: An iterated local search to find many solutions of the 6-states firing squad synchronization problem. Appl. Soft Comput. **66**, 449–461 (2018)
3. Duprat, J.: Proof of correctness of the Mazoyer's solution of the firing squad problem in Coq. Research Report LIP RR-2002-14, Laboratoire de l'informatique du parallélisme (2002)
4. Gerken, H.D.: Über Synchronisationsprobleme bei Zellularautomaten. Diplomarbeit, Institut fur Theoretische Informatik, Technische Universität Braunschweig, 50 (1987)

5. Maignan, L., Yunès, J.-B.: A spatio-temporal algorithmic point of view on firing squad synchronisation problem. In: Sirakoulis, G.C., Bandini, S. (eds.) ACRI 2012. LNCS, vol. 7495, pp. 101–110. Springer, Heidelberg (2012). https://doi.org/10.1007/978-3-642-33350-7_11

6. Maignan, L., Yunès, J.-B.: Experimental finitization of infinite field-based generalized FSSP solution. In: Wąs, J., Sirakoulis, G.C., Bandini, S. (eds.) ACRI 2014. LNCS, vol. 8751, pp. 136–145. Springer, Cham (2014). https://doi.org/10.1007/978-3-319-11520-7_15

7. Maignan, L., Yunès, J.-B.: Finitization of infinite field-based multi-general FSSP solution. J. Cell. Autom. **12**(1–2), 121–139 (2016)

8. Mazoyer, J.: A six-state minimal time solution to the firing squad synchronization problem. Theor. Comput. Sci. **50**, 183–238 (1987)

9. Tien Thao Nguyen and Luidnel Maignan: Some cellular fields interrelations and optimizations in FSSP solutions. J. Cell. Autom. **15**(1–2), 131–146 (2020)

10. Noguchi, K.: Simple 8-state minimal time solution to the firing squad synchronization problem. Theor. Comput. Sci. **314**(3), 303–334 (2004)

11. Sanders, P.: Massively parallel search for transition-tables of polyautomata. In: Jesshope, C.R., Jossifov, V., Wilhelmi, W. (eds.) Parcella 1994, VI. International Workshop on Parallel Processing by Cellular Automata and Arrays, Potsdam, Germany, September 21–23, 1994. Proceedings. Mathematical Research, vol. 81, pp. 99–108. Akademie Verlag, Berlin (1994)

12. Umeo, H., Hirota, M., Nozaki, Y., Imai, K., Sogabe, T.: A new reconstruction and the first implementation of Goto's FSSP algorithm. Appl. Math. Comput. **318**, 92–108 (2018)

13. Umeo, H., Hisaoka, M., Sogabe, T.: A survey on optimum-time firing squad synchronization algorithms for one-dimensional cellular automata. IJUC **1**(4), 403–426 (2005)

14. Waksman, A.: An optimum solution to the firing squad synchronization problem. Inf. Control **9**(1), 66–78 (1966)

Non-maximal Sensitivity to Synchronism in Periodic Elementary Cellular Automata: Exact Asymptotic Measures

Pedro Paulo Balbi[1], Enrico Formenti[2], Kévin Perrot[3], Sara Riva[2(✉)],
and Eurico L. P. Ruivo[1]

[1] FCI, Universidade Presbiteriana Mackenzie, São Paulo, Brazil
[2] CNRS, I3S, Université Côte d'Azur, Sophia Antipolis, France
riva@i3s.unice.fr
[3] Université publique, Marseille, France

Abstract. In [10] and [12] the authors showed that elementary cellular automata rules 0, 3, 8, 12, 15, 28, 32, 34, 44, 51, 60, 128, 136, 140, 160, 162, 170, 200 and 204 (and their conjugation, reflection, reflected-conjugation) are not maximum sensitive to synchronism, *i.e.,* they do not have a different dynamics for each (non-equivalent) block-sequential update schedule (defined as ordered partitions of cell positions). In this work we present exact measurements of the sensitivity to synchronism for these rules, as functions of the size. These exhibit a surprising variety of values and associated proof methods, such as the special pairs of rule 128, and the connection to the bissection of Lucas numbers of rule 8.

1 Introduction

Cellular automata (CAs) are discrete dynamical systems with respect to time, space and state variables, which have been widely studied both as mathematical and computational objects as well as suitable models for real-world complex systems. The dynamics of a CA is locally-defined: every agent (*cell*) computes its future state based upon its present state and those of its neighbors, that is, the cells connected to it. In spite of their apparent simplicity, CAs may display non-trivial global emergent behavior, some of them even reaching computational universality [3,7]. Originally, CAs are updated in a synchronous fashion, that is, every cell of the lattice is updated simultaneously. However, over the last decade, *asynchronous* cellular automata have attracted increasing attention in its associated scientific community. A comprehensive and detailed overview of asynchronous CAs is given in [6]. There are different ways to define asynchronism in CAs, be it deterministically or stochastically. Here, we deal with a deterministic version of asynchronism, known as *block-sequential*, coming from the model of Boolean networks and first characterized for this more general model in [1,2]. Under such an update scheme, the lattice of the CA is partitioned into blocks of cells, each one is assigned a priority of being updated, and this priority ordering

© IFIP International Federation for Information Processing 2020
Published by Springer Nature Switzerland AG 2020. All Rights Reserved
H. Zenil (Ed.): AUTOMATA 2020, LNCS 12286, pp. 14–28, 2020.
https://doi.org/10.1007/978-3-030-61588-8_2

is kept fixed throughout the time evolution. For the sake of simplicity, from now on, whenever we refer to *asynchronism*, we will mean *block-sequential*, deterministic asynchronism.

In previous works ([10,12]), the notion of *maximum sensitivity to asynchronism* was established. Basically, a CA rule was said to present maximum sensitivity to asynchronism when, for any two different block-sequential update schedules, the rule would yield different dynamics. Out of the 256 elementary cellular automata rules (ECAs), 200 possess maximum sensitivity to asynchronism, while the remaining 56 rules do not. Therefore, it is natural to try and define a *degree* of sensitivity to asynchronism to the latter.

Here, such a notion of a measure to the sensitivity to asynchronism is presented and general analytical formulas for sensitivities of the non-maximal sensitive rules are provided. The results (to be presented on Table 1 at the end of Sect. 2) exhibit an interesting range of values requiring the introduction of various techniques, from measures tending to 0 (insensitive rules) to measures tending to 1 (almost max-sensitive), with one rule tending to some surprising constant between 0 and 1.

This paper is organized as follows. In Sect. 2, fundamental definitions and results on Boolean networks, update digraphs and elementary cellular automata are given. In Sect. 3, formal expressions for the sensitivity to asynchronism of non-max sensitive ECA rules are provided for configurations of arbitrary size. Finally, concluding remarks are made in Sect. 4.

For lack of space most of the proofs are omitted, we refer the reader to [4].

2   Definitions

Elementary cellular automata will be presented in the more general framework of Boolean automata networks, for which the variation of update schedule benefits from useful considerations already studied in the literature. Figure 1 illustrates the definitions.

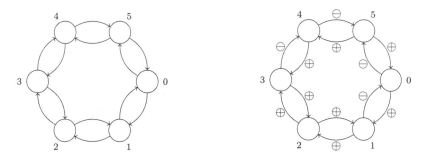

Fig. 1. Left: interaction digraph G_6^{ECA} of the ECA rule 128 for $n = 6$, with local functions $f_i(x) = x_{i-1} \wedge x_i \wedge x_{i+1}$ for all $i \in \{0, \dots, 5\}$. Right: update digraph corresponding to the update schedules $\Delta = (\{1,2,3\}, \{0,4\}, \{5\})$ and $\Delta' = (\{1,2,3\}, \{0\}, \{4\}, \{5\})$, which are therefore equivalent ($\Delta \equiv \Delta'$). For example, $f^{(\Delta)}(111011) = 110000$ whereas for the synchronous update schedule we have $f^{(\Delta^{\mathrm{sync}})}(111011) = 110001$.

2.1   Boolean Networks

A Boolean Network (BN) of size n is an arrangement of n finite Boolean automata (or components) interacting each other according to a *global rule* $f : \{0,1\}^n \rightarrow \{0,1\}^n$ which describes how the global state changes after one time step. Let $[\![n]\!] = \{0, \ldots, n-1\}$. Each automaton is identified with a unique integer $i \in [\![n]\!]$ and x_i denotes the current state of the automaton i. A *configuration* $x \in \{0,1\}^n$ is a snapshot of the current state of all automata and represents the global state of the BN.

For convenience, we identify configurations with words on $\{0,1\}^n$. Hence, for example, 01111 or 01^4 both denote the configuration $(0,1,1,1,1)$. Remark that the global function $f : \{0,1\}^n \rightarrow \{0,1\}^n$ of a BN of size n induces a set of n *local functions* $f_i : \{0,1\}^n \rightarrow \{0,1\}$, one per each component, such that $f(x) = (f_0(x), f_1(x), \ldots, f_{n-1}(x))$ for all $x \in \{0,1\}^n$. This gives a static description of a discrete dynamical system, and it remains to set the order in which components are updated in order to get a dynamics. Before going to update schedules, let us first introduce interaction digraphs.

The component i *influences* the component j if $\exists x \in \{0,1\}^n : f_j(x) \neq f_j(\overline{x}^i)$, where $\overline{x}^i$ is the configuration obtained from x by flipping the state of component i. Note that in literature one may also consider *positive* and *negative* influences, but they will not be useful for the present study. The *interaction digraph* $G_f = (V, A)$ of a BN f represents the effective dependencies among its set of components $V = [\![n]\!]$ and $A = \{(i, j) \mid i \text{ influences } j\}$. It will turn out to be pertinent to consider $\check{G}_f = (V, A)$, obtained from G_f by removing the loops (arcs of the form (i, i)).

For $n \in \mathbb{N}$, denote $\mathcal{P}_n$ the set of ordered partitions of $[\![n]\!]$ and $|f|$ the size of a BN f. A *block-sequential update schedule* $\Delta = (\Delta_1, \ldots, \Delta_k)$ is an element of $\mathcal{P}_{|f|}$. It defines the following dynamics $f^{(\Delta)} : \{0,1\}^n \rightarrow \{0,1\}^n$,

$$f^{(\Delta)} = f^{(\Delta_k)} \circ \cdots \circ f^{(\Delta_2)} \circ f^{(\Delta_1)} \quad \text{with} \quad f^{(\Delta_j)}(x)_i = \begin{cases} f_i(x) & \text{if } i \in \Delta_j, \\ x_i & \text{if } i \notin \Delta_j. \end{cases}$$

In words, the components are updated in the order given by Δ: sequentially part after part, and in parallel within each part. The *parallel* or *synchronous* update schedule is $\Delta^{\mathtt{sync}} = ([\![n]\!])$ and we have $f^{(\Delta^{\mathtt{sync}})} = f$. In this article, since only block-sequential update schedules are considered, they are simply called *update schedule* for short. They are

- "*fair*" in the sense that all components are updated the exact same number of times,
- "*periodic*" in the sense that the same ordered partition is repeated.

Given a BN f of size n and an update schedule Δ, the *transition digraph* $D_{f^{(\Delta)}} = (V, A)$ is such that $V = \{0,1\}^n$ and $A = \{(x, f^{(\Delta)}(x)) \mid x \in \{0,1\}^n\}$. It describes the *dynamics* of f under the update schedule Δ. The set of all possible dynamics of the BN f, at the basis of the measure of sensitivity to synchronism, is then defined as $\mathcal{D}(f) = \{D_{f^{(\Delta)}} \mid \Delta \in \mathcal{P}_{|f|}\}$.

2.2   Update Digraphs and Equivalent Update Schedules

For a given BN, some update schedules always give the same dynamics. Indeed, if, for example, two components do not influence each other, their order of updating has no effect on the dynamics (see Example 1 for a detailed example). In [2], the notion of *update digraph* has been introduced in order to study update schedules. Given a BN f with loopless interaction digraph $\hat{G}_f = (V, A)$ and an update schedule $\Delta \in \mathcal{P}_n$, define $lab_\Delta : A \to \{\oplus, \ominus\}$ as

$$\forall (i,j) \in A : lab_\Delta((i,j)) = \begin{cases} \oplus & \text{if } i \in \Delta_a, j \in \Delta_b \text{ with } 1 \le b \le a \le k, \\ \ominus & \text{if } i \in \Delta_a, j \in \Delta_b \text{ with } 1 \le a < b \le k. \end{cases}$$

The *update digraph* $U_{f(\Delta)}$ of the BN f for the update schedule $\Delta \in \mathcal{P}_n$ is the loopless interaction digraph decorated with lab_Δ, i.e., $U_{f(\Delta)} = (V, A, lab_\Delta)$. Note that loops are removed because they bring no meaningful information: indeed, an edge (i,i) would always be labeled $\oplus$. Now we have that, if two update schedules define the same update digraph then they also define the same dynamics.

Theorem 1 ([2]). *Given a BN f and two update schedules Δ, Δ', if $lab_\Delta = lab_{\Delta'}$ then $D_{f(\Delta)} = D_{f(\Delta')}$.*

A very important remark is that not all labelings correspond to *valid* update digraphs, in the sense that there are update schedules giving these labelings. For example, if two arcs (i,j) and (j,i) belong to the interaction digraph and are both labeled $\ominus$, it would mean that i is updated prior to j and j is updated prior to i, which is contradictory. Fortunately, there is a nice characterisation of *valid* update digraphs.

Theorem 2 ([1]). *Given f with $\hat{G}_f = (V, A)$, the label function $lab : A \to \{\oplus, \ominus\}$ is valid if and only if there is no cycle $(i_0, i_1, \ldots, i_k)$, with $i_0 = i_k$ and $k > 0$, such that*

- $\forall 0 \le j < k : ((i_j, i_{j+1}) \in A \wedge lab((i_j, i_{j+1})) = \oplus) \vee ((i_{j+1}, i_j) \in A \wedge lab((i_{j+1}, i_j)) = \ominus)$,
- $\exists 0 \le i < k : lab((i_{j+1}, i_j)) = \ominus$.

In words, Theorem 2 states that a labeling is valid if and only if the multi-digraph where the labeling is unchanged but the orientation of arcs labeled $\ominus$ is reversed, does not contain a cycle with at least one arc label $\ominus$ (*forbidden cycle*). According to Theorem 1, update digraphs define equivalence classes of update schedules: $\Delta \equiv \Delta'$ if and only if $lab_\Delta = lab_{\Delta'}$. Given a BN f, the set of equivalence classes of update schedules is therefore defined as $\mathcal{U}(f) = \{U_{f(\Delta)} \mid \Delta \in \mathcal{P}_{|f|}\}$.

2.3   Sensitivity to Synchronism

The sensitivity to synchronism $\mu_s(f)$ of a BN f quantifies the proportion of distinct dynamics $w.r.t$ non-equivalent update schedules. The idea is that when two or more update schedules are equivalent then $\mu_s(f)$ decreases, while it increase when distinct update schedules bring to different dynamics. More formally, given a BN f we define

$$\mu_s(f) = \frac{|\mathcal{D}(f)|}{|\mathcal{U}(f)|}.$$

Obviously, it holds that $\frac{1}{|\mathcal{U}(f)|} \leq \mu_s(f) \leq 1$, and a BN f is as much sensible to synchronism as it has different dynamics when the update schedule varies. The extreme cases are a BN f with $\mu_s(f) = \frac{1}{|\mathcal{U}(f)|}$ that has always the same dynamics $D_{f(\Delta)}$ for any update schedule Δ, and a BN f with $\mu_s(f) = 1$ which has a different dynamics for different update schedules (for each $\Delta \not\equiv \Delta'$ it holds that $D_{f(\Delta)} \neq D_{f(\Delta')}$). A BN f is *max-sensitive* to synchronism iff $\mu_s(f) = 1$. Note that a BN f is max-sensitive if and only if

$$\forall \Delta \in \mathcal{P}_{|f|} \forall \Delta' \in \mathcal{P}_{|f|} \, (\Delta \not\equiv \Delta') \Rightarrow \exists x \in \{0,1\}^n \exists i \in [\![n]\!] \, f^{(\Delta)}(x)_i \neq f^{(\Delta')}(x)_i \, . \tag{1}$$

2.4   Elementary Cellular Automata

In this study we investigate the sensitivity to synchronism of *elementary cellular automata* (ECA) over periodic configurations. Indeed, they are a subclass of BN in which all components (also called *cells* in this context) have the same local rule, as follows. Given a size n, the ECA of local function $h : \{0,1\}^3 \to \{0,1\}$ is the BN f such that $\forall i \in [\![n]\!] : f_i(x) = h(x_{i-1}, x_i, x_{i+1})$, where components are taken modulo n (this will be the case throughout all the paper without explicit mention). We use *Wolfram numbers* [13] to designate each of the 256 ECA local rule $h : \{0,1\}^3 \to \{0,1\}$ as the number

$$w(h) = \sum_{(x_1, x_2, x_3) \in \{0,1\}^3} h(x_1, x_2, x_3) 2^{2^2 x_1 + 2^1 x_2 + 2^0 x_3}.$$

Given a Boolean function $h : \{0,1\}^3 \to \{0,1\}$, consider the following transformations over local rules: $\tau_i(h)(x,y,z) = h(x,y,z)$, $\tau_r(h)(x,y,z) = h(z,y,x)$, $\tau_n(h)(x,y,z) = 1-h(1-z,1-y,1-x)$ and $\tau_{rn}(h)(x,y,z) = 1-h(1-z,1-y,1-x)$ for all $x,y,z \in \{0,1\}$. In our context, they preserve the sensitivity to synchronism. For this reason we consider only 88 ECA rules up to τ_i, τ_r, τ_n and τ_{rn}.

The definitions of Subsect. 2.3 are applied to ECA rules as follows. Given a size n, the *ECA interaction digraph of size n* $G_n^{\mathrm{ECA}} = (V,A)$ is such that $V = [\![n]\!]$ and $A = \{(i+1,i),(i,i+1) \mid i \in [\![n]\!]\}$.

In [10,12], it is proved that $|\mathcal{U}^{\mathrm{ECA}}(n)| = 3^n - 2^{n+1} + 2$, where $\mathcal{U}^{\mathrm{ECA}}(n)$ is the set of valid labelings of G_n^{ECA}. The sensitivity to synchronism of ECAs is measured relatively to the family of ECAs, and therefore relatively to this count of valid labelings of G_n^{ECA}, even for rules where some arcs do not correspond to effective influences (one may think of rule 0). Except from this subtlety, the measure is correctly defined by considering, for an ECA rule number α and a size n, that $h_\alpha \colon \{0,1\}^3 \to \{0,1\}$ is its local rule, and that $f_{\alpha,n} \colon \{0,1\}^n \to \{0,1\}^n$ is its global function on periodic configurations of size n, $\forall x \in \{0,1\}^n$ $f_{\alpha,n}(x)_i = h_\alpha(x_{i-1}, x_i, x_{i+1})$. Then, the sensitivity to synchronism of ECA rule number α is given by

$$\mu_s(f_{\alpha,n}) = \frac{|\mathcal{D}(f_{\alpha,n})|}{3^n - 2^{n+1} + 2}.$$

A rule α is ultimately *max-sensitive to synchronism* when $\lim\limits_{n \to +\infty} \mu_s(f_{\alpha,n}) = 1$.

The following result provides a first overview of sensitivity to synchronism.

Theorem 3 ([10,12]). *For any size $n \geq 7$, the nineteen ECA rules 0, 3, 8, 12, 15, 28, 32, 34, 44, 51, 60, 128, 136, 140, 160, 162, 170, 200 and 204 are not max-sensitive to synchronism. The remaining sixty nine other rules are max-sensitive to synchronism.*

Theorem 3 gives a precise measure of sensitivity for the sixty nine maximum sensitive rules, for which $\mu_s(f_{\alpha,n}) = 1$ for all $n \geq 7$, but for the nineteen that are not maximum sensitive it only informs that $\mu_s(f_{\alpha,n}) < 1$ for all $n \geq 7$. In the rest of this paper we study the precise dependency on n of $\mu_s(f_{\alpha,n})$ for these rules, filling the huge gap between $\frac{1}{3^n - 2^{n+1} + 2}$ and $\frac{3^n - 2^{n+1} + 1}{3^n - 2^{n+1} + 2}$. This will offer a finer view on the sensitivity to synchronism of ECA. The results are summarized in Table 1.

Table 1. The rules are divided into four classes (ϕ is the golden ratio).

Class	Rules (α)	Sections	Sensitivity ($\mu_s(f_{\alpha,n})$)
I	$0, 51, 200, 204$	3.1	$\frac{1}{3^n - 2^{n+1} + 2}$ for any $n \geq 3$
II	$3, 12, 15, 34, 60, 136, 170$	3.2	$\frac{2^n - 1}{3^n - 2^{n+1} + 2}$ for any $n \geq 4$
	$28, 32, 44, 140$		
III	8	3.3	$\frac{\phi^{2n} + \phi^{-2n} - 2^n}{3^n - 2^{n+1} + 2}$ for any $n \geq 5$
IV	$128, 160, 162$	3.4	$\frac{3^n - 2^{n+1} - cn + 2}{3^n - 2^{n+1} + 2}$ for any $n \geq 5$

3   Theoretical Measures of Sensitivity to Synchronism

This section contains the main results of the paper, regarding the dependency on n of $\mu_s(f_{\alpha,n})$ for ECA rules that are not max-sensitive to synchronism. As illustrated in Table 1, the ECA rules can be divided into four classes according to their sensitivity functions. Each class will requires specific proof techniques but all of them have interaction digraphs as a common denominator.

As a starting point, one can consider the case of ECA rules have an interaction digraph which is a proper subgraph of G_n^{ECA}. Indeed, when considering them as BN many distinct update schedules give the same labelings and hence, by Theorem 1 and the definition of $\mu_s(f_{\alpha,n})$, they cannot be max-sensitive. This is the case of the following set of ECA rules $\mathcal{S} = \{0, 3, 12, 15, 34, 51, 60, 136, 170, 204\}$. Indeed, denoting $G_{f_{\alpha,n}} = (\llbracket n \rrbracket, A_{f_{\alpha,n}})$ the interaction digraph of ECA rule α of size n for $\alpha \in \mathcal{S}$, one finds $\forall n \geq 3$ and $\forall i \in \llbracket n \rrbracket$:

- $(i+1, i), (i-1, i) \notin A_{f_{0,n}}$,
- $(i+1, i) \notin A_{f_{3,n}}$,
- $(i+1, i) \notin A_{f_{12,n}}$,
- $(i+1, i) \notin A_{f_{15,n}}$,
- $(i, i+1) \notin A_{f_{34,n}}$,

- $(i+1, i), (i-1, i) \notin A_{f_{51,n}}$,
- $(i+1, i) \notin A_{f_{60,n}}$,
- $(i, i+1) \notin A_{f_{136,n}}$,
- $(i, i+1) \notin A_{f_{170,n}}$,
- $(i+1, i), (i-1, i) \notin A_{f_{204,n}}$.

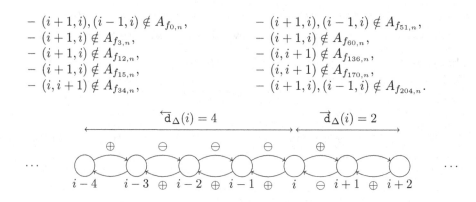

Fig. 2. Illustration of the chain of influences for some update schedule Δ.

Let us now introduce some useful results and notations that will be widely used in the sequel. Given an update schedule Δ, in order to study the chain of influences involved in the computation of the image at cell $i \in \llbracket n \rrbracket$, define

$$\overleftarrow{\mathsf{d}}_\Delta(i) = \max\{k \in \mathbb{N} \mid \forall j \in \mathbb{N} : 0 < j < k \implies lab_\Delta((i-j, i-j+1)) = \ominus\}$$

$$\overrightarrow{\mathsf{d}}_\Delta(i) = \max\{k \in \mathbb{N} \mid \forall j \in \mathbb{N} : 0 < j < k \implies lab_\Delta((i+j, i+j-1)) = \ominus\}.$$

These quantities are well defined because $k = 1$ is always a possible value, and moreover, if $\overleftarrow{\mathsf{d}}_\Delta(i)$ or $\overrightarrow{\mathsf{d}}_\Delta(i)$ is greater than n, then there is a forbidden cycle in the update digraph of schedule Δ (Theorem 2). Note that for any $\Delta \in \mathcal{P}_n$, $lab_\Delta((i - \overleftarrow{\mathsf{d}}_\Delta(i), i - \overleftarrow{\mathsf{d}}_\Delta(i) + 1)) = \oplus$ and $lab_\Delta((i + \overrightarrow{\mathsf{d}}_\Delta(i), i + \overrightarrow{\mathsf{d}}_\Delta(i) - 1)) = \oplus$. See Fig. 2 for an illustration. The purpose of these quantities is that it holds for any $x \in \{0, 1\}^n$,

$$f_\alpha^{(\Delta)}(x)_i = r_\alpha(\underbrace{\underbrace{r_\alpha(\quad, x_{i-1}, x_i)}_{\cdots}, x_i, \underbrace{r_\alpha(x_i, x_{i+1}, \quad)}_{\cdots}}_{})$$

$$\underbrace{r_\alpha(x_{i-\overleftarrow{d}_\Delta(i)}, x_{i-\overleftarrow{d}_\Delta(i)+1}, x_{i-\overleftarrow{d}_\Delta(i)+2})}_{} \quad \underbrace{r_\alpha(x_{i+\overrightarrow{d}_\Delta(i)-2}, x_{i+\overrightarrow{d}_\Delta(i)-1}, x_{i+\overrightarrow{d}_\Delta(i)})}_{} \tag{2}$$

i.e., the quantities $\overleftarrow{d}_\Delta(i)$ and $\overrightarrow{d}_\Delta(i)$ are the lengths of the chain of influences at cell i for the update schedule Δ, on both sides of the interaction digraph. If the chains of influences at some cell i are identical for two update schedules, then the images at i we be identical for any configuration, as stated in the following lemma.

Lemma 1. *For any ECA rule α, any $n \in \mathbb{N}$, any $\Delta, \Delta' \in \mathcal{P}_n$ and any $i \in [\![n]\!]$, it holds that*

$$\overleftarrow{d}_\Delta(i) = \overleftarrow{d}_{\Delta'}(i) \wedge \overrightarrow{d}_\Delta(i) = \overrightarrow{d}_{\Delta'}(i) \text{ implies } \forall x \in \{0,1\}^n \ f_{\alpha,n}^{(\Delta)}(x)_i = f_{\alpha,n}^{(\Delta')}(x)_i.$$

Proof. This is a direct consequence of Eq. 2, because the nesting of local rules for Δ and Δ' are identical at cell i. □

For any rule α, size n, and update schedules $\Delta, \Delta' \in \mathcal{P}_n$, it holds that

$$\forall i \in [\![n]\!] : \overleftarrow{d}_\Delta(i) = \overleftarrow{d}_{\Delta'}(i) \wedge \overrightarrow{d}_\Delta(i) = \overrightarrow{d}_{\Delta'}(i) \quad \Longleftrightarrow \quad \Delta \equiv \Delta' \tag{3}$$

and this implies $D_{f_{\alpha,n}^{(\Delta)}} = D_{f_{\alpha,n}^{(\Delta')}}$. Remark that it is possible that $\overleftarrow{d}_\Delta(i) + \overrightarrow{d}_\Delta(i) \geq n$, in which case the image at cell i depends on the whole configuration. Moreover the previous inequality may be strict, meaning that the dependencies on both sides may overlap for some cell. This will be a key in computing the dependency on n of the sensitivity to synchronism for rule 128 for example. Let $d_\Delta(i) = \{j \leq i \mid i - j \leq \overleftarrow{d}_\Delta(i)\} \cup \{j \geq i \mid j - i \leq \overrightarrow{d}_\Delta(i)\}$ be the set of cells that i depends on under update schedule $\Delta \in \mathcal{P}_n$. When $d_\Delta(i) \neq [\![n]\!]$ then cell i does not depend on the whole configuration, and $d_\Delta(i)$ describes precisely Δ, as stated in the following lemma.

Lemma 2. *For any $\Delta, \Delta' \in \mathcal{P}_n$, it holds that $\forall i \in [\![n]\!] \ d_\Delta(i) = d_{\Delta'}(i) \neq [\![n]\!]$ implies $\Delta \equiv \Delta'$.*

Proof. If $d_\Delta(i) \neq [\![n]\!]$ then $\overleftarrow{d}_\Delta(i)$ and $\overrightarrow{d}_\Delta(i)$ do not overlap. Moreover, remark that $\overleftarrow{d}_\Delta(i)$ and $\overrightarrow{d}_\Delta(i)$ can be deduced from $d_\Delta(i)$. Indeed, $\overleftarrow{d}_\Delta(i) = \max\{j \mid \forall k \in [\![j]\!], i - j + k \in d_\Delta(i)\}$ and $\overrightarrow{d}_\Delta(i) = \max\{j \mid \forall k \in [\![j]\!], i + j - k \in d_\Delta(i)\}$. The result follows since knowing $\overleftarrow{d}_\Delta(i)$ and $\overrightarrow{d}_\Delta(i)$ for all $i \in [\![n]\!]$ allows to completely reconstruct lab_Δ, which would be the same as $lab_{\Delta'}$ if $d_\Delta(i) = d_{\Delta'}(i)$ for all $i \in [\![n]\!]$ (Formula 3). □

3.1   Class I: Insensitive Rules

This class contains the simplest dynamics with sensitivity function $\frac{1}{3^n - 2^{n+1} + 2}$.

Theorem 4. $\mu_s(f_{0,n}) = \frac{1}{3^n - 2^{n+1} + 2}$ for any $n \geq 1$ and for $\alpha \in \{0, 51, 204\}$.

Proof. The result for ECA rule 0 is obvious since $\forall n \geq 1 : \forall x \in \{0,1\}^n : f_{0,n}(x) = 0^n$. The ECA Rule 51 is based on the boolean function $r_{51}(x_{i-1}, x_i, x_{i-1}) = \neg x_i$ and ECA rule 204 is the identity. Therefore, similarly to ECA rule 0, for any n their interaction digraph has no arcs. Hence, there is only one equivalence class of update digraph, and one dynamics.   □

The ECA rule 200 also belongs to Class I and it is based on the following local function $r_{200}(x_1, x_2, x_3) = x_2 \wedge (x_1 \vee x_3)$. Indeed, it is almost equal to the identity (ECA rule 204), except for $r_{200}(0, 1, 0) = 0$. It turns out that, even if its interaction digraph has all of the $2n$ arcs, this rule produces always the same dynamics, regardless of the update schedule.

Theorem 5. $\mu_s(f_{200,n}) = \frac{1}{3^n - 2^{n+1} + 2}$ for any $n \geq 1$.

Proof. We prove that $f_{200,n}^{(\Delta)}(x) = f_{200,n}^{(\Delta^{\text{sync}})}(x)$ for any configuration $x \in \{0,1\}^n$ and for any update schedule $\Delta \in \mathcal{P}_n$. For any $i \in [\![n]\!]$ such that $x_i = 0$, the ECA rule 200 is the identity, therefore it does not depend on the states of its neighbors which may have been updated before itself, *i.e.*, $f_{200,n}^{(\Delta)}(x)_i = 0 = f_{200,n}^{(\Delta^{\text{sync}})}(x)_i$. Moreover, for any $i \in [\![n]\!]$ such that $x_i = 1$, if its two neighbors x_{i-1} and x_{i+1} are both in state 0 then they will remain in state 0 and $f_{200,n}^{(\Delta)}(x)_i = 0 = f_{200,n}^{(\Delta^{\text{sync}})}(x)_i$; otherwise, the ECA 200 is the identity map and the two neighbors of cell i also apply the identity, thus again $f_{200,n}^{(\Delta)}(x)_i = 1 = f_{200,n}^{(\Delta^{\text{sync}})}(x)_i$.   □

3.2   Class II: Low Sensitivity Rules

This class contains rules whose sensitivity function equals $\frac{2^n - 1}{3^n - 2^{n+1} + 2}$. This is a very interesting class that demands the development of specific arguments and tools. However, the starting point is always the interaction digraph.

One-Way ECAs. The following result counts the number of equivalence classes of update schedules for ECA rules α having only arcs of the form $(i, i + 1)$, or only arcs of the form $(i + 1, i)$ in their interaction digraph $G_{f_{\alpha,n}}$.

Lemma 3. For the ECA rules $\alpha \in \{3, 12, 15, 34, 60, 136, 170\}$, it holds that $|\mathcal{U}(f_{\alpha,n})| \leq 2^n - 1$.

Proof. The interaction digraph of these rules is the directed cycle on n vertices (with n arcs). There can be only a forbidden cycle of length n in the case that all arcs are labeled $\ominus$ (see Theorem 2). Except for the all $\oplus$ labeling (which is valid), any other labeling prevents the formation of an invalid cycle, since the orientation of at least one arc is unchanged (labeled $\oplus$), and the orientation of at least one arc is reversed (labeled $\ominus$).   □

In the sequence, we are going to exploit Lemma 3 to obtain one of the main results of this section. The ECA rule 170, which is based on the following Boolean function: $r_{170}(x_{i-1}, x_i, x_{i+1}) = x_{i+1}$, shows the pathway.

Theorem 6. $\mu_s(f_{170,n}) = \frac{2^n - 1}{3^n - 2^{n+1} + 2}$ *for any* $n \geq 2$.

Proof. Let $f = f_{170,n}$ and $n \geq 2$. By definition, one finds that for any two non-equivalent update schedules $\Delta \not\equiv \Delta'$ it holds that $\exists i_0 \in [\![n]\!]$ $lab_\Delta((i_0+1, i_0)) = \oplus$ and $lab_{\Delta'}((i_0 + 1, i_0)) = \ominus$. Furthermore, since having $lab_{\Delta'}((i + 1, i)) = \ominus$ for all $i \in [\![n]\!]$ creates an invalid cycle of length n, there exists a minimal $\ell \geq 1$ such that $lab_{\Delta'}((i_0 + \ell + 1, i_0 + \ell)) = \oplus$ (this requires $n > 1$). A part of the update digraph corresponding to Δ' is pictured below.

By definition of the labels and the minimality of ℓ we have that for all $0 \leq k < \ell$ it holds that $f^{(\Delta')}(x)_{i_0+k} = x_{i_0+\ell+1}$. Since for the update schedule Δ we have $f^{(\Delta)}(x)_{i_0} = x_{i_0+1}$, it is always possible to construct a configuration x with $x_{i_0+1} \neq x_{i_0+\ell+1}$ such that the two dynamics differ, *i.e.*, $f^{(\Delta)}(x)_{i_0} \neq f^{(\Delta')}(x)_{i_0}$. The result holds by Formula 1.   □

Generalizing the idea behind the construction used for ECA rule 170 one may prove that ECA rules $3, 12, 15, 34, 60, 136$ have identical sensitivity function.

Exploiting Patterns in the Update Digraph. We are now going to develop a proof technique which characterizes the number of non-equivalent update schedules according to the presence of specific patterns in their interaction digraph. This will concern ECA rules $28, 32, 44$ and 140. When n is clear from the context, we will simply denote f_α instead of $f_{\alpha,n}$ with $\alpha \in \{28, 32, 44, 140\}$. We present ECA rule 32 which is based on the Boolean function $r_{32}(x_1, x_2, x_3) = x_1 \wedge \neg x_2 \wedge x_3$, the reasoning for rules $28, 44$ and 140 are analogous.

Lemma 4. *Fix* $n \in \mathbb{N}$. *For any update schedule* $\Delta \in \mathcal{P}_n$, *for any configuration* $x \in \{0, 1\}^n$ *and for any* $i \in [\![n]\!]$, *the following holds:* $f_{32}^{(\Delta)}(x)_i = 1$ *iff* $lab_\Delta((i + 1, i)) = lab_\Delta((i - 1, i)) = \oplus$ *and* $(x_{i-1}, x_i, x_{i+1}) = (1, 0, 1)$.

Corollary 1. *Fix* $n \in \mathbb{N}$. *For any update schedule* $\Delta \in \mathcal{P}_n$, *for any configuration* $x \in \{0, 1\}^n$ *and* $i \in [\![n]\!]$, *if* $lab_\Delta((i - 1, i)) = \ominus$ *or* $lab_\Delta((i + 1, i)) = \ominus$, *then* $f_{32}^{(\Delta)}(x)_i = 0$.

Lemma 5. *For any* $n \in \mathbb{N}$, *consider* $\Delta, \Delta' \in \mathcal{P}_n$. *Then,* $D_{f_{32,n}^{(\Delta)}} \neq D_{f_{32,n}^{(\Delta')}}$ *if and only if there exists* $i \in [\![n]\!]$ *such that one of the following holds:*

1. $lab_\Delta((i + 1, i)) = lab_\Delta((i - 1, i)) = \oplus$ *and either* $lab_{\Delta'}((i + 1, i)) = \ominus$ *or* $lab_{\Delta'}((i - 1, i)) = \ominus$;
2. $lab_{\Delta'}((i + 1, i)) = lab_{\Delta'}((i - 1, i)) = \oplus$ *and either* $lab_\Delta((i + 1, i)) = \ominus$ *or* $lab_\Delta((i - 1, i)) = \ominus$.

Theorem 7. $\mu_s(f_{\alpha,n}) = \frac{2^n-1}{3^n-2^{n+1}+2}$ *for any $n > 3$ and for all ECA rules $\alpha \in \{28, 32, 44, 140\}$.*

Proof. Given a configuration of length $n > 3$, the patterns in Lemma 4 may be present in k cells out of n with $1 \leq k \leq n$ (it must be present in at least one cell because otherwise we would have a $\ominus$ cycle). Therefore, there are $\sum_{k=1}^{n} \binom{n}{i} = 2^n - 1$ different dynamics. The proof for the ECA rules $28, 44, 140$ is similar. $\square$

3.3   Class III: Medium Sensitivity Rules

This subsection is concerned uniquely with ECA Rule 8 which is based on the following Boolean function $r_8(x_1, x_2, x_3) = \neg x_1 \wedge x_2 \wedge x_3$. As will be seen, finding the expression of sensitivity function for this rule is somewhat peculiar and requires to develop specific techniques. The sensitivity function obtained tends to $\frac{1+\phi}{3}$, where ϕ is the golden ratio.

Remark 1. For any $x_1, x_3 \in \{0, 1\}$, it holds that $r_8(x_1, 0, x_3) = 0$. Hence, for any update schedule a cell that is in state 0 will remain in state 0 forever.

We will first see in Lemma 6 that as soon as two update schedules differ on the labeling of an arc $(i, i-1)$, then the two dynamics are different. Then, given two update schedules Δ, Δ' such that $lab_\Delta((i, i-1)) = lab_{\Delta'}((i, i-1))$ for all $i \in [\![n]\!]$, Lemmas 7 and 8 will respectively give sufficient and necessary conditions for the equality of the two dynamics.

Lemma 6. *Consider two update schedules $\Delta, \Delta' \in \mathcal{P}_n$ for $n \geq 3$. If there exists $i \in [\![n]\!]$ such that $lab_\Delta((i, i-1)) \neq lab_{\Delta'}((i, i-1))$, then $D_{f_{8,n}^{(\Delta)}} \neq D_{f_{8,n}^{(\Delta')}}$.*

Now consider two update schedules Δ, Δ' whose labelings are equal on all *counter-clockwise* arcs (*i.e.*, of the form $(i, i-1)$). Lemma 7 states that, if Δ and Δ' differ only on one arc $(i-1, i)$ such that $lab_\Delta((i+1, i)) = lab_{\Delta'}((i+1, i)) = \ominus$, then the two dynamics are identical. By transitivity, if there are more differences but only on arcs of this form, then the dynamics are also identical.

Lemma 7. *Suppose Δ and Δ' are two update schedules over a configuration of length $n \geq 3$ and there is $i \in [\![n]\!]$ such that*

- $lab_\Delta((i+1, i)) = lab_{\Delta'}((i+1, i)) = \ominus;$
- $lab_\Delta((i-1, i)) \neq lab_{\Delta'}((i-1, i));$
- $lab_\Delta((j_1, j_2)) = lab_{\Delta'}((j_1, j_2))$, *for all* $(j_1, j_2) \neq (i-1, i).$

Then $D_{f_{8,n}^{(\Delta)}} = D_{f_{8,n}^{(\Delta')}}$.

Lemma 8 states that, as soon as Δ and Δ' differ on arcs of the form $(i-1, i)$ such that $lab_\Delta((i+1, i)) = lab_{\Delta'}((i+1, i)) = \oplus$, then the two dynamics are different (remark that in this case we must have $lab_\Delta((i, i-1)) = lab_{\Delta'}((i, i-1)) = \oplus$, otherwise one of Δ or Δ' has an invalid cycle of length two between the nodes $i-1$ and i). This lemma can be applied if at least one cell of the configuration contains the pattern.

Lemma 8. *For* $n \geq 5$, *consider two update schedules* $\Delta, \Delta' \in \mathcal{P}_n$. *If there exists (at least one cell)* $i \in [\![n]\!]$ *such that*

- $lab_\Delta((i+1, i)) = lab_{\Delta'}((i+1, i)) = \oplus;$
- $lab_\Delta((i-1, i)) \neq lab_{\Delta'}((i-1, i));$
- $lab_\Delta((j, j-1)) = lab_{\Delta'}((j, j-1)),$ *for all* $j \in [\![n]\!];$

then $D_{f_{8,n}^{(\Delta)}} \neq D_{f_{8,n}^{(\Delta')}}$.

Lemmas 6, 7 and 8 characterize completely for rule 8 the cases when two update schedules Δ, Δ' lead to the same dynamics (*i.e.*, $\mathcal{D}(f_{8,n}^{(\Delta)}) = \mathcal{D}(f_{8,n}^{(\Delta')})$), or different dynamics (*i.e.*, $\mathcal{D}(f_{8,n}^{(\Delta)}) \neq \mathcal{D}(f_{8,n}^{(\Delta')})$). Indeed, Lemma 6 shows that counting $|\mathcal{D}(f_{8,n})|$ can be partitioned according to the word given by $lab_\Delta((i, i-1))$ for $i \in [\![n]\!]$, and then for each labeling of the n arcs of the form $(i, i-1)$, Lemmas 7 and 8 provide a way of counting the number of dynamics.

Theorem 8. $\mu_s(f_{8,n}) = \frac{\phi^{2n} + \phi^{-2n} - 2^n}{3^n - 2^{n+1} + 2}$ *for any* $n \geq 5$, *with* $\phi = \frac{1+\sqrt{5}}{2}$.

3.4 Class IV: Almost Max-Sensitive Rules

This last class contains three ECA rules, namely 128, 160 and 162, for which the sensitivity function tends to 1. The study of sensitivity to synchronism for these rules is based on the characterization of pairs of update schedule leading to the same dynamics. A pair of update schedules $\Delta, \Delta' \in \mathcal{P}_n$ is *special for rule* α if $\Delta \neq \Delta'$ but $D_{f_{\alpha,n}^{(\Delta)}} = D_{f_{\alpha,n}^{(\Delta')}}$. We will count the special pairs for rules 128 (the reasoning for 160 and 162 is similar). Given an update schedule $\Delta \in \mathcal{P}_n$, define the *left rotation* $\sigma(\Delta)$ and the *left/right exchange* $\rho(\Delta)$, such that, $\forall i \in [\![n]\!]$ it holds that $lab_{\sigma(\Delta)}((i, j)) = lab_\Delta((i+1, j+1))$ and $lab_{\rho(\Delta)}((i, j)) = lab_\Delta((j, i))$. It is clear that if a pair of update schedules $\Delta, \Delta' \in \mathcal{P}_n$ is special then $\sigma(\Delta), \sigma(\Delta')$ is also special. Furthermore, when rule α is left/right symmetric (meaning that $\forall x_1, x_2, x_3 \in \{0, 1\}$ we have $r_\alpha(x_1, x_2, x_3) = r_\alpha(x_3, x_2, x_1)$, which is the case of rules 128 and 162, but not 160) then $\rho(\Delta), \rho(\Delta')$ is also special. We say that special pairs in a set S are *disjoint* when no update schedule belongs to more than one pair *i.e.*, if three update schedules $\Delta, \Delta', \Delta'' \in S$ are such that both (Δ, Δ') and (Δ, Δ'') are special pairs then $\Delta' = \Delta''$. When it is clear from the context, we will omit to mention the rule relative to which some pairs are special.

ECA Rule 128. The Boolean function associated with the ECA rule 128 is $r_{128}(x_1, x_2, x_3) = x_1 \wedge x_2 \wedge x_3$. Its simple definition will allow us to better illustrate the role played by special pairs. When $d_\Delta(i) = [\![n]\!]$ for some cell i, the only possibility to get $f_{128}^{(\Delta)}(x)_i = 1$ is $x = 1^n$. However for $x = 1^n$ we have $f_{128}^{(\Delta)}(x)_i = 1$ for any Δ. The previous remark combined with an observation in the spirit of Lemma 2, gives the next characterization. Let us introduce the notation $d_\Delta = d_{\Delta'}$ for cases in which $d_\Delta(i) = d_{\Delta'}(i)$ holds in every cell $i \in [\![n]\!]$.

Lemma 9. *For any $n \in \mathbb{N}$, choose $\Delta, \Delta' \in \mathcal{P}_n$ such that $\Delta \not\equiv \Delta'$. Then, $d_\Delta = d_{\Delta'}$ if and only if $D_{f_{128,n}^{(\Delta)}} = D_{f_{128,n}^{(\Delta')}}$.*

Lemma 9 characterizes exactly the pairs of non-equivalent update schedules for which the dynamics of rule 128 differ, *i.e.*, the set of special pairs for rule 128, which are the set pairs $\Delta, \Delta' \in \mathcal{P}_n$ such that $\Delta \not\equiv \Delta'$ but $d_\Delta = d_{\Delta'}$. Computing $\mu_s(f_{128,n})$ is now the combinatorial problem of computing the number of possible d_Δ for $\Delta \in \mathcal{P}_n$. However, remark that Lemma 9 does not hold for all rules, since some of them are max-sensitive, even though there exists $\Delta \not\equiv \Delta'$ with $d_\Delta(i) = d_{\Delta'}(i)$ for all $i \in [\![n]\!]$.

We prove that for any $n > 6$, there exist $10n$ disjoint special pairs of schedules of size n (Lemma 12). We first state that special pairs differ in the labeling of exactly one arc (Lemma 11), then establish the existence of $10n$ special pairs of schedules of size n (which come down to five cases up to rotation and left/right exchange) and finally prove that these pairs are disjoint. This gives Theorem 9. These developments make heavy use of the following lemma (see Fig. 3).

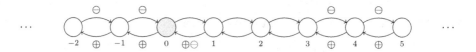

Fig. 3. Illustration of Lemma 10, with Δ in blue and Δ' in red: hypothesis on the labelings of arc $(1,0)$ imply many $\ominus$ (resp. $\oplus$) labels on arcs of the form $(j, j+1)$ (resp. $(j+1, j)$), for Δ. (Color figure online)

Lemma 10. *For any $n \geq 4$, consider a special pair $\Delta, \Delta' \in \mathcal{P}_n$ for rule 128 s. t. $lab_\Delta((i+1,i)) = \oplus$ and $lab_{\Delta'}((i+1,i)) = \ominus$ for some $i \in [\![n]\!]$. For all $j \in [\![n]\!] \setminus \{i, i+1, i+2\}$, it holds that $lab_\Delta((j, j+1)) = \ominus$ and $lab_\Delta((j+1, j)) = \oplus$.*

Lemma 11. *For any $n > 6$, if $\Delta, \Delta' \in \mathcal{P}_n$ is a special pair for rule 128, then Δ and Δ' differ on the labeling of exactly one arc.*

Lemma 12. *For any $n > 6$, there exist $10n$ disjoint special pairs of size n for rule 128.*

As a consequence of Lemma 12 we have $|\{d_\Delta \mid \Delta \in \mathcal{P}_n\}| = 3^n - 2^{n+1} - 10n + 2$ for any $n > 6$, and the result follows from Lemma 9. For the ECA rule 160 (resp., 162) the number of special pairs is $12n$ (resp., n).

Theorem 9. $\mu_s(f_{\alpha,n}) = \frac{3^n - 2^{n+1} - c_\alpha n + 2}{3^n - 2^{n+1} + 2}$ *for any $n > 6$ and $\alpha \in \{128, 160, 162\}$, with $c_{128} = 10$, $c_{160} = 12$ and $c_{162} = 1$.*

4   Conclusion and Perspectives

Asynchrony highly impacts the dynamics of CAs and new original dynamical behaviors are introduced. In this new model, the dynamics become dependent from the update schedule of cells. However, not all schedules produce original dynamics. For this reason, a measure to quantify the sensitivity of ECA *w.r.t* to changes of the update schedule has been introduced in [12]. All ECA rules were then classified into two classes: max-sensitive and non-max sensitive.

This paper provides a finer study of the sensitivity measure *w.r.t* the size of the configurations. Indeed, we found that there are four classes (see Table 1). In particular, it is interesting to remark that the asymptotic behavior is not dichotomic, *i.e.*, the sensitivity function does not always either go to 0 or to 1 when the size of configurations grows. The ECA rule 8 when considered as a classical ECA (*i.e.*, when all cells are updated synchronously) has a very simple dynamical behavior but its asynchronous version has a sensitivity to asynchronism function which tends to $\frac{1+\phi}{3}$ when n tends to infinity (ϕ being the golden ratio). Remark that in the classical case, the limit set of the ECA rule 8 is the same as ECA rule 0 after just two steps. It would be interesting to understand which are the relations between the limit set (both in the classical and in the asynchronous cases) and the sensitivity to asynchronism. Indeed, remark that in our study the sensitivity is defined on one step of the dynamics. It would be interesting to compare how changes the sensitivity function of an ECA when the limit set is considered. This idea has been investigated in works on *block-invariance* [8,9], with the difference that it concentrates only on the set of configurations in attractors, and discards the transitions within these sets.

Remark also that this study focus on block-sequential updating schemes. However, block-parallel update schedules are gaining growing interest [5]. It is a promising research direction to investigate how the sensitivity functions change when block-parallel schedules are considered. Another interesting research direction would consider the generalization of our study to arbitrary CA in order to verify if a finer grained set of classes appear or not. Maybe, the set of possible functions is tightly related to the structure of the neighborhood. Finally, another possible generalization would consider infinite configurations in the spirit of [11]. However, it seems much more difficult to come out with precise asymptotic results in this last case.

Acknowledgments. The work of KP was funded mainly by his salary as a French State agent, affiliated to Aix-Marseille Univ, Univ. de Toulon, CNRS, LIS, France, and to Univ. Côte d'Azur, CNRS, I3S, France, and secondarily by ANR-18-CE40-0002 FANs project, ECOS-Sud C16E01 project, STIC AmSud CoDANet 19-STIC-03 (Campus France 43478PD) project. P.P.B. thanks the Brazilian agencies CAPES and CNPq for the projects CAPES 88881.197456/2018-01, CAPES-Mackenzie PrInt project 88887.310281/2018-00 and CNPq-PQ 305199/2019-6.

References

1. Aracena, J., Fanchon, E., Montalva, M., Noual, M.: Combinatorics on update digraphs in boolean networks. Discr. Appl. Math. **159**(6), 401–409 (2011)
2. Aracena, J., Goles, E., Moreira, A., Salinas, L.: On the robustness of update schedules in boolean networks. Biosystems **97**, 1–8 (2009)

3. Cook, M.: Universality in elementary cellular automata. Complex Syst. **15**(1), 1–40 (2004)

4. de Oliveira, P.P.B ., Formenti, E., Perrot, K., Riva, S., Ruivo, E.L.P.: Non-maximal sensitivity to synchronism in periodic elementary cellular automata: exact asymptotic measures. Preprint on arXiv:2004.07128 (2020)

5. Demongeot, J., Sené, S.: About block-parallel boolean networks: a position paper. Nat. Comput. **19**(1), 5–13 (2020)

6. Fatès, N.: A guided tour of asynchronous cellular automata. J. Cell. Autom. **9**(5–6), 387–416 (2014)

7. Gardner, M.: Mathematical games: the fantastic combinations of John Conway's new solitaire game "Life". Sci. Am. **223**(4), 120–123 (1970)

8. Goles, E., Montalva-Medel, M., Maclean, S., Mortveit, H.S.: Block invariance in a family of elementary cellular automata. J. Cell. Autom. **13**(1–2), 15–32 (2018)

9. Chacc, E.G., Montalva-Medel, M., Mortveit, H.S., Ramírez-Flandes, S.: Block invariance in elementary cellular automata. J. Cell. Autom. **10**(1—-2), 119–135 (2015)

10. Perrot, K., Montalva-Medel, M., de Oliveira, P.P.B., Ruivo, E.L.P.: Maximum sensitivity to update schedule of elementary cellular automata over periodic configurations. Nat. Comput. **19**, 51–90 (2019)

11. Ruivo, E.L.P., de Oliveira, P.P.B., Montalva-Medel, M., Perrot, K.: Maximum sensitivity to update schedules of elementary cellular automata over infinite configurations. Inf. Comput. **274**, 104538 (2019)

12. Ruivo, E.L.P., Montalva-Medel, M., de Oliveira, P.P.B.: Characterisation of the elementary cellular automata in terms of their maximum sensitivity to all possible asynchronous updates. Chaos, Solitons Fractals **113**, 209–220 (2018)

13. Wolfram, S.: A New Kind of Science. Wolfram Media (2002)

Cycle Based Clustering Using Reversible Cellular Automata

Sukanya Mukherjee[1]([✉]), Kamalika Bhattacharjee[2], and Sukanta Das[3]

[1] Department of Computer Science and Engineering, Institute of Engineering and Management, Kolkata 700091, West Bengal, India
sukanya.mukherjee@iemcal.com
[2] Department of Computer Science and Engineering, Indian Institute of Information Technology Ranchi, Ranchi 834010, Jharkhand, India
kamalika.it@gmail.com
[3] Department of Information Technology, Indian Institute of Engineering Science and Technology, Shibpur, Howrah 711103, West Bengal, India
sukanta@it.iiests.ac.in

Abstract. This work proposes cycle based clustering technique using reversible cellular automata (CAs) where 'closeness' among objects is represented as objects belonging to the same cycle, that is *reachable* from each other. The properties of such CAs are exploited for grouping the objects with minimum intra-cluster distance while ensuring that limited number of cycles exist in the configuration-space. The proposed algorithm follows an iterative strategy where the clusters with *closely reachable* objects of previous level are *merged* in the present level using an unique *auxiliary* CA. Finally, it is observed that, our algorithm is at least at par with the best algorithm existing today.

Keywords: Reversible cellular automata · Reachability · Large length cycle · Level-wise clustering · Connectivity · Silhouette score · Dunn index

1 Introduction

Clustering technique [10,12,13] is a well studied research topic when no class information is provided for grouping the available objects (data records) based on some closeness measuring metric. It also exploits the inherent anatomy of data objects for partitioning the dissimilar objects into separate clusters. Till date, a varied collection of well accepted algorithms for clustering [10,12] have been developed. Such clustering techniques aim to gather alike data objects for producing 'good' clusters where intra-cluster and inter-cluster isolation, based on feature space should be lower and higher respectively. Maintaining less intra-cluster distance between any two objects intrinsically means the alike objects are *interconnected*. This interconnectivity in clustering motivates us to use cellular automata (CAs) as *natural* clusters.

© IFIP International Federation for Information Processing 2020
Published by Springer Nature Switzerland AG 2020. All Rights Reserved
H. Zenil (Ed.): AUTOMATA 2020, LNCS 12286, pp. 29–42, 2020.
https://doi.org/10.1007/978-3-030-61588-8_3

In a cellular automaton (CA), the configurations within a cycle are *reachable* from one another, whereas the configurations of different cycles are *not-reachable*. Moreover, the *locality* property of CA influences that the *related* configurations are reachable. This 'reachability' is the key of clustering using CA as reachable configurations form cycle(s). Therefore, CA can act as a function that maintains bijective mapping among the configurations which are reachable or connected and gathers similar objects (configurations) into same cluster (cycle). This work reports reversible non-uniform CAs as the proposed model, where each configuration x (object) is reachable (connected) from the remaining configurations of that cycle (cluster) where x belongs to. Hereafter, if not otherwise mentioned, by a 'CA', we shall mean a reversible non-uniform CA under null-boundary condition which uses Wolfram's rules [11].

Ideally, a CA of size n can distribute 2^n configurations among m cycles where m ranges from 1 to 2^n. To an extreme degree, a CA based clustering can attract all target objects in one cluster or distribute among m clusters where the count of target objects is m ($\leq 2^n$) – both of which are not desirable for good clustering. Therefore, a CA is said to be *effective* for clustering if it can distribute the target objects among a *limited number of clusters*. This limited number of clusters is not necessarily the only primary objective for efficient CA based clustering – the feature based distances among the reachable configurations of each cluster should also be as minimum as possible. So, clustering can be viewed as an optimization problem where there is a trade-off between these two facets.

To incorporate this idea in CA based clustering technique, this work proposes an intelligent *arrangement* of CA rules for generating an n-cell *candidate* CA which is capable of maintaining less intra-cluster distance among objects and generates limited number of cycles. (Here, n is determined based on the number of features owned by the target objects which is always finite.) For ensuring that this CA has limited number of cycles, we use the framework of a related problem – CA with large cycles (introduced in [1]). However, to guarantee that for the candidate CA, the configurations inside a cycle maintain minimum possible *hamming distance* (as binary CA is considered for this research), we propose a scheme to select *significant* rules which contribute minimum change in cell's state value when transition occurs between configurations (Sect. 3.2). Next, the *proportion* of such significant rules for designing an n-cell (*non-uniform*) CA for clustering is evaluated to ensure optimal number of clusters (Sect. 3.3).

Definitely, generating a CA for a fixed n maintaining less intra-cluster distance and limited number of clusters is a very challenging problem; even if the desired number of clusters is given, it is difficult to determine the corresponding CA which can produce *good* clusters for the given dataset. The inherent hardness of this problem motivates us to take an iterative strategy which distributes the target objects in m clusters. In the proposed algorithm, the clusters of level i are generated by *merging* a set of clusters of level $i-1$ which are *closely reachable* (Sect. 4). To measure the quality (goodness) of clusters, some benchmark *cluster validation indices* (internal) [2] are used. Section 5 presents the performance analysis of our proposed cycle based clustering algorithm on some real datasets taken from ML repository (http://archive.ics.uci.edu/ml/index.php). Finally, we compare our proposed algorithm with some traditional benchmark clustering algorithms like *centroid based clusterings, hierarchical clusterings* [2,12]. Our results indicate that, performance of our CA-based clustering technique is at least as good as the best known clustering algorithm existing today.

2   Basics of CAs

In this work, we use one-dimensional three-neighborhood n-cell CAs under null boundary condition, where each cell takes any of the states $S = \{0, 1\}$. The next state of each cell is updated following an *elementary cellular automaton* (ECA) rule. The present state of all cells at a given time is called the *configuration* of the CA. Thus, evolution of a CA is determined by a *global transition function* G such that $G : C \rightarrow C$ where $C = \{0, 1\}^n$ represents the configuration space. Hence, if the next configuration of $\mathbf{x} = (x_i)_{\forall i \in n}$ is $\mathbf{y}$, then $\mathbf{y} = G(\mathbf{x})$ where $\mathbf{x}, \mathbf{y} \in C$, $\mathbf{y} = (y_i)_{\forall i \in n}$ and x_i, y_i are the present and next state values of cells i respectively. Therefore, $y_i = \mathcal{R}_i(x_{i-1}, x_i, x_{i+1})$ where $\mathcal{R}_i$ is the rule corresponding to cell i and x_{i-1}, x_i, x_{i+1} is the *neighborhood combination* for cell i. This neighborhood combination is named as the *Rule Min Term* (RMT) and represented by its decimal equivalent $r = 2^2 \times x_{i-1} + 2^1 \times x_i + x_{i+1}$. A *rule vector* $\mathcal{R} = (\mathcal{R}_0, \mathcal{R}_1, \cdots, \mathcal{R}_{n-1})$ of length n is used to represent any arbitrary n-cell non-uniform CA, where $\mathcal{R}_i \neq \mathcal{R}_j$ for some i and j.

Table 1. An 4-cell CA $(9, 150, 45, 65)$.

Present state	111	110	101	100	011	010	001	000	Rule
(i) Next state	i	i	i	i	1	0	0	1	$9(\mathcal{R}_0)$
(ii) Next state	1	0	0	1	0	1	1	0	$150(\mathcal{R}_1)$
(iii) Next state	0	0	1	0	1	1	0	1	$45(\mathcal{R}_2)$
(iv) Next state	i	1	i	0	i	0	i	1	$65(\mathcal{R}_3)$

Let us now present the rules in tabular form (see Table 1). Obviously, there are $2^8 = 256$ distinct rules. These rules are traditionally named by their decimal equivalents. Since we are using null boundary condition, $x_{-1} = x_n = 0$. Therefore, for the first cell, $y_0 = \mathcal{R}_0(0, x_0, x_1)$, and for the last cell, $y_{n-1} = \mathcal{R}_{n-1}(x_{n-2}, x_{n-1}, 0)$. So, for each of these terminal cells, only $2^4 = 16$ distinct rules are considered as valid. For these rules, next state values for the present states $(1, x_0, x_1)$ and $(x_{n-2}, x_{n-1}, 1)$ respectively, are undefined and marked as *invalid* (i) (see, for example, first row of Table 1).

In a CA, if $\mathcal{R}_i(x_{i-1}x_ix_{i+1}) = x_i$, the corresponding RMT of rule $\mathcal{R}_i$ is called a *self-replicating* RMT. If all RMTs of a configuration $\mathbf{x}$ is self-replicating, then its next configuration $\mathbf{y}$ is *identical* to it and they form *a cycle of length one*. The number of self replicating RMTs for a rule plays a major role in cycle formation

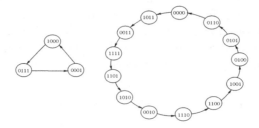

Fig. 1. Transition diagram of the 4-cell reversible CA $(9, 150, 45, 65)$.

– number of cycles and lengths of cycles. Let $C_i \subseteq C = \{0, 1\}^n$ be a set of configurations such that $G^l(\mathbf{x}) = \mathbf{x}$, $\forall \mathbf{x} \in C_i$, where $l \in \mathbb{N}$ and $|C_i| = l$. Then, all configurations $\mathbf{x} \in C_i$ are *cyclic* and *reachable* from each other. The set of l configurations which forms a single cycle is named as a *cycle space*. So, C_i is a cycle space of the CA. For instance, in Fig. 1, the configurations 1000, 0111 and 0001 are reachable from one another as they form a cycle space of length 3. A CA is called *reversible*, if all configurations are part of some cycle. Fig. 1 represents a reversible CA. Therefore, configuration space of a CA can be represented as a collection of cycle spaces.

To synthesize an n-cell reversible CAs, we use the methodology described in [4]. For ease of reference, the table describing the class information of the participating rule $\mathcal{R}_i$, $0 \le i \le n - 1$, is reproduced here (see Table 2). The generation of an n-cell reversible CA is guided by the rule of cell i and the class information of the rule of cell $i + 1$ (see [4] for more details). The following example illustrates the process of synthesis.

Example 1. Let us design a 4-cell reversible CA. To select an arbitrary $\mathcal{R}_0$, the first column of Table 2(b) is taken into consideration. Let rule 9 be selected as $\mathcal{R}_0$ from Table 2(b) (the third row and first column of Table 2(b)). As the class information of the next rule of rule 9 is class III (the second column and third row of Table 2(b)), therefore, $\mathcal{R}_1$ is to be anyone from the pool of CA rules of class III from Table 2(a). Let rule 150 be chosen as $\mathcal{R}_1$ (the first column of Table 2(a) for rule 150 is class III). Now, the third column and the row corresponding to rule 150 in Table 2(a) is class II, therefore, $\mathcal{R}_2$ is to be selected from class II from Table 2(a). By repeating the same process, let us choose $\mathcal{R}_2$ as 45. Therefore, the class information for rule $\mathcal{R}_3$ is class I. However, as, this is the last rule, we need to select this rule from Table 2(c). Let $\mathcal{R}_3$ is 65 (second column and first row of Table 2(c)). Therefore, the reversible CA is $(9, 150, 45, 65)$ (see Fig. 1).

3   The Mapping Between CA and Clustering

This section introduces how an n-cell reversible CA can be used for clustering problem with k target objects having p distinct features. As binary CA is to be used as a tool, each target object needs to be mapped to a *configuration*. To do that, *data discretization* should be done *effectively*.

3.1   The Encoding Technique

Let $\mathbb{X} = \{X_1, X_2, \cdots, X_k\}$ be the set of target objects which are to be distributed among m clusters and $A_1, A_2, \cdots, A_p$ are p distinct attributes (features) of the objects where each A_j is a quantifiable property. This A_j is a finite set depicting the range of values of each feature has. To measure closeness among the target objects using hamming distance [12], each object (X) is converted into a binary string x (where $x \in \{0,1\}^n$ and $n \in \mathbb{N}$). Now, let $X = (x^1 x^2 \cdots x^p)$ where $x^j \in A_j$.

If A_j is *continuous* attribute, the range can be partitioned into v disjoint subsets $A_{j1}, A_{j2}, \cdots, A_{jv}$ such that $A_{j1} \cap A_{j2} \cap \cdots \cap A_{jv} = \emptyset$. Using *frequency based* encoding [5] for each A_j, let the encoding function be $M : A_j \mapsto A_j^{-1}$, where A_j^{-1} is a finite set of discretized elements. Here, M is *surjective* and $|A_j| \ll |A_j^1|$. As we use binary CA, therefore, $A_j^{-1} \in \{0,1\}^i$ (where $i > 1$). In this work, we consider $v = 3$, that is, three intervals, so, two bit representation is needed to maintain a *minimum* hamming distance. Therefore, $A_j^{-1} \subset \{0,1\}^2$; we use binary strings 00, 01 and 11 to refer the intervals $[a_1, a_s]$, $[a_{s+1}, a_w]$ and $[a_{w+1}, a_t]$ respectively, where $a_1 < a_s < a_{s+1} < a_w < a_{w+1} < a_t$. However, if A_j is *categorical* attribute, then the length of the substring for encoding each element of A_j is $\log_2 u$ where $|A_j| = u$ and each element of A_j is represented as a way where there is only one 1 at some unique position. Therefore, the hamming

Table 2. Rules to generate a Reversible CA.

Class of $\mathcal{R}_i$	$\mathcal{R}_i$	Class of $\mathcal{R}_{i+1}$
I	51, 204, 60, 195	I
	85, 90, 165, 170	II
	102, 105, 150, 153	III
	53, 58, 83, 92, 163, 172, 197, 202	IV
	54, 57, 99, 108, 147, 156, 198, 201	V
	86, 89, 101, 106, 149, 154, 166, 169	VI
II	15, 30, 45, 60, 75, 90, 105, 120, 135, 150, 165, 180, 195, 210, 225, 240	I
III	51, 204, 15, 240	I
	85, 105, 150, 170	II
	90, 102, 153, 165	III
	23, 43, 77, 113, 142, 178, 212, 232	IV
	27, 39, 78, 114, 141, 177, 216, 228	V
	86, 89, 101, 106, 149, 154, 166, 169	VI
IV	60, 195	I
	90, 165	IV
	105, 150	V
V	51, 204	I
	85, 170	II
	102, 153	III
	86, 89, 90, 101, 105, 106, 149, 150, 154, 165, 166, 169	VI
VI	15, 240	I
	105, 150	IV
	90, 165	V

(a) Class relationship of $\mathcal{R}_i$ and $\mathcal{R}_{i+1}$

Rules for $\mathcal{R}_0$	Class of $\mathcal{R}_1$
3, 12	I
5, 10	II
6, 9	III

(b) First Rule Table

Rule class for $\mathcal{R}_{n-1}$	Rule set for $\mathcal{R}_{n-1}$
I	17, 20, 65, 68
II	5, 20, 65, 80
III	5,17, 68, 80
IV	20, 65
V	17, 68
VI	5, 80

(c) Last Rule Table

Table 3. Encoding a set of hypothetical books into CA configurations

#Object	Continuous attribute				Categorical attribute		Encoded CA configuration
	#Pages	Encoding	Ratings	Encoding	Binding type	Encoding	
1	300	01	9	11	Hard	01	011101
2	325	11	8	11	Soft	10	111110
3	40	00	9.5	11	Soft	10	001110
4	200	01	4	00	Hard	01	010001
5	129	01	4.5	01	Soft	10	010110
6	65	00	7	01	Hard	01	000101
7	319	11	6.8	01	Soft	10	110110
8	110	00	3	00	Soft	10	000010
9	400	11	2.6	00	Soft	10	110010
10	350	11	9.3	11	Soft	10	111110

distance between any pair of elements for such qualitative A_j is always fixed i.e. *two*. At a glance, to convert a target object with p features (where p_{q_n} and p_{q_l} are the count of quantitative and qualitative attributes [10]) into a configuration of n-cell CA, the following mechanism is considered: For each quantitative attribute, as *two* bits are used, therefore, $n = (2 * p_{q_n}) + (u_1 + u_2 + \cdots + u_{p_{q_l}})$. If all attributes are quantitative, then $n = 2 * p_{q_n}$.

Example 2. Let us take a hypothetical set of *books*, where each book is identified by three attributes – *number of pages, ratings by reviewers* and *type of binding*. The first two attributes are *continuous* whereas, the last one is categorical. Table 3 shows the detailed encoding scheme for ten such objects into CA configurations.

Here, the categorical attribute values are encoded as 01 (hard) or 10 (soft). Whereas, the continuous attribute values are divided into three sub-intervals to be represented by 00, 01 and 11 respectively. For example, values in *Ratings* are divided into sub-intervals $[2.6, 4]$, $[4.5, 7]$ and $[8, 9.5]$ depicted by 00, 01 and 11 respectively. Therefore, each object is mapped to a 6-bit string which can be shown as a configurations of a 6-cell CA.

Hence, using the encoding function M, the set of target objects ($\mathbb{X}$) is mapped to the configurations $C = \{0, 1\}^n$ of an n-cell CA. This work also supports *hard clustering* [3,10] where each target object is assigned to a fixed cluster. Next, the significance of CA rules in designing the desired clusters is depicted.

3.2   CA Rules to Maintain Minimum Intra-cluster Distance

For our present objective, we need to select such rules where minimum changes occur during state transition. Ideally, it means all RMTs of any configuration is *self-replicating*. The intrinsic property of such an n-cell CA is that each cell follows a special rule where *all* RMTs are *self replicating* - this is rule 204. However, this CA is not *effective* as number of clusters is 2^n. Therefore, we have to restrict on the count of self-replicating RMTs for any configuration. If CA size is n, it is expected that more number of cycles possess configuration pairs that maintains as minimum as possible hamming distances, which eventually leads to enrich preservation of less intra-cluster distance. To detect such *significant* rules, we rank each rule of Table 2 based on the number of self replicating RMTs it possesses when used in designing the rule vector of a reversible CA. If all 8 RMTs (resp. the 4 valid RMTs, if used in cell 0 or cell $n-1$) are self-replicating, the rule is *ranked* 1. Similarly, a CA rule is *ranked* 2, 3, 4 or 5 depending on whether it possess 6, 4 (resp. 2 for cells 0 and $n-1$), 2 or 0 self-replicating RMTs respectively. Table 4 shows this ranking. This *rank* determines how a rule can act as an influencing factor for designing a cluster with more similar (less hamming distance) data.

Evidently, rule 204 is ranked *first* (8 self-replicating RMTs), but as it is already mentioned, if rule 204 is applied to every cell of an n-cell CA, then each target object belongs to an unique cycle which is not desirable for clustering. Similarly, rule 51 is the *least significant* rule for clustering (no self-replicating RMTs), as, for an n-cell CA with rule 51 as the only rule, each cluster consists of a pair of configuration with hamming distance n. Therefore, we need to select rule 204 for as many cells as possible and just opposite strategy should be used for rule 51. However, CAs with only rules 204 and 51 are not *effective* for clustering. Hence, to design clusters of objects with less intra-cluster distance, we take the following strategy of choosing rules for synthesizing a reversible CA:

1. *Discard all rules with Rank 4 and 5 (that is, less than 4 self-replicating RMTs) from Table 2.* **Seventeen** *rules (51, 53, 58, 83, 163, 54, 57, 99, 147, 23, 43, 113, 178, 27, 39, 114, 177) are discarded by this condition. Therefore, currently, the rule space is reduced to 45.*
2. *For the $n-2$ non-terminal cell positions (cell 1 to cell $n-2$), at most 50% rules with rank 2 (6 self-replicating RMTs) are to be selected.*

If we process in this way, the configurations with lesser hamming distances are placed on the same cycle. However, this scheme can not restrict the number of cycles. Next, we focus on the design of CA with limited number of cycles.

3.3 Designing CA with Optimal Number of Clusters

From the above discussion, it is obvious that, the consecutive configurations of a cycle maintain minimum distance in feature space if *more* significant rules are used in an n-cell CA. That is, the same cycle connects alike objects. However, it may increase the number of cycles. So, there is a trade-off between these two aspects of clustering technique - maintaining less number of cycles (clusters) and less intra-cluster distance among the objects, that is, configurations with less hamming distances are in the same cycle. In this section, we discuss a technique to generate CAs with limited number of cycles, that is, more configurations are to be placed on the same cycle. This requirement matches with an existing problem statement, *generation of large cycle CA*, already studied in [1]. For ease of understanding, we briefly recall the idea.

Table 4. Categories of reversible CA rules on the parameter P.

Category	$\mathcal{R}_i$	Rank
Completely Dependent	90, 165, 150, 105	3
Partially Dependent	30, 45, 75, 120, 135, 180, 210, 225, 86, 89, 101, 106, 149, 154, 166, 169	3
Weakly Dependent	92,172, 197, 202, 108, 156, 198, 201, 77, 142, 212, 232, 78, 141, 216, 228,	2
	53, 58, 83, 163, 54, 57, 99, 147, 23, 43, 113, 178, 27, 39, 114, 177	4
Independent	51,	5
	85, 170, 102, 153, 60, 195, 15, 240	3
	204	1

(a) Categories of reversible CA rules

Category	$\mathcal{R}_0$	Rank	$\mathcal{R}_{n-1}$	Rank
Completely Dependent	5, 6, 9, 10	3	5, 20, 65, 80	3
Independent	3,	5	17,	5
	12	1	68	1

(b) Categories of $\mathcal{R}_0$ and $\mathcal{R}_{n-1}$

A CA is expected to have a cycle of large length, if its rules are dependent on both of the left and right neighbors. To measure this dependence, a *parameter* (P), called *degree of dependence on both the neighbors*, is defined which determines how much a cell is dependent on its neighbors for updating its state. For a rule $\mathcal{R}_i$, $P(\mathcal{R}_i) = P_r(\mathcal{R}_i) * P_l(\mathcal{R}_i)$. Here, $P_r(\mathcal{R}_i)$ (resp. $P_l(\mathcal{R}_i)$) is the *degree of right (resp. left) dependence*, defined as the ratio of the number of combinations of values of x_i and x_{i-1} (resp. x_{i+1}) for which the next state function on x_i depends on x_{i-1} (resp. x_{i+1}). Evidently, $P(\mathcal{R}_i)$ can take values 0, 0.25, 0.5 or 1. Based on these values, the rules of reversible CAs are classified into *four* categories – *completely dependent* (P = 1), *partially dependent* (P = 0.5), *weakly dependent* (P = 0.25) and *independent* (P = 0) (see Table 4). It is observed that in a CA with large cycle(s), majority of the participating rules are from the *completely dependent* category, some are from the *partially dependent* category and a few are from the category of *weakly dependent*, whereas, none are from the *Independent* category. For more detailed discussion, please see [1].

Obviously, following the strategy mentioned in Sect. 3.2, sixteen rules from *weakly dependent* category and all rules from *independent* categories are rejected for clustering purpose as they produce more pair of configurations with high hamming distances. The remaining sixteen rules of *weakly dependent* category have *rank* 2, whereas, the rules of *completely dependent* and *partially dependent* categories have *rank* 3. In the following section, our proposed clustering technique, cycle based clustering using these CAs, is described in detail.

4   Cycle Based Clustering

Generating an n-cell CA with large number of cycles having less intra-cluster distance is itself a very challenging problem. Moreover, even if desired number of clusters are generated, then also it is difficult to ascertain that the produced clusters are *good* for the given dataset. To deal with this issue, this section describes a CAs based iterative algorithm which efficiently generates *desired* number of *good* clusters.

In this algorithm, more than one CA can participate in designing the clusters for a given dataset. However, any arbitrary CA is not *acceptable* as candidate; such CAs need to maintain the necessary conditions described in Sect. 3. Therefore, in our CA based clustering approach, the following characteristics are to be maintained:

- **Property 1**: Participating CA of size n maintains rules at all cells from a subset of *rank 3* and at most *one* rule from *rank 2*.
- **Property 2**: Our technique *converges* by *merging* the clusters. To do that, a hierarchy of levels has to be maintained.
- **Property 3**: Only *closely reachable* clusters of level $i - 1$ are to be merged to generate the updated clusters of level i.

Let $M(\mathbb{X})$ be the set of *encoded* target objects where $M(\mathbb{X}) \subset C$ and $\mathbb{X} = \{X_1, X_2, \cdots, X_k\}$ is the set of target objects. These encoded target objects are named as *target configurations*. Let $|M(\mathbb{X})| = k'$ where $k' \leq k$. At any level, a target configuration $\mathbf{x} \in M(\mathbb{X})$ is member of a distinct cluster $\mathbf{c}$ (a set of encoded target objects) such that $|\bigcup c| = |M(\mathbb{X})|$.

Let m_i be the number of *primary* clusters at level i. For level 0, the primary clusters are $c_1^0, c_2^0, \cdots, c_{m_0}^0$, where each cluster is a singleton set. Therefore, $k' = m_0$. In general, for any level i, the primary clusters are $c_1^i, c_2^i, \cdots, c_{m_i}^i$. To form these primary clusters of level i from level $i - 1$, a CA of size n is selected *uniformly random without replacement* from a pool of candidate CAs maintaining **property 1**. This process is maintained at every level i. Such a CA is named as an *auxiliary* CA. This CA plays a major role in clustering. Firstly, it is needed to compute the number of *auxiliary clusters* of such a CA, in which the *target* configurations (k') *strictly belong to*.

Definition 1. *Let x be a target configuration and $G : C \mapsto C$ be an auxiliary CA. If $x \in C_j$ where $C_j \subset C$ is a cycle space of G, then x strictly belongs to the auxiliary cluster C_j.*

Let the target configurations *strictly belong* to m' number of *auxiliary* clusters $C_1^i, C_2^i, \cdots, C_{m'}^i$ of level i. Our *second* step is to follow **property 2**, that is, *merging* the primary clusters $c_1^{i-1}, c_2^{i-1}, \cdots, c_{m_0}^{i-1}$ of level $i - 1$ using these auxiliary clusters to get the resultant primary clusters of level i where $m_i \leq m_{i-1}$. However, these clusters can not be merged arbitrarily; a pair of primary clusters can be merged depending on their *degree of membership of participation*.

Definition 2. *Let c_j^{i-1} be a primary cluster of level $i - 1$ where $|c_j^{i-1}| = v_j$. Let C_t^i be an auxiliary cluster of level i. The degree of membership of participation of c_j^{i-1} in C_t^i, denoted by $\mu(C_t^i, c_j^{i-1})$, is defined as the availability of configurations of c_j^{i-1} in C_t^i. It is computed as v'_j / v_j where v'_j refers to the count of target configurations from primary cluster c_j^{i-1} in auxiliary cluster C_t^i.*

The configurations of $c_j{}^{i-1}$ can *strictly belong to* more than one auxiliary cluster. Similarly, C_t^i can possess target configurations from different clusters of level $i-1$. Let $c_1{}^{i-1}$ and $c_j{}^{i-1}$ be two primary clusters of level $i-1$. These two clusters may be merged if they are necessarily *closely reachable* (**property 3**).

Definition 3. *Let $c_j{}^{i-1}$, $c_1{}^{i-1}$ and $c_s{}^{i-1}$ be the clusters whose members strictly belong to C_t^i. Now, clusters $c_j{}^{i-1}$ and $c_1{}^{i-1}$ are said to be* closely reachable *in C_t^i if $|(\mu(C_t^i, c_j{}^{i-1}) - \mu(C_t^i, c_1{}^{i-1}))| < |(\mu(C_t^i, c_j{}^{i-1}) - (\mu(C_t^i, c_s{}^{i-1}))|$.*

Therefore, for every C_t^i, we can get pairs of closely reachable clusters. The *degree of participation* plays a vital role for selecting the closely reachable clusters which are then merged. Next, we discuss the algorithm in detail.

1. Let $c_1{}^0, c_2{}^0, \cdots, c_{m_0}{}^0$ (resp. $c_1{}^{i-1}, c_2{}^{i-1}, \cdots, c_{m_{i-1}}{}^{i-1}$) be the primary clusters of level 0 (resp. $i-1$) where the count of clusters is m_0 (resp. m_{i-1}). Also let $C_1^1, C_2^1, \cdots, C_{m'}^1$ (resp. $C_1^i, C_2^i, \cdots, C_{m'}^i$) be the auxiliary clusters of level 1 (resp. i) where the count of auxiliary clusters is m'. For all t, $1 \le t \le m'$, compute $\mu(C_t^1, c_j{}^0)$ (resp. $\mu(C_t^i, c_j{}^{i-1})$). For any given $c_j{}^0$ (resp. $c_j{}^{i-1}$), find the auxiliary cluster of level 1 (resp. i) in which it has *maximum* participation, that is, its *degree of participation* is maximum. Obviously, for some value of t, maximum participation of $c_j{}^0$ (resp. $c_j{}^{i-1}$) is in C_t^1 (resp. C_t^i).
2. Let $C_{t_1}^1$ (resp. $C_{t_1}^i$) be the auxiliary cluster having maximum configurations belonging from $c_j{}^0$ (resp. $c_j{}^{i-1}$). Therefore, $c_j{}^0$ (resp. $c_j{}^{i-1}$) can merge with some of the clusters which have also participated in $C_{t_1}^1$ (resp. $C_{t_1}^i$). However, only those clusters are to be merged with $c_j{}^0$ (resp. $c_j{}^{i-1}$), which are closely reachable to $c_j{}^0$ (resp. $c_j{}^{i-1}$). Hence, a new primary cluster $c_j{}^1$ (resp. $c_j{}^i$) is formed as $c_j{}^i = c_j{}^{i-1} \cup c_1{}^{i-1}$ if and only if $|(\mu(C_{t_1}^i, c_j{}^{i-1}) - \mu(C_{t_1}^i, c_1{}^{i-1}))| < |(\mu(C_{t_1}^i, c_j{}^{i-1}) - \mu(C_{t_1}^i, c_s{}^{i-1}))|$, for any $s \ne l$ where $c_s{}^{i-1}$ is another participating cluster in $C_{t_1}^i$ and $max\{\mu(C_t^i, c_j{}^{i-1})_{(\forall t)}\} = \mu(C_{t_1}^i, c_j{}^{i-1})$. Therefore, the newly generated cluster $c_j{}^i$ constitutes of a set of target configurations, out of which some strictly belongs to a cluster (cycle) of the auxiliary CA of level i. This instigates to name our approach as *cycle based clustering*.
3. If for any primary cluster $c_j{}^0$ (resp. $c_j{}^{i-1}$), there is no closely reachable primary cluster in all auxiliary clusters, then the new primary cluster of level i is $c_j{}^i = c_j{}^{i-1}$. Therefore, $m_i \le m_{i-1}$.
4. The algorithm stops when we reach the *optimal* number of clusters (m). The test of optimality is determined either by arriving at the desired number of clusters given by user or if $m_i = m_{i-1}$ after a fixed number of attempts.

Algorithm 1: Cycle based clustering algorithm

Input : A set of target objects $\mathbb{X} = \{X_1, X_2, \cdots, X_k\}$, number of quantitative and qualitative attributes p_{q_n} and p_{q_l} respectively, optimal number of clusters (m) and an auxiliary CA space of size w

Output: The clusters $\{c_1{}^v, c_2{}^v, \cdots, c_m{}^v\}$ where $c_1{}^v \cup c_2{}^v \cup \cdots \cup c_m{}^v = \mathbb{X}$

Step 1 Set $n \leftarrow (2 * p_{q_n}) + (u_1 + u_2 + \cdots + u_{p_{q_l}})$;

    foreach $j = 1$ to k **do** *Encode* X_j into an n-bit binary string Let $M(\mathbb{X})$ be the set of *encoded* target objects $\{x_1, x_2, \cdots, x_{k'}\}$ where $|M(\mathbb{X})| = k'$;

Step 2 Construct a set of n-cell CAs R from the given auxiliary CA space ;

Step 3 Set $m_0 \leftarrow k'$, $i \leftarrow 1$ and $z \leftarrow 1$;

    for $j = 1$ to m_0 **do**

        ⌊ Set $c_j{}^0 \leftarrow \{x_j\}$; // Initialize primary clusters of level 0

Step 4 **while** $(m_i \neq m_{i-1}) || (m_i \neq m)$ **do**

        Select $\mathcal{R} \in$ R and Set R $\leftarrow$ R $\setminus \{\mathcal{R}\}$ // Auxiliary CA is selected randomly at uniform without replacement

        Generate auxiliary clusters $C_1^i, C_2^i, \cdots, C_{m'}^i$ for the CA $\mathcal{R}$;

        Initialize a matrix $A[a_{tj}]_{m' \times m_{i-1}}$ to 0;

        for $t = 1$ to m' **do**

            ⌊ **for** $j = 1$ to m_{i-1} **do** Set $a_{tj} \leftarrow \mu(C_t^i, c_j{}^{i-1})$

        foreach $j = 1$ to m_{i-1} **do**

            // For each of the primary clusters of previous level

            Let $a_{t'j}$ = maximum of a_{tj} where $1 \leq t \leq m'$; // Find the auxiliary cluster with maximum participation of $c_j{}^{i-1}$

            for $(j_1 = 1$ to $m_{i-1}) \&\&(j_1 \neq j)$ **do**

                ⌊ Find $a_{t'j'}$ = maximum of a_{tj_1} such that $a_{t'j'} \neq 0$;

            if *no such* $a_{t'j'}$ *exists* **then**   *continue*

            else

                | Set $c_z{}^i \leftarrow c_j{}^{i-1} \cup c_{j'}{}^{i-1}$ and $z \leftarrow z + 1$;

                | Mark $c_j{}^{i-1}$ and $c_{j'}{}^{i-1}$ as *modified* ;

            Remove row t' from A;

        foreach unmodified *clusters* $c_y{}^{i-1}$ **do**

            Set $c_z{}^i \leftarrow c_y{}^{i-1}$ and $z \leftarrow z + 1$; // move the unmodified primary cluster(s) of previous level $i1$ to get a new primary cluster of level i and update cluster number

        Set $m_i \leftarrow z$ and $i \leftarrow i + 1$;

Step 5 Report $c_1{}^i, c_2{}^i, \cdots, c_{m_i}{}^i$ as the final clusters at level i and *Exit* ;

Example 3. Let us consider the Iris dataset (http://archive.ics.uci.edu/ml/index.php, see Table 5) where $\mathbb{X} = \{X_1, X_2, \cdots, X_{150}\}$ and each object has four quantitative (p_{q_n}) and no qualitative attributes (p_{q_l}). Hence, size of the CA for this data set is $n = 2 * 4 = 8$. Now, let the desired number of clusters (m) is **two**. Using the encoding technique, we get $M(\mathbb{X}) = \{x_1, x_2, \cdots, x_{24}\}$.

Initially, at level 0, there exist **twenty four** primary clusters such that $c_1{}^0 = \{x_1\}, c_2{}^0 = \{x_2\}, \cdots, c_{24}{}^0 = \{x_{24}\}$, where $m_0 = 24$. As $m_0 \neq m$, we select an auxiliary CA $\mathcal{R}$ from the set of candidate CAs (satisfying **Property 1**) uniformly random without replacement. Let $\mathcal{R} = (9, 169, 150, 150, 165, 105, 165, 20)$. This CA generates **four** auxiliary clusters - $C_1^0, C_2^0, C_3^0, C_4^0$. Next, we find the degree of participation of each $c_j{}^0$ in these clusters. As we are at level 1, $\mu(C_1^1, c_{j_1}{}^0) = 100\%$ $(\forall j_1 \in \{1, 3, 4, 22, 13, 14\})$, $\mu(C_2^1, c_{j_2}{}^0) = 100\%$ $(\forall j_2 \in \{2, 5, 6, 7, 8, 9, 10, 11, 12, 15, 17, 19, 20, 21, 23, 24\})$, $\mu(C_3^1, c_{16}{}^0) = 100\%$

Table 5. Description of real datasets used for cycle based clustering.

Name	# of p	# of p_{q_n}	# of p_{q_l}	# of target objects	CA size (n)
Iris	4	4	0	150	8
BuddyMove	6	6	0	249	12
Wholesale Customers	8	6	2	440	16
Seed	7	7	0	210	14

and $\mu(C_4^1, c_{18}{}^0) = 100\%$. So, we can merge the closely reachable primary clusters of level 0 to form the primary clusters of level 1. Here, auxiliary cluster C_1^1 has maximum (and equal) participation of primary clusters $c_1{}^0$, $c_3{}^0$, $c_4{}^0$, $c_{22}{}^0$, $c_{13}{}^0$ and $c_{14}{}^0$. Similarly, C_2^1 has maximum participation of $c_2{}^0$, $c_5{}^0$, $c_6{}^0$, $c_7{}^0$, $c_8{}^0$, $c_9{}^0$, $c_{10}{}^0$, $c_{11}{}^0$, $c_{12}{}^0$, $c_{15}{}^0$, $c_{17}{}^0$, $c_{19}{}^0$, $c_{20}{}^0$, $c_{21}{}^0$, $c_{23}{}^0$ and $c_{24}{}^0$. Therefore, the newly generated primary cluster of level 1 is $c_1{}^1 = c_1{}^0 \cup c_3{}^0 \cup c_4{}^0 \cup c_{22}{}^0 \cup c_{13}{}^0 \cup c_{14}{}^0$. Similarly, $c_2{}^1$ can be generated. For the remaining two auxiliary clusters, new primary clusters are formed as $c_3{}^1 = c_{16}{}^0$ and $c_4{}^1 = c_{18}{}^0$. As, the number of primary clusters at level 1 (m_1) is $4 \neq m$, we move from level 1 to level 2.

Let, at level 2, the selected auxiliary CA is $(6, 232, 90, 90, 165, 90, 90, 20)$. This CA generates **six** auxiliary clusters C_1^2, C_2^2, C_3^2, C_4^2, C_5^2 and C_6^2. Like level 1, here also, we compute the maximum participation of each primary cluster of level 1 in auxiliary cluster C_t^2, $(1 \leq t \leq 6)$. It is found that $\mu(C_1^2, c_1{}^1) = 16\%$, $\mu(C_2^2, c_1{}^1) = 33\%$, $\mu(C_2^2, c_2{}^1) = 62\%$, $\mu(C_2^2, c_3{}^1) = 100\%$, $\mu(C_3^2, c_1{}^1) = 16\%$, $\mu(C_3^2, c_2{}^1) = 12\%$, $\mu(C_3^2, c_4{}^1) = 100\%$, $\mu(C_4^2, c_1{}^1) = 33\%$, $\mu(C_5^2, c_2{}^1) = 18\%$ and $\mu(C_6^2, c_2{}^1) = 6\%$. Hence, we can merge $c_2{}^1$ and $c_3{}^1$ with respect to the closeness in the auxiliary cluster C_2^2. Similarly, $c_1{}^1$ and $c_4{}^1$ can be merged with respect C_3^2. Hence, the newly generated primary clusters of level 2 are $c_1{}^2 = c_2{}^1 \cup c_3{}^1 = \{2, 5, 6, 7, 8, 9, 10, 11, 12, 15, 16, 17, 19, 20, 21, 23, 24\}$ and $c_2{}^2 = c_1{}^1 \cup c_4{}^1 = \{1, 3, 4, 22, 13, 14, 18\}$. Therefore, $m_2 = 2$. As desired number of clusters is achieved at level 2, the algorithm exists.

Hence, our algorithm can not only generate the requirement based clusters, but also it gives the direction of optimal count of the clusters. Our technique uses v auxiliary CAs if the optimal number of clusters is achieved at level v. Next, we test the competency of our proposed algorithm on real dataset.

5   Results and Discussion

This section reports the performance of our proposed cycle based clustering algorithm on some real datasets (http://archive.ics.uci.edu/ml/index.php) using some benchmarks validation techniques [8,12]. Here, we use *four* datasets **Iris**, **BuddyMove, Wholesale Customers, Seed** where each of them has mostly *quantitative* attributes (see Table 5 for details).

Table 6. Comparison of clustering techniques based on internal validation indices for each of the available datasets of Table 5.

Dataset	Algorithm	Connectivity		Dunn index		Silhouette score	
		Score	m	Score	m	Score	m
Iris	Hierarchical	0.0000	2	0.3389	2	0.6867	2
	K-means	6.1536	2	0.1365	4	0.6810	2
	DIANA	6.1536	2	0.1302	5	0.6810	2
	PAM	3.9623	2	0.1235	5	0.6858	2
	SOTA	11.5016	2	0.0582	5	0.6569	2
	Proposed algorithm	**0.0000**	**2**	**0.3389**	**2**	**0.6867**	**2**
BuddyMove	Hierarchical	2.9290	2	0.3146	2	0.4764	2
	K-means	30.0881	2	0.0193	5	0.3492	3
	DIANA	27.1242	2	0.0476	6	0.3020	2
	PAM	41.6647	2	0.0178	3	0.3819	3
	SOTA	44.4111	2	0.0666	3	0.3134	2
	Proposed algorithm	**2.9289**	**2**	**0.3146**	**2**	**0.4763**	**2**
Wholesale customers	Hierarchical	2.9290	2	0.3853	2	0.7957	2
	K-means	35.2032	2	0.0900	6	0.3492	3
	DIANA	34.3694	2	0.0870	6	0.3020	2
	PAM	38.3802	2	0.0511	5	0.3310	4
	SOTA	43.8266	2	0.0061	2	0.3134	2
	Proposed algorithm	**3.7329**	**2**	**0.0508**	**2**	**0.5257**	**2**
Seed	Hierarchical	8.7861	2	0.1089	6	0.5248	2
	K-means	21.3698	2	0.0855	3	0.5229	2
	DIANA	19.1714	2	0.0743	6	0.5218	2
	PAM	20.6762	2	0.0788	5	0.5175	2
	SOTA	16.0179	2	0.0566	4	0.5049	2
	Proposed algorithm	**3.6**	**2**	**0.09**	**2**	**0.5288**	**2**

To measure the performance of our proposed cycle based clustering algorithm on these datasets, we use the package **clValid** in **R**, using the implementation available in the package [2]. Table 6 records the performance of this algorithm. In Table 6, columns III & IV, V & VI and VII & VIII represent the optimal scores and the optimal number of clusters (m) of the validation indices - *connectivity* [9], *silhouette score* [7] and *Dunn index* [6] respectively. Our algorithm gives the optimal score in each of the internal validation indices for the *Iris* dataset in just 2 levels using the CA (10, 75, 166, 105, 105, 166, 150, 20) for level 0 and CA (6, 166, 165, 154, 105, 165, 165, 65) for level 1. Similarly, the optimal results for the *BuddyMove* dataset is found in 4 levels. For *Wholesale* dataset, the optimal result on connectivity, Dunn index and silhouette score are observed in 2, 5 and 3 levels respectively. Whereas, for the *Seed* dataset, the optimal score is recorded in just 1 level for Dunn index, whereas in 3 and 7 levels for silhouette score and connectivity respectively.

To compare the performance of our algorithm, these datasets are tested on five benchmark clustering algorithms – *K-means* (centroid based clustering) [2], *hierarchical* (agglomerative hierarchical clustering) [2], *DIANA* (divisive hierarchical clustering) [2], *PAM (Partitioning around medoids)* (centroid based clustering) [2] and *SOTA (Self-organizing tree algorithm)* (unsupervised network with a divisive hierarchical clustering) [2] using the implementation in **R** [2]. Table 6 also reports result of this comparison. It can be observed that, among the existing algorithms, performance of *hierarchical* algorithm is best with respect to all datasets. However, our algorithm performs at par with this algorithm, and even beats it for the **Seed** dataset. Therefore, from this table, it can be concluded that our algorithm can easily compete with the *highly* efficient benchmark algorithms and performance of our proposed cycle based clustering algorithm is at least as good that of the best algorithm existing today.

References

1. Adak, S., Mukherjee, S., Das, S.: Do there exist non-linear maximal length cellular automata? A study. In: Mauri, G., El Yacoubi, S., Dennunzio, A., Nishinari, K., Manzoni, L. (eds.) ACRI 2018. LNCS, vol. 11115, pp. 289–297. Springer, Cham (2018). https://doi.org/10.1007/978-3-319-99813-8_26
2. Brock, G., Pihur, V., Datta, S., Datta, S.: clValid: an R package for cluster validation. J. Stat. Softw. **25**(4), 1–22 (2008)
3. Carvalho, F., Lechevallier, Y., Melo, F.: Partitioning hard clustering algorithms based on multiple dissimilarity matrices. Pattern Recogn. **45**(1), 447–464 (2012)
4. Das, S.: Theory and applications of nonlinear cellular automata in VLSI design. PhD thesis, Bengal Engineering and Science University, Shibpur, India (2006)
5. Dougherty, J., Kohavi, R., Sahami, M.: Supervised and unsupervised discretization of continuous features. In: Machine Learning Proceedings 1995, pp. 194–202. Elsevier (1995)
6. Dunn, J.C.: Well separated clusters and fuzzy partitions. J. Cybern. **4**, 95–104 (1974)
7. Dunn, J.C.: Silhouettes: a graphical aid to the interpretation and validation of cluster analysis. J. Comput. Appl. Math. **20**, 53–65 (1987)
8. Estivill-Castro, V.: Why so many clustering algorithms - a position paper. ACM SIGKDD Explor. Newslett. **4**, 65–75 (2002)
9. Handl, J., Knowles, J., Kell, D.B.: Computational cluster validation in post-genomic data analysis. Bioinformatics **21**(15), 3201–3212 (2005)
10. Jain, A.K., Murthy, M.N., Flynn, P.J.: Data clustering: a review. ACM Comput. Surv. **31**(3), 165–193 (1999)
11. Wolfram, S.: Theory and applications of cellular automata. World Scientific, Singapore (1986). ISBN 9971-50-124-4 pbk
12. Xu, D., Tian, Y.: A comprehensive survey of clustering algorithms. Ann. Data Sci. **2**(2), 165–193 (2015). https://doi.org/10.1007/s40745-015-0040-1
13. Xu, R., Wunsch, D.: Survey of clustering algorithms. IEEE Trans. Neural Net. **16**(3), 645–678 (2005)

Commutative Automata Networks

Florian Bridoux[1], Maximilien Gadouleau[2(✉)], and Guillaume Theyssier[3]

[1] Aix-Marseille Université, Université de Toulon, CNRS, LIS, Marseille, France
`florian.bridoux@lis-lab.fr`
[2] Department of Computer Science, Durham University,
South Road, Durham DH1 3LE, UK
`m.r.gadouleau@durham.ac.uk`
[3] Université d'Aix-Marseille, CNRS, Centrale Marseille, I2M, Marseille, France
`guillaume.theyssier@cnrs.fr`

Abstract. Automata networks are mappings of the form $f : Q^Z \to Q^Z$, where Q is a finite alphabet and Z is a set of entities; they generalise Cellular Automata and Boolean networks. An update schedule dictates when each entity updates its state according to its local function $f_i : Q^Z \to Q$. One major question is to study the behaviour of a given automata networks under different update schedules. In this paper, we study automata networks that are invariant under many different update schedules. This gives rise to two definitions, locally commutative and globally commutative networks. We investigate the relation between commutativity and different forms of locality of update functions; one main conclusion is that globally commutative networks have strong dynamical properties, while locally commutative networks are much less constrained. We also give a complete classification of all globally commutative Boolean networks.

Keywords: Automata networks · Boolean networks · Commutativity · Update schedules

1 Introduction

Automata networks are mappings of the form $f : Q^Z \to Q^Z$, where Q is a finite alphabet and Z is a set of entities; they generalise Cellular Automata and Boolean networks. An update schedule dictates when each entity updates its state according to its local function $f_i : Q^Z \to Q$.

One major question is to study the behaviour of a given automata network under different update schedules. A lot is known about the relation between synchronous and asynchronous dynamics of finite or infinite interaction networks (see [3,4] and references therein). In particular, there is a stream of work that focuses on networks with the most "asynchronous power," i.e. networks which can asynchronously simulate a large amount of parallel dynamics [1,2].

In this paper, we study automata networks that are "robust to asynchronicity," i.e. invariant under many different update schedules. This gives rise to

© IFIP International Federation for Information Processing 2020
Published by Springer Nature Switzerland AG 2020. All Rights Reserved
H. Zenil (Ed.): AUTOMATA 2020, LNCS 12286, pp. 43–58, 2020.
https://doi.org/10.1007/978-3-030-61588-8_4

two definitions, locally commutative and globally commutative networks. A network is globally commutative if applying f in parallel is equivalent to updating different parts of Z sequentially, for any possible ordered partition of Z. A network is locally commutative if applying f in parallel is equivalent to updating different elements of Z sequentially, for any possible ordered partition of Z into singletons. (Formal definitions will be given in Sect. 2.)

In this paper, we investigate the relation between commutativity (defined in Sect. 2) and different forms of locality of update functions, namely: finiteness properties of the influences of some nodes on some other ones (Sect. 3), dynamical locality (Sect. 4), and idempotence (Sect. 5); one main conclusion is that globally commutative networks have strong dynamical properties, while locally commutative networks are much less constrained. We also determine the transition graphs of all globally commutative Boolean networks (Sect. 6).

2　Commutativity Properties

Let Q be a finite alphabet of size $q \geq 2$, and let Z be a countable set. We refer to any element $x \in Q^Z$ as a **configuration**. An automata network, or simply **network**, is any mapping $f : Q^Z \to Q^Z$.

We denote the set of all subsets of Z as $\mathcal{P}(Z)$ and the set of all finite subsets of Z as $\mathcal{FP}(Z)$. For all $j \in \mathbb{N}$, we denote $[j] = \{1, \dots, j\}$. For any $x \in Q^Z$ and any $s \in \mathcal{P}(Z)$, we will use the shorthand notation $x_s = (x_i : i \in s)$ and $x = (x_s, x_{Z \setminus s})$ (the ordering of the elements of s will be immaterial). We will extend these notations to networks as well, i.e. $f = (f_i : i \in Z)$ and $f_s = (f_i : i \in s)$. For any $a \in Q$ and $s \in \mathcal{P}(Z)$, we denote the configuration $x \in Q^s$ with $x_i = a$ for all $i \in s$ as a_s (we shall commonly use examples such as 0_Z and 1_Z). If $Q = \{0, 1\}$ and $Z = \mathbb{N}$, then the **density** of $x \in \{0, 1\}^{\mathbb{N}}$ is

$$\delta(x) := \limsup_{n \to \infty} \frac{w_H(x_1, \dots, x_n)}{n},$$

where the Hamming weight $w_H(x_1, \dots, x_n)$ is the number of nonzero elements of $(x_1, \dots, x_n)$.

For any $s \in \mathcal{P}(Z)$, the update of s according to f is $f^{(s)} : Q^Z \to Q^Z$ such that $f^{(s)}(x) = (f_s(x), x_{Z \setminus s})$. We denote $f^{(s_1, \dots, s_k)} = f^{(s_k)} \circ \cdots \circ f^{(s_1)}$ for any finite sequence $s_1, \dots, s_k \in \mathcal{P}(Z)$. We consider the following commutativity properties.

(C1) $f^{(i,j)} = f^{(j,i)}$ for all $i, j \in Z$.
(C2) $f^{(b,c)} = f^{(c,b)}$ for all $b, c \in \mathcal{FP}(Z)$.
(C3) $f^{(s,t)} = f^{(t,s)}$ for all $s, t \in \mathcal{P}(Z)$.

We say that a network satisfying **(C1)** is **locally commutative**, while a network satisfying **(C3)** is **globally commutative**. We remark that if f is locally (respectively, globally) commutative, then $f^{(s)}$ is locally (respectively, globally) commutative for any $s \in \mathcal{P}(Z)$. Global commutativity has another definition, given below.

Lemma 1. *Global commutativity is equivalent to:* $f^{(\sigma,\tau)} = f^{(\tau,\sigma)}$ *for all* $\sigma, \tau \in$ $\mathcal{P}(Z)$ *with* $\sigma \cap \tau = \emptyset$.

Proof. In the latter case, for any $s, t \in \mathcal{P}(Z)$, we have $f^{(s \cap t, s \setminus t)} = f^{(s \setminus t, s \cap t)} = f^{(s)}$ and symmetrically for $f^{(t)}$ so that

$$f^{(s,t)} = f^{(s \cap t, s \setminus t, t \setminus s, s \cap t)} = f^{(s \cap t, t \setminus s, s \setminus t, s \cap t)} = f^{(t,s)}.$$

Throughout this paper, we use notation $(\mathbf{X}) \implies (\mathbf{Y})$ to mean that if a network satisfies Property $(\mathbf{X})$, then it satisfies Property $(\mathbf{Y})$ as well. We use shorthand notation such as $(\mathbf{X}) \implies (\mathbf{Y}) \implies (\mathbf{Z})$ with the obvious meaning, and we use the notation $(\mathbf{X}) \not\Longrightarrow (\mathbf{Y})$ to mean that there exists a network satisfying $(\mathbf{X})$ but not $(\mathbf{Y})$. For instance, we have $(\mathbf{C3}) \implies (\mathbf{C2}) \implies (\mathbf{C1})$.

The commutativity properties above have alternative definitions. An **enumeration** of Z is an ordered partition of Z, i.e. a sequence $Y = (y_\tau : \tau \in \mathbb{N})$, where $\bigcup_{\tau \in \mathbb{N}} y_\tau = Z$ and $y_\tau \cap y_\sigma = \emptyset$ for all $\tau \neq \sigma$. If each y_τ is either a singleton or the empty set, then Y is a sequential enumeration; if each y_τ is finite, then Y is a finite-block enumeration. For any enumeration Y and any $t \in \mathbb{N}$, we denote $Y_t = (y_1, \ldots, y_t)$. We then define $f^Y : Q^Z \to Q^Z$ by $f^Y_{y_\tau} := f^{Y_\tau}_{y_\tau}$ for all $\tau \in \mathbb{N}$. Since all the y_τ are disjoint, we see that $f^{Y_t}_{y_\tau} = f^{Y_\tau}_{y_\tau} = f^Y_{y_\tau}$ for any $t \geq \tau$. We then consider the following alternative commutativity properties.

(C1a) $f^I = f^J$ for any two sequential enumerations I and J of Z.
(C2a) $f^B = f^C$ for any two finite-block enumerations B and C of Z.
(C3a) $f^S = f^T$ for any two enumerations S and T of Z.

We also consider the following alternative properties, which at first sight are stronger than those listed just above.

(C1b) $f = f^I$ for any sequential enumeration I of Z.
(C2b) $f = f^B$ for any finite-block enumeration B of Z.
(C3b) $f = f^S$ for any enumeration S of Z.

We prove that in fact, those three versions are equivalent. This helps us show that $(\mathbf{C1})$ and $(\mathbf{C2})$ are also equivalent.

Theorem 1. *Commutativity properties are related as follows:*

$$(C1) \iff (C1a) \iff (C1b). \tag{1}$$
$$(C2) \iff (C2a) \iff (C2b). \tag{2}$$
$$(C3) \iff (C3a) \iff (C3b). \tag{3}$$

$$(C1) \iff (C2) \not\Longrightarrow (C3). \tag{4}$$

Proof. (1), (2) and (3). We only prove the equivalence (3) for $(\mathbf{C3})$; the other equivalences are similarly proved. Firstly, $(\mathbf{C3b}) \implies (\mathbf{C3a})$. Secondly, if f satisfies $(\mathbf{C3a})$, then for any disjoint $s, t \in \mathcal{P}(Z)$,

$$f_t^{(s,t)} = f_t^{(s,t,Z \setminus (s \cup t))} = f_t^{(t,s,Z \setminus (s \cup t))} = f_t^{(t,s)},$$

and by symmetry $f_s^{(s,t)} = f_s^{(t,s)}$, thus $f^{(s,t)} = f^{(t,s)}$. Thus, by Lemma 1 f satisfies **(C3)**. Thirdly, if $f^{(s,t)} = f^{(t,s)}$ for all s, t, then let $S = (s_\tau : \tau \in \mathbb{N})$; we have

$$f_{s_\tau}^S = f_{s_\tau}^{S_\tau} = f_{s_\tau}^{(s_\tau, s_1, \ldots, s_{\tau-1})} = f_{s_\tau}$$

for any τ and hence $f^S = f$.

(4). We first prove **(C1)** $\implies$ **(C2)**. If f satisfies **(C1)**, then for any finite subsets $b = \{b_1, \ldots, b_k\}$ and $c = \{c_1, \ldots, c_l\}$, the equivalence in (1) yields

$$f^{(b,c)} = f^{(b_1, \ldots, b_k, c_1, \ldots, c_l)} = f^{(c_1, \ldots, c_l, b_1, \ldots, b_k)} = f^{(c,b)}.$$

We now prove **(C1)** $\nRightarrow$ **(C3)** by exhibiting a network satisfying **(C1)** but not **(C3)**. Let $Q = \{0, 1\}$ and $Z = \mathbb{N}$, then let $f(x) = 1_Z$ if $\delta(x) \le 1/2$ and $f(x) = 0_Z$ otherwise. Since $\delta(f^{(i)}(x)) = \delta(x)$ for any $i \in Z$, we easily obtain that $f^{(i)}$ and $f^{(j)}$ commute. On the other hand, let $x = 0_Z$ and s a set of density $1/3$ (e.g. all multiples of 3). Then $f_s^{(s,Z \setminus s)}(x) = 1_s$ while $f_s^{(Z \setminus s, s)}(x) = 0_s$. $\square$

3   Commutativity and Finiteness Properties

The example of a network f that satisfies **(C1)** but not **(C3)** used the fact that f, though it depended on all the variables x_i "globally", did not depend on each x_i "individually": changing only the value of any x_i could not change the value of $f_j(x)$. We thus consider various finiteness properties for the local functions.

For any $\phi : Q^Z \to Q$ and any ordered pair $(x, y) \in Q^Z \times Q^Z$, we say $u \subseteq Z$ is an **influence** of ϕ for (x, y) if

$$\phi(x_{Z \setminus u}, y_u) = \phi(y), \text{ and } \phi(x_{Z \setminus t}, y_t) \ne \phi(y) \; \forall t \subset u.$$

Lemma 2. *Let $\phi : Q^Z \to Q$ and $x, y \in Q^Z$.*

(1) If there exists $v \in \mathcal{FP}(Z)$ such that $\phi(x_{Z \setminus v}, y_v) = \phi(y)$, then there exists a finite influence of ϕ for (x, y).

Let $u \subseteq Z$ be an influence of ϕ for (x, y).

(2) $u \subseteq \Delta(x, y) := \{i \in Z : x_i \ne y_i\}$.
(3) $u = \emptyset$ if and only if $\phi(x) = \phi(y)$.
(4) For any $t \subseteq u$, there exists $z \in Q^Z$ such that t is an influence of ϕ for (z, y).

Proof. (1). Consider the family of sets $w \subseteq Z$ such that $\phi(x_{Z \setminus w}, y_w) = \phi(y)$. This family contains a finite set (i.e. v), thus it contains a set u of minimum cardinality; it is clear that u is then an influence for (x, y).

(2). If $u \not\subseteq \Delta(x, y)$, then $t := u \cap \Delta(x, y)$ satisfies $t \subset u$ and $\phi(x_{Z \setminus t}, y_t) = \phi(x_{Z \setminus u}, y_u) = \phi(y)$, which is the desired contradiction.

(3). If $u = \emptyset$, then $\phi(x) = \phi(x_{Z \setminus u}, y_u) = \phi(y)$. Conversely, if $\phi(x) = \phi(y)$, then $\phi(x_{Z \setminus \emptyset}, y_\emptyset) = \phi(y)$ and there is no $t \subset \emptyset$, thus the empty set is an influence of ϕ for (x, y).

(4). Let $v = u \setminus t$ and $z := (x_{Z \setminus v}, y_v)$, then $(x_{Z \setminus u}, y_u) = (z_{Z \setminus t}, y_t)$, from which we easily obtain that t is an influence of ϕ for (z, y). $\square$

We then consider three finiteness properties for a function $\phi : Q^Z \to Q$.

(F1) For any $x, y \in Q^Z$, there exists an influence of ϕ for (x, y).
(F2) For any $x, y \in Q^Z$, there exists a finite influence of ϕ for (x, y).
(F3) There exists $b \in \mathcal{FP}(Z)$ such that for any $x, y \in Q^Z$, there exists an influence of ϕ for (x, y) contained in b.

By extension, we say a network $f : Q^Z \to Q^Z$ satisfies **(F1)** (**(F2)**, **(F3)**, respectively) if for all $i \in Z$, f_i satisfies **(F1)** (**(F2)**, **(F3)**, respectively). Clearly, **(F3)** $\implies$ **(F2)** $\implies$ **(F1)**.

In order to emphasize the role of different commutativity properties, we introduce the following notation for our results: **(C)** $\vdash$ **(Y)** $\implies$ **(Z)** means that the implication **(Y)** $\implies$ **(Z)** holds when we restrict ourselves to networks with Property **(C)**. This notation will be combined with the other ones introduced so far.

Theorem 2. *The commutativity and finiteness properties are related as follows.*

$$(C3) \vdash (F1) \not\Longrightarrow (F2). \tag{5}$$

$$(C3) \vdash (F2) \not\Longrightarrow (F3). \tag{6}$$

$$(C1) \vdash (F1) \not\Longrightarrow (C3). \tag{7}$$

$$(C1) \vdash (F2) \Longrightarrow (C3). \tag{8}$$

Proof. For the first two items, we only need to exhibit counterexamples for $Q = \{0, 1\}$ and $Z = \mathbb{N}$ of the form $f_1(x) = \phi(x)$ and $f_i(x) = x_i$ for all $i \geq 2$, which always verify **(C3)**.

(5). Let $\phi(x) = \bigwedge_{i \in \mathbb{N}} x_i$. We verify that ϕ satisfies **(F1)** but does not satisfy **(F2)**. Indeed, if $x \neq 1_\mathbb{N}$, say $x = (0_s, 1_t)$ and $y = 1_\mathbb{N}$, then s is an influence for (x, y) and any $i \in s$ is an influence for (y, x).

(6). For any nonzero $x \in \{0, 1\}^\mathbb{N}$, let $a(x) = \min\{j : x_j = 1\}$, and let

$$\phi(x) = \begin{cases} 0 & \text{if } x = 0_\mathbb{N}, \\ x_{a(x)+1} & \text{otherwise.} \end{cases}$$

We verify that ϕ satisfies **(F2)**; we shall use Lemma 2(1) repeatedly. If $y \neq 0_\mathbb{N}$, then for any x, $\phi(x_{\mathbb{N} \setminus [a(y)+1]}, y_{[a(y)+1]}) = \phi(y)$. If $y = 0_\mathbb{N}$, then for any $x \neq 0_\mathbb{N}$, $\phi(x_{\mathbb{N} \setminus \{a(x)+1\}}, y_{\{a(x)+1\}}) = \phi(y)$. So ϕ satisfies **(F2)** but the case $y = 0_\mathbb{N}$ shows that it does not satisfy **(F3)**.

(7). Let $Q = \{0, 1\}$, $Z = \mathbb{N}$, and for all $i \in \mathbb{N}$,

$$f_i(x) = x_i \vee \bigvee_{k > i} \neg x_k.$$

In other words, $f_i(x) = x_i$ if $x_k = 1$ for all $k > i$ and $f_i(x) = 1$ whenever there exists $k > i$ with $x_k = 0$. It is clear that f satisfies **(F1)**. We now prove that

f satisfies **(C1)**. Let $i, j \in \mathbb{N}$ be distinct and $x \in \{0,1\}^{\mathbb{N}}$. Clearly, if $i > j$, then $f_i(x) = f_i(f^{(j)}(x))$, so suppose $i < j$. If there exists $k > j$ with $x_k = 0$, then $f_i(x) = f_i(f^{(j)}(x)) = 1$; otherwise, $f^{(j)}(x) = x$ and $f_i(x) = f_i(f^{(j)}(x))$ and we are done. We finally prove that f does not satisfy **(C3)**. Let $x = 0_{\mathbb{N}}$, then $f_1(x) = 1$, while $f_1(f^{(\mathbb{N}\backslash 1)}(x)) = f_1(0, 1_{\mathbb{N}\backslash 1}) = 0$.

(8). Suppose f satisfies **(F2)** and **(C1)**, but not **(C3)**. Then by Lemma 1 there exist s, t and x for which $s \cap t = \emptyset$ and $f_t^{(s,t)}(x) \neq f_t^{(t,s)}(x) = f_t(x)$. In particular, there exists $i \in t$ such that $f_i(f^{(s)}(x)) \neq f_i(x)$. Denoting $y = f^{(s)}(x)$, there exists a finite influence $b \subseteq \Delta(x, y) \subseteq s$ such that $f^{(b)}(x) = (x_{Z\backslash b}, y_b)$ verifies $f_i(f^{(b)}(x)) = f_i(y) \neq f_i(x)$. This implies $f^{(i,b)} \neq f^{(b,i)}$, which is the desired contradiction. $\qquad\square$

4   Commutativity and Dynamical Locality

Let X be a set, and $\alpha : X \to X$. A **cycle** of α is a finite sequence $x^1, \ldots, x^l \in X$ such that $\alpha(x^i) = x^{i+1}$ for $1 \leq i \leq l-1$ and $\alpha(x^l) = x^1$. The integer l is the length of the cycle; the **period** of α is the least common multiple of all the cycle lengths of α. (If α has no cycles, or if it has cycles of unbounded lengths, then its period is infinite.) The transient length of x is the smallest $k \geq 0$, such that $\alpha^k(x)$ belongs to a cycle of α. The **transient length** of α is the maximum over all transient lengths. (Again, if α has no cycles, or if α has unbounded transient lengths, then the transient length is infinite.)

Here is an example of α where every trajectory leads to a cycle, but α has infinite period and infinite transient length. Let $X = \mathbb{N}$, then for any prime number p, let

$$\alpha(p^i) = \begin{cases} p^{i+1} & \text{if } 0 \leq i \leq 2p - 2, \\ p^p & \text{if } i = 2p - 1, \end{cases}$$

and $\alpha(n) = n$ for any other $n \in \mathbb{N}$. Then the trajectory of the prime number p has transient length p and period p.

We note that for any $m > n \geq 0$, $\alpha^m = \alpha^n$ if and only if α has transient length $\leq n$ and period dividing $m - n$. In particular, any $\alpha : Q \to Q$ has transient length at most $q - 1$ and period at most q. Thus, for $\pi_q := \mathrm{lcm}(1, 2, \ldots, q)$, any $\alpha : Q \to Q$ satisfies

$$\alpha^{\pi_q + q - 1} = \alpha^{q-1}. \tag{9}$$

Moreover, this is the minimum equation satisfied by all $\alpha : Q \to Q$, in the sense that any equation of the form $\alpha^m = \alpha^n$ for $m > n \geq 0$ must have $m \geq \pi_q + q - 1$ and $n \geq q - 1$. We then consider the dynamical property

(D) f has transient length at most $q - 1$ and period dividing π_q, i.e. $f^{\pi_q + q - 1} = f^{q-1}$.

We shall refer to Property **(D)** as being **dynamically local**, as it implies that f behaves almost like a function $Q \to Q$. We naturally also consider its analogues for updates.

(D1) $f^{(i)}$ is dynamically local for all $i \in Z$.
(D2) $f^{(b)}$ is dynamically local for all $b \in \mathcal{FP}(Z)$.
(D3) $f^{(s)}$ is dynamically local for all $s \in \mathcal{P}(Z)$.

We shall prove that globally commutative networks are dynamically local, and in particular that their period is at most π_q. On the other hand, it is straightforward to exhibit examples of globally commutative networks whose period is equal to π_q. For instance, for any $q \geq 2$ let $Z = \{2, 3, \ldots, q\}$ and $f : Q^Z \to Q^Z$ where

$$f_i(x) = \begin{cases} x_i + 1 \mod i & \text{if } 0 \leq x_i \leq i - 1 \\ x_i & \text{otherwise.} \end{cases}$$

It is clear that f is globally commutative, and that its period is exactly π_q.

Property **(D1)** is actually trivial, as it is satisfied by any network. Indeed, $f^{(i)}$ can be decomposed into a family of mappings from Q to itself (one for each value of $x_{Z \setminus i}$): for any $a \in Q^{Z \setminus i}$, let $g^a : Q \to Q$ be $g^a(x_i) := f_i(x_i, a)$, then

$$f^{(i)^m}(x_i, a) = ((g^a)^m(x_i), a)$$

for all $m \geq 1$, thus $f^{(i)}$ verifies Eq. (9).

Theorem 3. *Commutativity and dynamical locality are related as follows.*

$$(C3) \implies (D3). \tag{10}$$
$$(C1) \implies (D2). \tag{11}$$

$$(C1) \not\implies (D). \tag{12}$$

$$(C1) \vdash (D) \not\implies (D3). \tag{13}$$

Proof. (10). If f is globally commutative, then so is $f^{(s)}$ for any s; therefore, we only need to prove that **(C3)** $\implies$ **(D)**. Now, let f satisfy **(C3)**, $i \in Z$, then for any $m \geq 1$,

$$f_i^m = \left(f^{(i, Z \setminus i)^m}\right)_i = \left(f^{(i)^m}(Z \setminus i)^m\right)_i = f_i^{(i)^m}.$$

Thus,

$$f_i^{\pi_q + q - 1} = f_i^{(i)^{\pi_q + q - 1}} = f_i^{(i)^{q-1}} = f_i^{q-1}.$$

Since this holds for any i, we obtain $f^{\pi_q + q - 1} = f^{q-1}$.

(11). Let f satisfy **(C1)** and let $b = \{b_1, \ldots, b_k\} \in \mathcal{FP}(Z)$. Then for $m = \pi_q + q - 1$ and $n = q - 1$, we have

$$f^{(b)^m} = f^{(b_1, \ldots, b_k)^m} = f^{((b_1)^m, \ldots, (b_k)^m)} = f^{((b_1)^n, \ldots, (b_k)^n)} = f^{(b_1, \ldots, b_k)^n} = f^{(b)^n}.$$

We delay the proofs of (12) and (13) until Theorem 5, where we prove stronger statements. □

If $f : Q^Z \to Q^Z$ is dynamically local, then the following are equivalent: f is bijective; f is injective; f is surjective; $f^{\pi_q} = \text{id}$. We thus consider the property

(B) f is bijective.

Again, we consider its counterparts for updates.

(B1) $f^{(i)}$ is bijective for all $i \in Z$.
(B2) $f^{(b)}$ is bijective for all $b \in \mathcal{FP}(Z)$.
(B3) $f^{(s)}$ is bijective for all $s \in \mathcal{P}(Z)$.

By using dynamical locality and similar arguments to those used in the proof of Theorem 3, we obtain that all versions of bijection are equivalent for globally commutative networks; however, locally commutative networks are not so well behaved.

Theorem 4. *Bijection properties and commutativity properties are related as follows.*

$$(\textbf{C3}) \vdash (\textbf{B}) \iff (\textbf{B1}) \iff (\textbf{B2}) \iff (\textbf{B3}). \tag{14}$$
$$(\textbf{C1}) \vdash (\textbf{B3}) \implies (\textbf{B}) \implies (\textbf{B1}) \iff (\textbf{B2}). \tag{15}$$

$$(\textbf{C1}) \vdash (\textbf{B}) \wedge (\textbf{D3}) \nRightarrow (\textbf{B3}). \tag{16}$$

$$(\textbf{C1}) \vdash (\textbf{B1}) \wedge (\textbf{D3}) \nRightarrow (\textbf{B}). \tag{17}$$

Proof. (14). We only need to prove $(\textbf{C3}) \vdash (\textbf{B1}) \implies (\textbf{B}) \implies (\textbf{B3})$. We first prove $(\textbf{C3}) \vdash (\textbf{B1}) \implies (\textbf{B})$. In that case, we have for all $i \in Z$,

$$f_i^{\pi_q} = f_i^{(i)^{\pi_q}(Z \setminus i)^{\pi_q}} = f_i^{(Z \setminus i)^{\pi_q}} = \mathrm{id}_i,$$

and hence $f^{\pi_q} = \mathrm{id}$. We now prove $(\textbf{C3}) \vdash (\textbf{B}) \implies (\textbf{B3})$. In that case, we have for all $s \in \mathcal{P}(Z)$,

$$f_s^{(s)^{\pi_q}} = f_s^{(s)^{\pi_q}(Z \setminus s)^{\pi_q}} = f_s^{\pi_q} = \mathrm{id}_s,$$

and hence $f^{(s)^{\pi_q}} = \mathrm{id}$.

(15). We first prove $(\textbf{C1}) \vdash (\textbf{B1}) \implies (\textbf{B2})$. If f satisfies $(\textbf{C1})$ and $(\textbf{B1})$, then for any $b = \{b_1, \ldots, b_k\} \in \mathcal{FP}(Z)$,

$$f^{(b)^{\pi_q}} = f^{(b_1)^{\pi_q}, \ldots, (b_k)^{\pi_q}} = \mathrm{id}.$$

We now prove $(\textbf{C1}) \vdash (\textbf{B1}) \implies (\textbf{B1})$. Suppose f satisfies $(\textbf{C1})$ but not $(\textbf{B1})$, then let $f^{(i)}$ be non-injective and $x, y \in Q^Z$ such that $f^{(i)}(x) = f^{(i)}(y)$. Then for any $j \in Z$,

$$f_j(x) = f_j(f^{(i)}(x)) = f_j(f^{(i)}(y)) = f_j(y),$$

and hence $f(x) = f(y)$. Thus f is not bijective.

(16). Let $Q = \{0, 1\}$, $Z = \mathbb{N}$ and

$$f(x) = \begin{cases} \neg x & \text{if } \delta(x) = 0 \text{ or } \delta(x) = 1, \\ x & \text{otherwise.} \end{cases}$$

It is easy to verify that f satisfies **(C1)**, **(B)** and **(D3)**. However, let $s \subseteq Z$ such that $y = (1_s, 0_{Z \setminus s})$ has density $1/2$, then $f^{(s)}(0_{\mathbb{N}}) = y = f^{(s)}(y)$ and hence $f^{(s)}$ is not bijective.

(17). Let $Q = \{0, 1\}$, $Z = \mathbb{N}$ and

$$f(x) = \begin{cases} \neg x & \text{if } \delta(x) = 0, \\ x & \text{otherwise.} \end{cases}$$

It is easy to verify that f satisfies **(C1)**, **(B1)** and **(D3)**, but $f(0_{\mathbb{N}}) = 1_{\mathbb{N}} = f(1_{\mathbb{N}})$ and hence f is not bijective. □

5 Commutativity and Idempotence

Let us now strengthen the commutativity properties as follows.

(IC1) $f^{(i,j)} = f^{(\{i,j\})}$ for all $i, j \in Z$.
(IC2) $f^{(b,c)} = f^{(b \cup c)}$ for all $b, c \in \mathcal{FP}(Z)$.
(IC3) $f^{(s,t)} = f^{(s \cup t)}$ for all $s, t \in \mathcal{P}(Z)$.

Intuitively, **(IC1)** means that updating i and j in series is equivalent to updating them in parallel; **(IC2)** and **(IC2)** then extend this property to updates of finite blocks and to any updates, respectively. This is closely related to **idempotence**:

(I) $f^2 = f$.

Dynamically, idempotence means that Q^Z is partitioned into gardens of Eden of f (configurations y such that $f^{-1}(y) = \emptyset$) and fixed points of f (configurations z such that $f(z) = z$). Again, we consider the counterparts of idempotence to updates.

(I1) $f^{(i)^2} = f^{(i)}$ for all $i \in Z$.
(I2) $f^{(b)^2} = f^{(b)}$ for all $b \in \mathcal{FP}(Z)$.
(I3) $f^{(s)^2} = f^{(s)}$ for all $s \in \mathcal{P}(Z)$.

For globally commutative networks, all four notions of idempotence are equivalent. This is far to be the case for locally commutative networks instead.

Theorem 5. *Idempotence properties and commutativity properties are related as follows.*

$$(C3) \vdash (I) \iff (I1) \iff (I3) \iff (IC3). \tag{18}$$
$$(C1) \vdash (I1) \iff (IC1) \iff (I2) \iff (IC2). \tag{19}$$
$$(C1) \vdash (I1) \not\Rightarrow (D). \tag{20}$$
$$(C1) \vdash (I) \wedge (D3) \not\Rightarrow (I1). \tag{21}$$
$$(C1) \vdash (I1) \wedge (I) \not\Rightarrow (D3). \tag{22}$$
$$(C1) \vdash (I1) \wedge (D3) \not\Rightarrow (I). \tag{23}$$
$$(C1) \vdash (I3) \not\Rightarrow (C3). \tag{24}$$

Proof. (18). Clearly, **(IC3)** $\implies$ **(C3)** $\wedge$ **(I3)**. We first prove that **(C3)** $\wedge$ **(I3)** $\implies$ **(IC3)**. For any $s, t \in \mathcal{P}(Z)$, let $u = s \cap t$, then we have

$$f^{(s,t)} = f^{(s \setminus t, u, u, t \setminus s)} = f^{(s \setminus t, u, t \setminus s)} = f^{(s \cup t)}.$$

We now prove that **(C3)** $\wedge$ **(I)** $\implies$ **(I3)**: for any $s \in \mathcal{P}(Z)$, we have

$$f_s^{(s)^2} = f_s^{(s,s,Z \setminus s, Z \setminus s)} = f_s^2 = f_s,$$

and hence $f^{(s)^2} = f^{(s)}$. We finally prove that **(C3)** $\wedge$ **(I1)** $\implies$ **(I3)**: for any $s \in \mathcal{P}(Z)$ and any $i \in s$, we have $f_i^{(s)^2} = f_i^{(i)^2(s \setminus i)^2} = f_i^{(i)^2} = f_i^{(i)} = f_i$, and hence $f^{(s)^2} = f^{(s)}$.

(19). Clearly, **(IC2)** $\implies$ **(IC1)** $\implies$ **(C1)** $\wedge$ **(I1)** on the one hand and **(IC2)** $\implies$ **(C2)** $\wedge$ **(I2)** on the other. We now prove **(C1)** $\wedge$ **(I1)** $\implies$ **(IC2)**. Let f satisfy **(C1)** $\wedge$ **(I1)**, and let $b, c \in \mathcal{FP}(Z)$. We denote $b \setminus c = \{b_1, \ldots, b_k\}$, $c \setminus b = \{c_1, \ldots, c_l\}$ and $b \cap c = \{d_1, \ldots d_m\}$. Then, by **(C2b)**,

$$
\begin{aligned}
f^{(b,c)} &= f^{(b_1, \ldots, b_k, d_1, \ldots, d_m, c_1 \ldots, c_l, d_1, \ldots, d_m)} \\
&= f^{(b_1, \ldots, b_k, c_1 \ldots, c_l, d_1, d_1, \ldots, d_m, d_m)} \\
&= f^{(b_1, \ldots, b_k, c_1 \ldots, c_l, d_1, \ldots, d_m)} \\
&= f^{(b \cup c)}.
\end{aligned}
$$

For the remaining claims, we let $Q = \{0, 1\}$ and $Z = \mathbb{N}$.

(20). Split Z into parts $\{Z_\omega : \omega \in \mathbb{N}\}$ of densities $2^{-\omega}$, and for any $\omega \in \mathbb{N}$, let

$$
f_{Z_\omega}(x) = \begin{cases} 1_{Z_\omega} & \text{if } \delta(x) \geq 1 - 2^{1-\omega}, \\ 0_{Z_\omega} & \text{otherwise.} \end{cases}
$$

It is easy to verify that f satisfies **(C1)** and **(I1)**. However, the initial configuration $x = 0_Z$ has an infinite trajectory, hence f does not satisfy **(D)**.

(21). Let

$$
f_1(x) = \begin{cases} \neg x_1 & \text{if } \delta(x) = 0, \\ x_1 & \text{otherwise.} \end{cases}
$$

and $f_i(x) = 1$ for all $i \geq 2$. It is easy to verify that f satisfies **(C1)**, **(I)**, and **(D3)**. However, $f^{(1)}(0_\mathbb{N}) = (1, 0_{\mathbb{N} \setminus 1})$ and $f^{(1)^2}(0_\mathbb{N}) = 0_\mathbb{N}$, hence f does not satisfy **(I1)**.

(22). Split Z as above, and this time $f_{Z_1} = 0_{Z_1}$ and for any $\omega \geq 2$,

$$
f_{Z_\omega}(x) = \begin{cases} 1_{Z_\omega} & \text{if } \delta(x) > 1 - 2^{1-\omega}, \\ x_{Z_\omega} & \text{otherwise.} \end{cases}
$$

Again, it is easy to verify that f satisfies **(C1)** and **(I1)**. Moreover, $\delta(f(x)) \leq 1/2$ for any $x \in Q^Z$, hence $f(x)$ is fixed, thus f satisfies **(I)**. On the other hand, if

$s = Z \setminus Z_1$, then $f^{(s)}$ has infinite trajectory for x such that $x_{Z_1} = 1_{Z_1}$ and $\delta(x_{Z_\omega}) = 2^{-\omega-1}$ for all $\omega \geq 2$.

(23). Let

$$f(x) = \begin{cases} 1_{\mathbb{N}} & \text{if } \delta(x) = 0, \\ 0_{\mathbb{N}} & \text{if } \delta(x) = 1, \\ x & \text{otherwise.} \end{cases}$$

Then it is clear that f satisfies **(C1)**, **(I1)** and **(D3)**; on the other hand, $f(0_{\mathbb{N}}) = 1_{\mathbb{N}}$ and $f^2(0_{\mathbb{N}}) = 0_{\mathbb{N}}$, hence f is not idempotent.

(24). Let

$$f_1(x) = \begin{cases} x_1 & \text{if } \delta(x) = 1, \\ 0 & \text{otherwise.} \end{cases}$$

$$f_i(x) = 1 \qquad \forall i \geq 2.$$

Then it is easy to verify that f satisfies **(C1)** and **(I3)**, but not **(C3)**.   □

6   Globally Commutative Boolean Networks

There are a plethora of globally commutative networks over non-Boolean alphabets. For instance, for $q = 4$, consider the following construction. Let f be a Boolean network, and view $Q = \{0,1\}^2 = \{a = (a^1, a^2) : a^1, a^2 \in \{0,1\}\}$, then the quaternary network g given by $g(x^1, x^2) = (f(x^2), x^2)$ satisfies **(C3)**. This can be easily generalised for any $q \geq 4$. For $q = 3$, let f be any Boolean network such that f_i does not depend on x_i for any i. Then let g be the ternary network defined by

$$g_i(x) = \begin{cases} 2 & \text{if } x_i = 2 \\ f_i(\hat{x}) & \text{otherwise,} \end{cases}$$

where $\hat{x}_i = \lfloor x_i/2 \rfloor$ for all i. Then it is easy to check that g satisfies **(C3)**. However, we can classify globally commutative Boolean networks (i.e. networks with $Q = \{0,1\}$ and that satisfy **(C3)**). Before we give our classification, we need the following concepts and notation. First, for any $x \in \{0,1\}^Z$ and any $s \subseteq Z$, we denote $\overline{x}^s = (\neg x_s, x_{Z \setminus s})$.

The **transition graph** of f is the directed graph $\Gamma(f)$ with vertex set $\{0,1\}^Z$ and an arc for every pair $(x, f^{(s)}(x))$ for any $x \in \{0,1\}^Z$ and $s \in \mathcal{P}(Z)$. We remark that $\Gamma(f)$ completely determines f.

A **subcube** of $\{0,1\}^Z$ is any set of the form $X[s,\alpha] := \{x \in \{0,1\}^Z, x_s = \alpha\}$ for some $s \subseteq Z$ and $\alpha \in \{0,1\}^s$. A family of subcubes $X = \{X_\omega : \omega \in \Omega\}$ is called an **arrangement** if $X_\omega \cap X_\xi \neq \emptyset$ for all $\omega, \xi \in \Omega$ and $X_\omega \not\subseteq X_\xi$ for all $\omega \neq \xi$.

We denote the **content** of X by $\hat{X} := \bigcup_{\omega \in \Omega} X_\omega$.

Lemma 3. Let $X = \{X_\omega : \omega \in \Omega\}$ be an arrangement, then $Y := \bigcap_{\omega \in \Omega} X_\omega$ is a non-empty subcube.

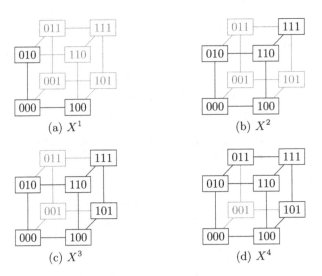

Fig. 1. Arrangements

Proof. Denote $X_\omega := X[s^\omega, \alpha^\omega]$ for all $\omega \in \Omega$. Then for any ω, ξ, we have $\alpha^\omega_{s^\omega \cap s^\xi} = \alpha^\xi_{s^\omega \cap s^\xi}$, therefore we can define $\sigma = \bigcup_{\omega \in \Omega} s^\omega$ and $\alpha \in \{0,1\}^\sigma$ with $\alpha_{s^\omega} = \alpha^\omega_{s^\omega}$ for all $\omega \in \Omega$. Then it is easy to verify that $Y = X[\sigma, \alpha]$. □

For any $C \subseteq \{0,1\}^Z$, we classify any $i \in Z$ as follows.

– If $x_i = y_i$ for any $x, y \in C$, then i is an **external** dimension of C. Otherwise, i is an **internal** dimension of C.
– If for any $x \in C$, $\overline{x}^i \in C$, then i is a **free** dimension of C.
– If i is an internal, non-free dimension of C, then i is a **tight** dimension of C. If i is a tight dimension, then there exists $z \notin C$ such that $\overline{z}^i \in C$; such z is called an i-**border** of C.

If $X = \{X_\omega = X[s^\omega, \alpha^\omega] : \omega \in \Omega\}$ is an arrangement, then (following the notation used in the proof of Lemma 3) the dimensions of $\hat{X}$ are as follows.

– Let $\tau := \bigcap_{\omega \in \Omega} s^\omega$, then τ is the set of external dimensions of $\hat{X}$. The smallest cube containing $\hat{X}$ is $K(\hat{X}) := X[\tau, \alpha_\tau]$.
– $\sigma := \bigcup_{\omega \in \Omega} s^\omega$ and $Z \setminus \sigma$ is the set of free dimensions of $\hat{X}$. The intersection subcube of X is $Y := \bigcap_{\omega \in \Omega} X_\omega = X[\sigma, \alpha]$.
– The other dimensions in $\sigma \setminus \tau$ are the tight dimensions of $\hat{X}$.

For instance, let $Z = [3]$ and consider the following arrangements:

$$X^1 = \{(x_1, x_3) = (0,0)\} \cup \{(x_2, x_3) = (0,0)\}$$
$$X^2 = \{x_3 = 0\} \cup \{(x_1, x_2) = (1,1)\}$$
$$X^3 = \{x_3 = 0\} \cup \{x_1 = 1\}$$
$$X^4 = \{x_3 = 0\} \cup \{x_1 = 1\} \cup \{x_2 = 1\}.$$

They are displayed in Fig. 1. The dimensions of the different arrangements are classified as follows: for X^1, 1 and 2 are tight and 3 is external; for X^2, all are tight; for X^3, 1 and 3 are tight and 2 is free; for X^3, all are tight.

Let $C \subseteq \{0,1\}^Z$ and $f : \{0,1\}^Z \to \{0,1\}^Z$. For any $i \in Z$, we say f_i is **trivial** on C if $f_i(x) = x_i$ for all $x \in C$. We say f_i is **uniform** on C if for any $x, y \in C$, $x_i = y_i \implies f_i(x) = f_i(y)$. We say f is **uniform nontrivial** on C if f_i is nontrivial and uniform on C for all i.

We can then define a class of globally commutative Boolean networks by their transition graphs. Let X be an arrangement. Outside of $\hat{X}$, f is trivial: $f(x) = x$ if $x \notin \hat{X}$. In $\hat{X}$, f satisfies the following:

1. $f_i(x) = \alpha_i$ for every tight dimension i of $\hat{X}$,
2. f_j is uniform nontrivial for any free dimension j of $\hat{X}$,
3. f_k is trivial on any external dimension k of $\hat{X}$.

Any such network is referred to as an **arrangement network**.

For instance, the arrangement X^3 on Fig. 1 has three arrangement networks, one for each choice of the uniform nontrivial f_2 on $\hat{X}^3$. One such network, with $f_2(x) = \neg x_2$, is displayed in Fig. 2.

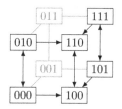

Fig. 2. Arrangement network for $\hat{X}^3$

We can combine families of globally commutative networks as follows. For any f, a singleton $\{x\}$ is a connected component of $\Gamma(f)$ if and only if x is an **unreachable fixed point** of f: $f^{(s)}(y) = x \iff y = x$ for all $s \in \mathcal{P}(X)$. Let $U(f)$ be the set of unreachable fixed points of f and $R(f) = \{0,1\}^Z \setminus U(f)$. If $\{f^a : a \in A\}$ is a family of networks with $R(f^a) \cap R(f^{a'}) = \emptyset$ for all $a, a' \in A$ (or equivalently, $x \in U(f^a)$ or $x \in U(f^{a'})$ for any $x \in \{0,1\}^Z$), we define their **union** as

$$F(x) := \bigcup_{a \in A} f^a(x) = \begin{cases} f^a(x) & \text{if } x \in R(f^a) \\ x & \text{otherwise.} \end{cases}$$

It is easy to see that in an arrangement network f for X, if $x \in X_\omega$ for some $\omega \in \Omega$, then so does $f^{(s)}(x)$ for any s. Therefore, the connected components of $\Gamma(f)$ are precisely $\hat{X}$ and all singletons $\{\{y\} : y \notin \hat{X}\}$. It follows that if f^a is an arrangement network for X^a, then the union $\bigcup_{a \in A} f^a$ is well defined if and only if $\hat{X}^a \cap \hat{X}^{a'} = \emptyset$ for all $a, a' \in A$.

It is then clear that f is a union of arrangement networks if and only if, for every connected component C of $\Gamma(f)$, the following holds:

1. C is the content of an arrangement,
2. f is uniform nontrivial on C,
3. $f_i = cst = \neg z_i$ for any tight dimension i and any i-border z of C.

Theorem 6. *A Boolean network is globally commutative if and only if it is a union of arrangement networks.*

The proof of Theorem 6 will follow from combining Lemmas 4 and 5.

Lemma 4. *Any union of arrangement networks satisfies* **(C3)**.

Proof. The proof is the conjunction of the following two claims.

Claim 1. *Any arrangement network is globally commutative.*

Proof. Let f be an arrangement network for X and $s', t' \in \mathcal{P}(Z)$. If $x \notin \hat{X}$, then x is fixed, and hence $f^{(s',t')}(x) = f^{(t',s')}(x) = x$. Therefore, let us assume $x \in \hat{X}$. We have $f_\sigma = cst = \alpha_\sigma$, thus we consider $s = (Z \setminus \sigma) \cap s'$ and $t = (Z \setminus \sigma) \cap t'$. Because f is uniform, we can express

$$f_{s \cap t}(x) = \lambda(x_{s \cap t}), \qquad f_{s \setminus t}(x) = \mu(x_{s \setminus t}), \qquad f_{t \setminus s}(x) = \nu(x_{t \setminus s}),$$

for $\lambda : \{0,1\}^{s \cap t} \to \{0,1\}^{s \cap t}$, $\mu : \{0,1\}^{s \setminus t} \to \{0,1\}^{s \setminus t}$, and $\nu : \{0,1\}^{t \setminus s} \to \{0,1\}^{t \setminus s}$. We obtain

$$f^{(s,t)}(x) = (\alpha_\sigma, \lambda^2(x_{s \cap t}), \mu(x_{s \setminus t}), \nu(x_{t \setminus s}), x_{(Z \setminus \sigma) \setminus (s \cup t)}) = f^{(t,s)}(x). \qquad \square$$

Claim 2. *If* $\{f^a : a \in A\}$ *is a family of globally commutative networks with* $R(f^a) \cap R(f^{a'}) = \emptyset$ *for all* $a, a' \in A$, *then their union is also globally commutative.*

Proof. Let $F = \bigcup_a f^a$, $x \in \{0,1\}^Z$ and $s, t \in \mathcal{P}(Z)$. If x belongs to $R(f^a)$, then so do $F^{(s)}(x)$ and $F^{(t)}(x)$, and hence $F^{(s,t)}(x) = (f^a)^{(s,t)}(x) = (f^a)^{(t,s)}(x) = F^{(t,s)}(x)$. If x does not belong to any $R(f^a)$, then by definition $x \in U(F)$ and $F^{(s,t)}(x) = F^{(t,s)}(x) = x$. $\qquad \square$

$\qquad\qquad\qquad\qquad\qquad\qquad\qquad\qquad\qquad\qquad\qquad\qquad\qquad\qquad\qquad\square$

Lemma 5. *If f is globally commutative, then it is a union of arrangement networks.*

Proof. In the sequel, f satisfies **(C3)** and C is a connected component of $\Gamma(f)$.

Claim 3. *If $f^w(x) = y$ for some finite word $w = (w_1, \ldots, w_k)$ with $w_i \in \mathcal{P}(Z)$, then $f^{(\Delta(x,y))}(x) = y$.*

Proof. Let $\Delta := \Delta(x, y)$. Suppose $f^{(\Delta)}(x) \neq y$, then there exists $i \in \Delta$ such that $f_i(x) = x_i$ or in other words, $f^{(i)}(x) = x$. But then, for any word $w = (w_1, \ldots, w_k)$ where i appears exactly l times, we have

$$f_i^{(w_1, \ldots, w_k)}(x) = f_i^{(i)^l (w_1 \setminus i, \ldots, w_k \setminus i)}(x) = f_i^{(w_1 \setminus i, \ldots, w_k \setminus i)}(x) = x_i,$$

and hence $f^w(x) \neq y$. $\qquad \square$

Claim 4. *If $x, y \in C$, then there exist $s, s' \in \mathcal{P}(Z)$ such that $f^{(s)}(x) = f^{(s')}(y)$.*

Proof. Since x and y belong to the same component, there exists a sequence of configurations $x = x^0, x^1, \ldots, x^k = y \in \{0, 1\}^Z$ and a corresponding sequence of subsets $s^0, \ldots, s^{k-1} \in \mathcal{P}(Z)$ such that either $f^{(s^i)}(x^i) = x^{i+1}$ or vice versa, in alternation. Suppose k is minimal. If $k = 1$, then $f^{(s^0)}(x) = f^{(\emptyset)}(y) = y$, and we are done. If $k = 2$, then either $f^{(s^0)}(x) = x^1 = f^{(s^1)}(y)$, or $x = f^{(s^0)}(x^1)$ and $y = f^{(s^1)}(x^1)$ in which case $f^{(s^1)}(x) = f^{(s^0)}(y)$. Now suppose $k \geq 3$. Without loss of generality, we have $f^{(s^0)}(x) = x^1 = f^{(s^1)}(x^2)$ and $f^{(s^2)}(x^2) = x^3$. But then $f^{(s^0, s^2)}(x) = f^{(s^1, s^2)}(x^2) = f^{(s^2)}(x^3) =: \tilde{x}$; denoting $\Delta := \Delta(x, \tilde{x})$, Claim 3 shows that $f^{(\Delta)}(x) = \tilde{x}$. Thus, the sequence $x, \tilde{x}, x^3, \ldots, x^k$ contradicts the minimality of k. $\qquad\square$

Claim 5. *f is uniform nontrivial on C.*

Proof. Firstly, let e be an external dimension of C, then $C \subseteq \{x_e = a\}$ for some $a \in \{0, 1\}$ and hence $f_e = cst = a$. Secondly, let i be an internal dimension of C. Then f_i is nontrivial on C for any i, for otherwise C could be split into two components, one for each value of the coordinate i. Let $x \in C$ with $f_i(x) \neq x_i$, and suppose $y \in C$ has $x_i = y_i$. By Claim 4, there exist $s, s' \in \mathcal{P}(Z)$ such that $f^{(s)}(x) = f^{(s')}(y)$, and since $x_i = y_i$ we can suppose that $i \notin s \cup s'$. Then

$$f_i(y) = f_i^{(i, s')}(y) = f_i^{(s', i)}(y) = f_i^{(s, i)}(x) = f_i^{(i, s)}(x) = f_i(x),$$

thus f_i is uniform. $\qquad\square$

Claim 6. *On C, $f_i = cst = \neg z_i$ for any tight dimension and any i-border z of C.*

Proof. Suppose $f_i(x) = z_i$ for some $x \in C$ with $x_i \neq z_i$. Let $y = \overline{z^i} \in C$, we then have $f_i(y) = f_i(x) = z_i$ and hence $z \in C$. Thus, $f_i(x) = \neg z_i$ for all $x \in C$ with $x_i = \neg z_i$. Now, if $f_i(x) = z_i$ for some $x_i = z_i$, then f_i is trivial, which contradicts Claim 5. $\qquad\square$

Claim 7. *C is the content of an arrangement.*

Proof. Suppose C is not the content of an arrangement. Consider the decomposition of C into maximal subcubes $C = \bigcup_{\omega \in \Omega} X_\omega$, then there exist X_0, X_1 and $i \in Z$ such that $X_0 \subseteq H_0 := \{x : x_i = 0\}$ and $X_1 \subseteq H_1 := \{x : x_i = 1\}$. We also consider the two subcubes $Y_0 = X_0 \cup \{\overline{x^i} : x \in X_0\}$ and $Y_1 = X_1 \cup \{\overline{x^i} : x \in X_1\}$. We note that i is an internal dimension of C. If i is a free dimension of C, then $Y_0 \subseteq C$, which contradicts the maximality of X_0. If i is a tight dimension of C, then by Claim 6, f_i is constant on C. If $f_i = 1$, then $f^{(i)}(x) = \overline{x^i}$ for any $x \in X_0$, and again $Y_0 \subseteq C$; if $f_i = 0$ we similarly obtain $Y_1 \subseteq C$. $\qquad\square$

Then Claims 5, 6 and 7 conclude the proof. $\qquad\square$

If X is an arrangement containing at least two subcubes, then X has a tight variable, and hence no network for that arrangement is bijective. Conversely, if $\{X\}$ is an arrangement containing only one subcube, then there is only one bijective arrangement network for X, i.e. $f(x) = \neg x$ if $x \in X$ and $f(x) = x$ otherwise, which we shall refer to as the negation on X. We obtain the following classification of globally commutative, bijective Boolean networks.

Corollary 1. *Let f be a globally commutative, bijective Boolean network. Then f is a union of negations on subcubes.*

Therefore, the number $A(n)$ of globally commutative, bijective Boolean networks is equal to the number of partitions of the cube $\{0, 1\}^n$ into subcubes. This, in turn, is equal to the number of minimally unsatisfiable cnfs on n variables. The first few values of $A(n)$ are given in OEIS A018926.

References

1. Bridoux, F., Castillo-Ramirez, A., Gadouleau, M.: Complete simulation of automata networks. J. Comput. Syst. Sci. **109**, 1–21 (2020)
2. Cameron, P.J., Fairbairn, B., Gadouleau, M.: Computing in permutation groups without memory. Chic. J. Theor. Comput. Sci. **2014**(07), 1–20 (2014)
3. Goles, E., Noual, M.: Disjunctive networks and update schedules. Adv. Appl. Math. **48**(5), 646–662 (2012)
4. Noual, M., Sené, S.: Synchronism versus asynchronism in monotonic Boolean automata networks. Nat. Comput. **17**, 393–402 (2017)

Cellular String Generators

Martin Kutrib[iD] and Andreas Malcher[(⊠)][iD]

Institut für Informatik, Universität Giessen, Arndtstr. 2, 35392 Giessen, Germany
{kutrib,andreas.malcher}@informatik.uni-giessen.de

Abstract. In contrast to many investigations of cellular automata with regard to their ability to *accept* inputs under certain time constraints, we are studying here cellular automata towards their ability to *generate* strings in real time. Structural properties such as speed-up results and closure properties are investigated. On the one hand, constructions for the closure under intersection, reversal, and length-preserving homomorphism are presented, whereas on the other hand the non-closure under union, complementation, and arbitrary homomorphism is obtained. Finally, decidability questions such as emptiness, finiteness, equivalence, inclusion, regularity, and context-freeness are addressed.

1 Introduction

Cellular automata (CA) are a widely used model to describe, analyze, and understand parallel processes. They are in particular applied for massive parallel systems, since they are arrays of identical copies of deterministic finite automata where, in addition, the single nodes are homogeneously connected to both their immediate neighbors. Furthermore, they work synchronously at discrete time steps processing a parallel distributed input, where every cell is fed with an input symbol in a pre-initial step.

A standard approach to measure the computational power of some model is to study its ability to accept formal languages (see, for example, [13]). In general, the given input is accepted if there is a time step at which a designated cell, usually the leftmost one, enters an accepting state. Commonly studied models are two-way cellular automata with time restrictions such as real time or linear time, which means that the available time for accepting an input is restricted to the length of the input or to a multiple of the length of the input. An important restricted class are the real-time one-way cellular automata [3], where every cell is connected with its right neighbor only. Hence, the flow of information is from right to left only. A survey on results concerning the computational capacity, closure properties, and decidability questions for these models and references to the literature may be found, for example, in [9,10].

In the language accepting approach each computation can be considered as producing a yes or no answer for every possible input within a certain time. A much broader view on cellular automata computations is taken in [4,11], where

© IFIP International Federation for Information Processing 2020
Published by Springer Nature Switzerland AG 2020. All Rights Reserved
H. Zenil (Ed.): AUTOMATA 2020, LNCS 12286, pp. 59–70, 2020.
https://doi.org/10.1007/978-3-030-61588-8_5

cellular automata computations are considered as transducing actions, that is, they produce an output of size n for every input of size n under time constraints such as real and linear time. Thus, the point of view changes from a parallel language accepting device to a parallel language transforming device. The paper [4] discusses for cellular automata the time constraints of linear time and real time. Moreover, the inclusion relationships based on these constraints, closure properties, and relations to cellular automata considered as formal language acceptors are established. An important technical result is a speed-up theorem stating that every computation beyond real time can be sped up by a linear factor. The paper [11] considers also cellular automata with sequential input mode, called iterative arrays, as transducing devices. In particular, these devices are compared with the cellular automata counterpart with parallel input mode. In addition, the cellular transducing models are compared with classical sequential transducing devices such as finite state transducers and pushdown transducers.

In this paper, we will look on computations with cellular automata from yet another perspective. Rather than computing a yes or no answer or computing an output we are considering cellular automata as generating devices. This means in detail that the cellular automaton starts with an arbitrary number of cells being all in a quiescent state and, subsequently, works by applying its transition function synchronously to all cells. Finally, if the configuration reaches a fixpoint the sequence of cell states is considered as the *string generated*. From this point of view cellular automata compute a (partial) function mapping an initial length n to a string of length n over some alphabet. First investigations for this model have been made in [12]. In particular, the real-time generation of unary patterns is studied in depth and a characterization by time-constructible functions and their corresponding unary formal languages is given. In this paper, we will continue these investigations for real-time cellular automata and study, in particular, speed-up possibilities, closure properties, and decidability questions of the model.

It should be remarked that the notion of pattern generation is used for cellular automata also in other contexts. For example, in [15] the sequence of configurations produced by a cellular automaton starting with some input is considered as a two-dimensional pattern generated. Kari [8] describes a cellular automaton as universal pattern generator in the sense that starting from a finite configuration all finite patterns over the state alphabet are generated which means here that these patterns occur as infixes in the sequence of configurations computed.

The paper is organized as follows. In Sect. 2, we formally define how cellular automata accept and generate formal languages and we present a detailed example generating prefixes of the Thue-Morse sequence. Section 3 is devoted to structural properties of cellular string generators. Two speed-up results are presented which are used in the subsequent constructions showing closure under intersection, reversal, and length-preserving homomorphism. In Sect. 4, we deal with the problems of deciding emptiness, finiteness, infiniteness, inclusion, equivalence, regularity, and context-freeness of real-time cellular string generators. By showing that suitably encoded computations of a Turing machine can be generated by cellular automata in real time, all decidability problems mentioned turn out to be not semidecidable.

2 Preliminaries

We denote the non-negative integers by $\mathbb{N}$. Let Σ denote a finite set of letters. Then we write Σ^* for the *set of all finite strings* consisting of letters from Σ. The *empty string* is denoted by λ, and we set $\Sigma^+ = \Sigma^* \setminus \{\lambda\}$. A subset of Σ^* is called a *language* over Σ. For the *length of a string* w we write $|w|$. In general, we use $\subseteq$ for *inclusions* and $\subset$ for *strict inclusions*. For convenience, we use $S_\#$ to denote $S \cup \{\#\}$.

A two-way cellular automaton is a linear array of identical finite automata, called cells, numbered $1, 2, \ldots, n$. Except for border cells each one is connected to its both nearest neighbors. The state transition depends on the current state of a cell itself and the current states of its two neighbors, where the outermost cells receive a permanent boundary symbol on their free input lines. The cells work synchronously at discrete time steps.

Formally, a *deterministic two-way cellular automaton* (CA, for short) is a system $M = \langle S, \Sigma, F, s_0, \#, \delta \rangle$, where S is the finite, nonempty set of *cell states*, $\Sigma \subseteq S$ is set of *input symbols*, $F \subseteq S$ is the set of *accepting states*, $s_0 \in S$ is the *quiescent state*, $\# \notin S$ is the permanent *boundary symbol*, and $\delta : S_\# \times S \times S_\# \to S$ is the *local transition function* satisfying $\delta(s_0, s_0, s_0) = s_0$.

A *configuration* c_t of M at time $t \geq 0$ is a mapping $c_t : \{1, 2, \ldots, n\} \to S$, for $n \geq 1$, occasionally represented as a word over S. Given a configuration c_t, $t \geq 0$, its successor configuration is computed according to the global transition function Δ, that is, $c_{t+1} = \Delta(c_t)$, as follows. For $2 \leq i \leq n-1$,

$$c_{t+1}(i) = \delta(c_t(i-1)), c_t(i), c_t(i+1)),$$

and for the outermost cells we set

$$c_{t+1}(1) = \delta(\#, c_t(1), c_t(2)) \quad \text{and} \quad c_{t+1}(n) = \delta(c_t(n-1), c_t(n), \#).$$

Thus, the global transition function Δ is induced by δ.

Here, a cellular automaton M can operate as decider or generator of strings.

A cellular automaton *accepts* a string (or word) $a_1 a_2 \cdots a_n \in \Sigma^+$, if at some time step during the course of the computation starting in the *initial configuration* $c_0(i) = a_i$, $1 \leq i \leq n$, the leftmost cell enters an accepting state, that is, the leftmost symbol of some reachable configuration is an accepting state. If the leftmost cell never enters an accepting state, the input is *rejected*. The *language accepted by* M is denoted by $L(M) = \{ w \in \Sigma^+ \mid w \text{ is accepted by } M \}$.

A cellular automaton *generates* a string $a_1 a_2 \cdots a_n$, if at some time step t during the computation on the initial configuration $c_0(i) = s_0$, $1 \leq i \leq n$, (i) the string appears as configuration (that is, $c_t(i) = a_i$, $1 \leq i \leq n$) and (ii) configuration c_t is a fixpoint of the global transition function Δ (that is, the configuration is stable from time t on). The *pattern generated by* M is

$$P(M) = \{ w \in S^+ \mid w \text{ is generated by } M \}.$$

Since the set of input symbols and the set of accepting states are not used when a cellular automaton operates as generator, we may safely omit them from its definition.

Let $t\colon \mathbb{N} \to \mathbb{N}$ be a mapping. If all $w \in L(M)$ are accepted with at most $t(|w|)$ time steps, or if all $w \in P(M)$ are generated with at most $t(|w|)$ time steps, then M is said to be of time complexity t. If $t(n) = n$ then M operates in *real time*. The family of all patterns generated by a cellular automaton in real time is denoted by $\mathscr{P}_{rt}(M)$.

We illustrate the definitions with an example.

Example 1. The Thue-Morse sequence is an infinite sequence over the alphabet $\{0, 1\}$. The well-known sequence has applications in numerous fields of mathematics and its properties are non-trivial. There a several ways of generating the Thue-Morse sequence one of which is given by a Lindenmayer system with axiom 0 and rewriting rules $0 \to 01$ and $1 \to 10$. The generation of strings can be described as follows: starting with the axiom every symbol 0 (symbol 1) is in parallel replaced by the string 01 (10). This procedure is iteratively applied to the resulting strings and yields the prefixes $p_0 = 0$, $p_1 = 01$, $p_2 = 0110$, $p_3 = 01101001$, $p_4 = 0110100110010110$, and so on. We remark that the length of the prefix p_i is 2^i.

The pattern $P_{Thue} = \{p_i \mid i \geq 0\}$ derived therefrom can be generated by some cellular automaton in real time [12]. However, this means that nothing is generated whenever the length of the cellular automaton is not a power of two. Here, we are going to generalize this construction and extend the pattern generated in such a way that also prefixes p_i of the Thue-Morse sequence are generated even when the length of the cellular automaton is not a power of two. The goal is to generate on initial length n the prefix p_i with $i = \lceil \log_2(n) \rceil$. Since the length of the generated prefix is larger than the number of cells if n is not a power of two, we will group two adjacent symbols $x, y \in \{0, 1\}$ of the sequence into states $x|y$ where appropriate. Note that in the special case of an input length being a power of two the construction described here is the construction given in [12].

The basic idea is to work with a real-time version of the FSSP based on the time optimal solution of Waksman [14]. The latter solution starts with one general at the left end of the array and it takes $n - 1$ time steps (n being the length of the array) to reach the right end. If we start instead with two generals at both ends, where the left general symmetrically behaves as the right general, we save $n - 1$ time steps. Since we need one additional time step to initialize the generals at both ends, we can realize the FSSP within $2n - 2 - (n - 1) + 1 = n$ time steps, that is, within real time.

In the construction of the FSSP, the initial length is iteratively divided into halves, whereby dependent on the arity one or two middle points and thus one or two new generals are generated. In the first case, here the single middle cell is virtually split into two. These cells will represent two grouped adjacent symbols of the sequence. Next, we identify these cells. The following recursive formula $f(n, m)$ gives 2, if the mth cell on initial length n contains a compressed symbol and, otherwise, gives 1.

$$f(n,m) = \begin{cases} 1 & n = 1 \text{ or } m \leq 1, \\ 2 & n > 1 \text{ odd and } m = \frac{n+1}{2}, \\ f\left(\frac{n+1}{2}, \left(m \bmod \frac{n+1}{2}\right) + \left(m \text{ div } \frac{n+1}{2}\right)\right), & n > 1 \text{ odd and } m \neq \frac{n+1}{2}, \\ f\left(\frac{n}{2}, m \bmod \frac{n}{2}\right), & n > 1 \text{ even.} \end{cases}$$

For example, in Fig. 1 we have $f(15,4) = f(8,4) = f(4,0) = 1$, $f(15,8) = 2$, and $f(15,13) = f(8,6) = f(4,2) = f(2,0) = 1$.

The function f can be used to define the generated compressed Thue-Morse sequence. Let $f_n(m) = \sum_{j=1}^{m} f(n,j)$ and $p_i = w_{i,1}w_{i,2}\cdots w_{i,2^i}$ be an enumeration of the symbols of prefix p_i. Then, the corresponding compressed prefix $p_i'(n)$ on initial length n with $i = \lceil \log_2(n) \rceil$ is $p_i'(n,1)p_i'(n,2)\cdots p_i'(n,n)$, where we define $p_i'(n,m) = w_{i,f_n(m)}$, if $f(n,m) = 1$, and $p_i'(n,m) = w_{i,f_n(m)-1}w_{i,f_n(m)}$, if $f(n,m) = 2$. For example, if $n = 15$, we have $f(15,8) = 2$ and $f(15,j) = 1$ if $j \neq 8$. Hence, $f_{15}(8) = 9$ and $f_{15}(13) = 14$ which gives $p_4'(15,8) = 11$ and $p_4'(15,13) = 1$, respectively.

The general generation procedure is as follows (see Fig. 1 for an example). Initially, at time $\lceil n/2 \rceil + 1$, the left new middle cell obtains the information 0 and the right new middle cell obtains the information 1, or the new single and grouped middle cell obtains the information 0|1. In the latter case, the cell simulates two cells from now on. The signals sent out from the new middle cells to the left and right, respectively, are attached with this information. If these signals meet some other signal so that another one or two new middle cell(s) is (are) generated, the left cell gets the information 0 and the right cell gets the information 1 if the signal carried the information 0. Otherwise, the left cell gets the information 1 and the right cell gets the information 0. This behavior is iterated up to the last but one time step in which all cells have become a

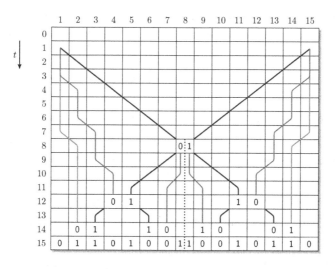

Fig. 1. Generation of the prefix $p_4 = 0110100110010110$ of the Thue-Morse sequence on initial length $n = 15$.

general. In the last time step, in which all cells are synchronized, a left signal 0
(1) in cell i at time $n-1$ leads to 0 (1) in cell $i-1$ and 1 (0) in cell i at time
n. Analogously, a right signal 0 (1) in cell i at time $n-1$ leads to 0 (1) in cell
i and 1 (0) in cell $i+1$ at time n. Note that here a split cell simulates two cells
that are counted to determine the numbers i. Finally, after the synchronization,
all states of the array represent the string generated and become permanent.

Let $\Sigma = \{0, 1, 0|0, 0|1, 1|0, 1|1\}$ be the alphabet and π be a projection to the
original letters, that is, $\pi(x) = x$ and $\pi(x|y) = xy$, for $x, y \in \{0, 1\}$. Then, the
pattern generated by the constructed real-time cellular automaton M has the
desired property $w \in P(M) \implies \pi(w) = p_i$ with $i = \lceil \log_2(|w|) \rceil$.   ∎

3   Structural Properties

For unary patterns of the form $P_\varphi = \{ a^n \mid \text{there is an } m \text{ with } n = \varphi(m) \}$, or
even $\hat{P}_\varphi = \{ x^n \mid x = a \text{ if there is an } m \text{ with } n = \varphi(m), \text{ and } x = b \text{ otherwise} \}$,
where $\varphi : \mathbb{N} \to \mathbb{N}$ is a time-constructible function, the three notions of language
acceptance, time-constructibility, and string generation are characterizing each
other, that is, they coincide. Here, we now turn to structural properties of the
string generators as speed-up and closures of the set of generated strings under
certain operations.

3.1   Speed-Up

Several types of cellular language acceptors can be sped-up as long as the remaining time complexity does not fall below real time. A proof in terms of trellis automata can be found in [2]. In [6,7] the speed-up results are shown for
deterministic and nondeterministic cellular and iterative language acceptors. The
proofs are based on sequential machine characterizations of the parallel devices.
In particular, for all $k \geq 1$, deterministic cellular automata can be sped-up from
$(n + t(n))$-time to $(n + \lceil t(n)/k \rceil)$-time [1,6,7]. The question of whether every
linear-time cellular language acceptor can be sped-up to real time is an open
problem.

The situation for string generators is more involved. While for language
acceptors usually only the states of one distinguished cell determine acceptance
or rejection, the states of all cells are the result of a string generation. So, these
known speed-up results do not apply here. However, in terms of transducers
that given an input of size n compute an output of size n, a speed-up result is
known [4] that can be adapted to our notion.

As a preliminary lemma we prove that cellular string generators working in
real time plus a constant amount of time can always be sped-up to real time.

Lemma 2. *Let M be a cellular string generator with time complexity $n + k$,
where $k \geq 1$ is a constant integer. Then an equivalent real-time string generator M' can effectively be constructed.*

Proof. The basic idea for the construction of M' is to have in every cell $k+1$ tracks such that at time t the tracks in M' are filled with states from M at time $t, t+1, \ldots, t+k$. Hence, time step $n+k$ in M is simulated at time n in M' in the last track. The construction works in two phases. In the first phase, we start the simulation of M at both ends, but we simulate $k+1$ time steps of M at once in every cell leaving the quiescent state s_0. In the remaining time steps, each cell shifts the contents of its ith track to its $(i-1)$st track for $2 \le i \le k+1$ and updates the entry in the $(k+1)$st track. Hence, every cell keeps track of the last $k+1$ time steps.

We have a left part and a right part of the computation in this first phase. For the left part we may assume that all missing information from the right can be replaced by the information s_0, since in the beginning all cells are in the quiescent state s_0. In addition, we have to provide each cell in the left part with the necessary information from the left, namely, with the states of the k cells to the left. This can be realized by using k additional tracks. Analogously, we can assume for the right part of the computation that missing information from the left can be replaced by s_0 and we can provide information about the states of the k cells to the right by using k tracks.

At time $n/2+1$ if the initial length n is even and at time $(n+1)/2$ if n is odd, the left and right part of the computation meet in the middle cell(s), from where the second phase starts. In this phase, all information to update the entries in the $(k+1)$st track is available taking into account both neighbors. Hence, the simulation of the last $k+1$ time steps can be continued. At time step n in M' we have eventually simulated the desired $(n+k)$th time step of M in the $(k+1)$st track. To extract this information in the nth time step of M' we start in the beginning in another track an instance of the FSSP. If the FSSP would fire at time step n, we just output the $(k+1)$st track that would be calculated at time step n. □

Next, we turn to show how to speed up the part of the time complexity beyond real time by a constant factor. As mentioned before, to this end we consider the involved and tricky construction shown for transductions in [4]. Before we turn to the adaption to our notion, we sketch the underlying idea of [4] to speed up the part of the time complexity beyond real time by a factor 2 (see Fig. 2). The basic idea is to compress the input of length n into the $\frac{n}{2}$ cells $\frac{1}{4}n+1, \frac{1}{4}n+2, \ldots, \frac{3}{4}n$, to simulate the given $(n+t(n))$-time cellular automaton with double speed on the compressed input, and to decompress the simulation result. The most involved part is the compression depicted in the red parts of the space-time diagram in Fig. 2. Roughly speaking, in these areas the compression takes place in addition to as many as possible simulation steps. The cells in the green area of the space-time diagram are in the quiescent state. The simulation in the blue area is with double speed. Concerning the time, once cell $\frac{1}{2}n$ has left the quiescent state it has to perform further $\frac{1}{2}n + t(n)$ steps. Since the simulation is with double speed, this takes $\frac{1}{4}n + \frac{1}{2}t(n)$ time. The decompression of the computation result takes another $\frac{1}{4}n$ time steps.

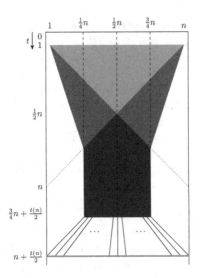

Fig. 2. Principle of speeding up the part of the time complexity beyond real time by a factor 2 according to [4].

Theorem 3. *Let M be a cellular string generator with time complexity $n + t(n)$, where $t\colon \mathbb{N} \to \mathbb{N}$ is a function such that M is synchronizable at time step $n + t(n)$. Then, for all $k \geq 1$, an equivalent string generator M' with time complexity $n + \lceil t(n)/k \rceil$ can effectively be constructed.*

Proof. The principle of the construction is as shown in [4] and has been described above. However, since a cellular string generator has to end a successful computation in a stable configuration there are differences with the transductions considered in [4]. So, basically, the simulation sketched in Fig. 2 has to be stopped synchronously at time $\frac{3}{4}n + \frac{1}{2}t(n)$, and the decompression has to be stopped synchronously at time $n + \frac{1}{2}t(n)$.

The first synchronization justifies the condition that M has to be synchronizable at time step $n + t(n)$. So, some FSSP that synchronizes M at this time is implemented on an extra track of M. Therefore, its simulation is finished by firing the cells $\frac{1}{4}n + 1, \frac{1}{4}n + 2, \dots, \frac{3}{4}n$ at time $\frac{3}{4}n + \frac{1}{2}t(n)$ as required. Additionally, the decompression phase is started synchronously.

The second synchronization is achieved by using two more extra tracks. On the first track an FSSP is implemented that synchronizes all cells at time step n. On the second track an FSSP is implemented that would synchronize all cells at time $n + t(n)$. But now this second FSSP runs with speed one until the first FSSP fires, and continues with half speed. So, it fires at time $n + \frac{1}{2}t(n)$ as required. □

3.2 Closure Properties

This subsection is devoted to investigating the closure properties of the family $\mathscr{P}_{rt}(\mathrm{CA})$. We start with the Boolean operations.

Proposition 4. *The family $\mathscr{P}_{rt}(CA)$ is closed under intersection. It is neither closed under union nor under complementation.*

Next, we look at the reversal operation. By interchanging the left hand and right hand entries of the local transition function, we immediately obtain that also the reversal of a real-time pattern can be generated by a real-time string generator.

Proposition 5. *The family $\mathscr{P}_{rt}(CA)$ is closed under reversal.*

Finally, we investigate homomorphisms and obtain that the family $\mathscr{P}_{rt}(\mathrm{CA})$ is not closed under arbitrary homomorphisms, whereas we can show that the family $\mathscr{P}_{rt}(\mathrm{CA})$ is closed under length-preserving homomorphisms.

Proposition 6. *The family $\mathscr{P}_{rt}(CA)$ is not closed under arbitrary homomorphism, but is closed under length-preserving homomorphism.*

Proof. For the non-closure under arbitrary homomorphism we consider the language $L = \{a, bb\}$, that can be generated by a real-time CA, and the homomorphism h which maps a to aa and b to b. Then, $h(L) = \{aa, bb\}$ which cannot be generated by any real-time CA.

Now, let $M = \langle S, s_0, \#, \delta \rangle$ be a real-time cellular automaton generating the pattern $P \subseteq \Sigma^*$, where $\Sigma \subseteq S$. Moreover, let $h \colon \Sigma^* \to \Gamma^*$ be a length-preserving homomorphism. For the construction of a cellular automaton that generates $h(P)$ in real time, we consider a primed version S' of the state set S, where the primed version of Σ is denoted by Σ', and we extend h to a length-preserving homomorphism h' mapping from S'^* to $(S' \cup \Gamma)^*$ such that $h'(a') = h(a)$, if $a' \in \Sigma'$, and $h'(s') = s'$, if $s' \in S' \setminus \Sigma'$.

Next, we will sketch the construction of a cellular automaton M' generating $P(M') = h'(P(M)) = h'(P) = h(P)$ in real time plus one that is subsequently sped up with Lemma 2 to work in real time. The basic idea is to work with three tracks and to start in the first track the simulation of M with state set S', and in the second track an instance of the FSSP. At time step n, when the FSSP fires, we generate in the third track the homomorphic image under h' of the first track. At time step $n + 1$, we check in every cell whether its state in the first track, that is in the simulated configuration of M at time n, would remain the same also in the next time step, that is, in the simulated configuration of M at time $n + 1$. If so, each such cell enters the state from the third track, that is the homomorphic image under h' of the state in the simulated configuration of M at time n. Otherwise, a new state p is entered that alternates with some other new state q. Furthermore, the transition function of M' is suitably complemented so that configurations containing only symbols from Γ remain stable. If the configuration of M at time n is stable, a string from Σ^* is generated by M and we obtain that the homomorphic image under h', which is equivalent to h on Σ, of this string is generated by M'. Otherwise, if M generates no string due to an instable configuration, then M' enters an instable configuration as well. Therefore, it is ensured that M' generates no string as well in such cases. $\square$

4   Decidability Problems

The first decidability problem we are dealing with is the question whether a given cellular automaton M generates a string at all, or whether the pattern $P(M)$ is empty. In order to show that the emptiness problem is not even semidecidable, even for cellular automata that generate patterns in real time, we reduce the problem to decide whether a Turing machine *does not halt* on empty input. It is well known that this problem is not semidecidable.

For the reduction, a technique from [5] is utilized. Basically, the history of a Turing machine computation is encoded into a string. It suffices to consider deterministic Turing machines with one single tape and one single read-write head. Without loss of generality and for technical reasons, we assume that the Turing machines can either print a symbol on the current tape square or move the head one square to the right or left. Moreover, they neither can print blanks nor leave a square containing a blank. Finally, a Turing machine is assumed to perform at least one transition. So, let Q be the state set of some Turing machine M, where q_0 is the initial state and $T \cap Q = \emptyset$ is the tape alphabet containing the blank symbol ⊔. Then a configuration of M can be written as a string of the form $T^*(Q, T)T^*$ such that $x_1 x_2 \cdots x_i(q, y)x_{i+1}x_{i+2}\cdots x_n$ is used to express that M is in state q, scanning tape symbol y, and $x_1 x_2 \cdots x_i y x_{i+1}x_{i+2}\cdots x_n$ is the support of the tape inscription.

Dependent on M we define the string v_M. Let $\$ \notin T \cup Q$, $m \geq 1$, and $w_i \in T^*(Q, T)T^*$, $0 \leq i \leq m$, be configurations of M. If M does not halt on empty input then $v_M = \lambda$. Otherwise we set $v_M = \$w_0\$w_1\$w_2\$\cdots\$w_m\$$, where w_0 is the initial configuration $(q_0, ⊔)$, w_m is a halting configuration, and w_i is the successor configuration of w_{i-1}, $1 \leq i \leq m$. Now we define a pattern as $P_M = \{v_M\} \setminus \{\lambda\}$.

Proposition 7. *Let M be a Turing machine. Then the pattern P_M is generated by some cellular automaton in real time.*

Basically, Proposition 7 is already the reduction of the problem to decide whether a Turing machine *does not halt* on empty input to our emptiness problem.

Theorem 8. *Given a real-time cellular automaton M, it is not semidecidable whether $P(M)$ is empty.*

Proof. Given an arbitrary Turing machine M', by Proposition 7 we construct a real-time cellular automaton M that generates the pattern $P_{M'}$. Pattern $P_{M'}$ is empty if and only if M' does not halt on empty input. So, if the emptiness of $P(M)$ were semidecidable then the problem to decide whether a Turing machine does not halt on empty input would be semidecidable, a contradiction.   □

From the undecidability of the emptiness problem the undecidability of the equivalence and inclusion problem follows immediately.

Corollary 9. *Given two real-time cellular automata M_1 and M_2, it is neither semidecidable whether $P(M_1) = P(M_2)$ nor whether $P(M_1) \subseteq P(M_2)$.*

Theorem 10. *Given a real-time cellular automaton M, it is neither semidecidable whether $P(M)$ is finite nor whether $P(M)$ is infinite.*

Proof. Let M' be an arbitrary Turing machine.

In order to show the assertion for finiteness, the pattern $P_{M'}$ is extended to $\hat{P}_{M'} = \{ v_{M'} a^n \mid n \geq 0 \} \setminus \{ a^n \mid n \geq 0 \}$. Since $\hat{P}_{M'}$ is empty and, thus, finite if and only if M' does not halt on empty input, the non-semidecidability of finiteness follows.

For infiniteness, the pattern $P_{M'}$ is changed differently. We set

$$\tilde{P}_{M'} = \{ \$w_0\$w_1\$ \cdots \$w_m\$ \mid m \geq 1, w_0 = (q_0, \sqcup), \text{ and } w_i \text{ is successor of } w_{i-1} \}.$$

Since pattern $\tilde{P}_{M'}$ is infinite if and only if M' does not halt on empty input, the non-semidecidability of infiniteness follows. $\square$

Next we turn to two decidability problems that, to some extent, relate pattern generation with language acceptance. It is of natural interest if a given language is regular or context free. So, here we can ask whether the strings of a pattern form a regular or context-free language.

Theorem 11. *Given a real-time cellular automaton M, it is neither semidecidable whether $P(M)$ forms a regular nor whether $P(M)$ forms a context-free language.*

Proof. Let L be an arbitrary recursively enumerable language. Then there is a Turing machine M' that enumerates the words of L, that is, it produces a list of not necessarily distinct words from L such that any word in L appears in the list. Modify M' as follows. Whenever a new word w is to be put into the list, the new machine M'' first checks if w already appears in the list. If yes, it is not put into the list again and M'' continues to enumerate the next word. If not, the word w is put into the list and after that M'' enters a state from some set Q_+ that indicates that a new word has been enumerated.

Similar as in the proof of Theorem 10 we set

$$\bar{P}_{M''} = \{ \$w_0\$w_1\$ \cdots \$w_m\$ \mid m \geq 1, w_0 = (q_0, \sqcup), w_i \text{ is successor of } w_{i-1},$$
$$\text{and the state in } w_m \text{ belongs to } Q_+ \}.$$

So, if L is finite, the pattern $\bar{P}_{M''}$ is finite and, thus, regular and context free. If L is infinite, the pattern $\bar{P}_{M''}$ is infinite and a simple application of the pumping lemma shows that it is not regular and not context free. In particular, pattern $\bar{P}_{M''}$ is regular and context-free if and only if L is finite. Since finiteness of recursively enumerable language is not semidecidable, the assertion follows. $\square$

Acknowledgements. The authors would like to thank the anonymous referees for their useful comments and remarks.

References

1. Bucher, W., Čulik II, K.: On real time and linear time cellular automata. RAIRO Inform. Théor. **18**, 307–325 (1984)
2. Choffrut, C., Čulik II, K.: On real-time cellular automata and trellis automata. Acta Inform. **21**, 393–407 (1984)
3. Dyer, C.R.: One-way bounded cellular automata. Inform. Control **44**, 261–281 (1980)
4. Grandjean, A., Richard, G., Terrier, V.: Linear functional classes over cellular automata. In: Formenti, E. (ed.) International workshop on Cellular Automata and Discrete Complex Systems and Journées Automates Cellulaires (AUTOMATA & JAC 2012). EPTCS, vol. 90, pp. 177–193 (2012)
5. Hartmanis, J.: On the succinctness of different representations of languages. In: Maurer, H.A. (ed.) ICALP 1979. LNCS, vol. 71, pp. 282–288. Springer, Heidelberg (1979). https://doi.org/10.1007/3-540-09510-1_22
6. Ibarra, O.H., Kim, S.M., Moran, S.: Sequential machine characterizations of trellis and cellular automata and applications. SIAM J. Comput. **14**, 426–447 (1985)
7. Ibarra, O.H., Palis, M.A.: Some results concerning linear iterative (systolic) arrays. J. Parallel Distrib. Comput. **2**, 182–218 (1985)
8. Kari, J.: Universal pattern generation by cellular automata. Theor. Comput. Sci. **429**, 180–184 (2012)
9. Kutrib, M.: Cellular automata - a computational point of view. In: Bel-Enguix, G., Jiménez-López, M.D., Martín-Vide, C. (eds.) New Developments in Formal Languages and Applications. SCI, vol. 113, pp. 183–227. Springer, Heidelberg (2008). https://doi.org/10.1007/978-3-540-78291-9_6
10. Kutrib, M.: Cellular automata and language theory. In: Meyers, R. (ed.) Encyclopedia of Complexity and Systems Science, pp. 800–823. Springer, New York (2009). https://doi.org/10.1007/978-0-387-30440-3_54
11. Kutrib, M., Malcher, A.: One-dimensional cellular automaton transducers. Fundam. Inform. **126**, 201–224 (2013)
12. Kutrib, M., Malcher, A.: One-dimensional pattern generation by cellular automata. LNCS. Springer (2020, to appear). Accepted at ACRI 2020
13. Smith III, A.R.: Cellular automata and formal languages. In: Symposium on Switching and Automata Theory, SWAT 1970, pp. 216–224. IEEE (1970)
14. Waksman, A.: An optimum solution to the firing squad synchronization problem. Inform. Control **9**, 66–78 (1966)
15. Wolfram, S.: Random sequence generation by cellular automata. Adv. Appl. Math. **7**, 123–169 (1986)

Everywhere Zero Pointwise Lyapunov Exponents for Sensitive Cellular Automata

Toni Hotanen$^{(\boxtimes)}$

University of Turku, Turku, Finland
`tonhot@utu.fi`

Abstract. Lyapunov exponents are an important concept in differentiable dynamical systems and they measure stability or sensitivity in the system. Their analogues for cellular automata were proposed by Shereshevsky and since then they have been further developed and studied. In this paper we focus on a conjecture claiming that there does not exist such a sensitive cellular automaton, that would have both the right and the left pointwise Lyapunov exponents taking the value zero, for each configuration. In this paper we prove this conjecture false by constructing such a cellular automaton, using aperiodic, complete Turing machines as a building block.

Keywords: Cellular automata · Sensitive · Lyapunov exponents

1 Introduction

Cellular automata are discrete dynamical systems, consisting of a set of configurations over a regular lattice of cells, a finite set of symbols, a neighbourhood vector of cells and a local update rule. The local update rule, together with the neighbourhood, defines a global rule. The global rule takes each cell to a state dictated by the local rule, when given the states of a given cell's neighbours as an input. The regular lattice we are interested in, is often a countable group. Classically the group is chosen to be $\mathbb{Z}^d$ for some $d \in \mathbb{Z}_+$, where d is called the dimension of the cellular automaton. The set of configurations is the set of all mappings from the selected group to the finite set of symbols. The global function is continuous with respect to the prodiscrete topology equipped to the set of configurations.

Lyapunov exponents are a measure for the rate of divergence of infinitesimally close trajectories in dynamical systems. They were first introduced in 1892 by Lyapunov in his doctoral thesis titled: The general problem of the stability of motion, English translation of which can be found in [11]. Since then they have been widely studied in the context of differentiable dynamical systems. Their importance in the study of non-linear dynamical systems, for example, can be

© IFIP International Federation for Information Processing 2020
Published by Springer Nature Switzerland AG 2020. All Rights Reserved
H. Zenil (Ed.): AUTOMATA 2020, LNCS 12286, pp. 71–85, 2020.
https://doi.org/10.1007/978-3-030-61588-8_6

found stated in [6]. In the context of cellular automata, the Lyapunov exponents were first considered by Wolfram in [14]. In Problem 2 of [15], the question to establish the exact connection between entropies and Lyapunov exponents is asked. A first formal definition of Lyapunov exponents for one-dimensional cellular automata is due to Shereshevsky in [12], which he defines as a shift-invariant measure of left and right perturbation speeds. In fact he proves an inequality connecting the measure-theoretical entropy of a cellular automaton and its shift-invariant Lyapunov exponents. Tisseur altered the definitions slightly and considers average Lyapunov exponents in [13], where he establishes a similar connection. Finally the pointwise Lyapunov exponents are defined in [2].

Connections between various dynamical properties of cellular automata and possible values of Lyapunov exponents have been studied for example in [5], [4] and [2]. In [4], a closed formula for calculating the value of the shift-invariant Lyapunov exponents, was presented in the setting of linear cellular automata. In [5], the authors proved that for a given positively expansive cellular automaton, the shift-invariant Lyapunov exponents are positive for each configuration. The result was later improved in [2], where it was shown that the same result holds for the pointwise Lyapunov exponents.

In [2], Bressaud and Tisseur construct a sensitive cellular automaton, for which the value of the left and right average Lyapunov exponents is zero, with respect to a specific measure. In the same paper the Conjecture 3 states, that for a given sensitive cellular automaton it is necessary, that there exists such a configuration, whose either left or right pointwise Lyapunov exponent has a positive value. The same conjecture is reinstated by Kůrka as a Conjecture 11 in [9]. Our aim is to prove this conjecture false, which we will do in Theorem 2. The result follows from the existence of complete, aperiodic Turing machines, established in [1] and [3], and their movement bounds proved in [8] and [7].

2   Preliminaries

An *alphabet* Σ is a finite set of *symbols*. A *word* of length n over an alphabet Σ is any element $w = (w_0, w_1, \ldots w_{n-1}) = w_0 w_1 \cdots w_{n-1}$ from the set $\Sigma^{[0,n)} = \Sigma^n$ and $|w| = n$ is the *length* of a word w. The *empty word* is denoted as ϵ and it is the unique word of length zero. A set of all finite words i.e. $\bigcup_{n \in \mathbb{N}} \Sigma^n$ is denoted as Σ^* and a set of all finite non-empty words $\Sigma^* \backslash \{\epsilon\}$ is denoted as Σ^+. A *concatenation* $\cdot : (\Sigma^*)^2 \to \Sigma^*$ is a mapping such that $u \cdot v = u_0 u_1 \ldots u_n v_0 v_1 \ldots v_m$, where $u = u_0 u_1 \ldots u_n$ and $v = v_0 v_1 \ldots v_m$. We will adapt the shorthand notation uv for the concatenation of any two words. Elements from the sets $\Sigma^{\mathbb{N}}$, $\Sigma^{\mathbb{Z}_-}$ and $\Sigma^{\mathbb{Z}}$ are called *right-infinite, left-infinite* and *bi-infinite* words, respectively. Furthermore we define a set $\Sigma^{\Omega} = \Sigma^+ \cup \Sigma^{\mathbb{N}} \cup \Sigma^{\mathbb{Z}_-} \cup \Sigma^{\mathbb{Z}}$. A concatenation of elements $u \in \Sigma^{\Omega}$ and $v \in \Sigma^{\Omega}$ is defined when u is finite or left-infinite and v is finite or right-infinite. Let $u \in \Sigma^{\Omega}$ and $w \in \Sigma^{\Omega}$, we will denote $u \sqsubseteq w$ if there exists such $j \in \mathbb{Z}$, that $u_{i+j} = w_i$ for each i in the domain of u, and say that u is a *subword* of w. If Σ and Γ are two alphabets, we will denote the set $\{uv \mid u \in \Sigma^{\alpha}, v \in \Gamma^{\beta}\}$ as $\Sigma^{\alpha} \Gamma^{\beta}$. where $\alpha \in \{\mathbb{Z}_-, *, +\} \cup \mathbb{N}$ and $\beta \in \{\mathbb{N}, *, +\} \cup \mathbb{N}$.

In this notation, if $\Sigma = \{a\}$, we will omit the brackets. Finally if $w \in \Sigma^*$, we will use the notation w^∞ for the right-infinite word $ww \cdots$.

A *Turing machine* is a 3-tuple (Q, Γ, δ), where Q is a finite set of *states*, Γ is a finite set of *symbols* and δ is a partial mapping $\delta : Q \times \Gamma \to Q \times \Gamma \times \Delta$ called a *transition rule*, where $\Delta = \{\leftarrow, \rightarrow\}$. A *configuration* is a 3-tuple (w, i, q), where $w \in \Gamma^{\mathbb{Z}}, i \in \mathbb{Z}$ and $q \in Q$. We will write $(w, i, q) \vdash (w', j, r)$ if $\delta(q, w_i) = (r, w'_i, d)$, where $w' \in \Gamma^{\mathbb{Z}}$, and $j = i+1$ if $d = \rightarrow$ and $j = i-1$ if $d = \leftarrow$ and $w'_k = w_k$ for each $k \neq i$. Inductively we define $\vdash^n$, where $\vdash$ is applied n times. Furthermore we will write $(w, i, q) \vdash^+ (w', j, r)$ if there exists such $n \in \mathbb{Z}_+$, that $(w, i, q) \vdash^n (w', j, r)$ holds. We will call a pair $(q, a) \in Q \times \Gamma$ an *error pair* if $\delta(q, a)$ is undefined. A Turing machine is called *complete* if it has no error pairs. We will call a configuration (w, i, q) *periodic* if $(w, i, q) \vdash^+ (w, i, q)$ and *weakly periodic* if there exists such $j \in \mathbb{Z}$, that $(w, i, q) \vdash^+ (w', i+j, q)$, where $w'_{k+j} = w_k$, for each $k \in \mathbb{Z}$. We will call a Turing machine *periodic* if all its configurations are periodic, and *aperiodic* if none of its configurations are weakly periodic.

A *topological dynamical system* is a pair (X, f), where X is a compact metric space and f is a continuous function $f : X \to X$.

A *shift dynamical system* is a dynamical system $(\Sigma^{\mathbb{Z}}, \sigma)$, where Σ is a finite set of symbols, $\Sigma^{\mathbb{Z}}$ is the space called the *full shift* and σ, called the *shift*, is defined in a way that $\sigma(x)_i = x_{i+1}$. The *metric* d of the space $\Sigma^{\mathbb{Z}}$ is defined as $d(x, y) = 2^{-\inf\{|i| \in \mathbb{N} | x_i \neq y_i\}}$. It is not difficult to see that the space $\Sigma^{\mathbb{Z}}$ is compact and that the function σ is continuous. An *endomorphism* is a continuous function $f : \Sigma^{\mathbb{Z}} \to \Sigma^{\mathbb{Z}}$, such that $f \circ \sigma = \sigma \circ f$.

A *one-dimensional cellular automaton* is a 3-tuple $\mathcal{A} = (\Sigma, N, h)$, where Σ is a finite set of symbols called *states*, N is a *neighbourhood* $(i_1, i_2, \ldots, i_n) \in \mathbb{Z}^n$ and $h : \Sigma^n \to \Sigma$ is a *local rule*. If $N = [-r, r]$, we call N a *radius-r* neighbourhood. In the context of cellular automata, we call the full shift $\Sigma^{\mathbb{Z}}$ a *configuration space* and refer to its elements as *configurations*. The local rule together with the neighbourhood induces a global rule $f : \Sigma^{\mathbb{Z}} \to \Sigma^{\mathbb{Z}}$, which is defined in such a way that $f(c)_i = h(c_{i+i_1}, c_{i+i_2}, \cdots, c_{i+i_n})$. We make no distinction between a cellular automaton and its global rule. By the Curtis-Hedlund-Lyndon theorem, the cellular automata, sometimes abbreviated as CA, are exactly the endomorphisms of the shift dynamical systems.

Definition 1. *A dynamical system (X, f) is sensitive if*

$$\exists \epsilon > 0 \colon \forall \delta > 0 \colon \forall x \in X \colon \exists y \in B_\delta(x) \colon \exists n \in \mathbb{N} \colon f^n(y) \notin B_\epsilon(f^n(x)).$$

Definition 2. *Let (Σ, N, h) be a one-dimensional cellular automaton, with a global rule $f : \Sigma^{\mathbb{Z}} \to \Sigma^{\mathbb{Z}}$. For every $c \in \Sigma^{\mathbb{Z}}$, we define*

$$W_m^+(c) = \{c' \in \Sigma^{\mathbb{Z}} \mid \forall i \geq m, c'_i = c_i\}$$

and

$$W_m^-(c) = \{c' \in \Sigma^{\mathbb{Z}} \mid \forall i \leq m, c'_i = c_i\}.$$

Furthermore we define

$$I_n^+(c) = \min\{m \in \mathbb{N} \mid f^i(W_{-m}^+(c)) \subseteq W_0^+(f^i(c)), \forall i \leq n\}$$

and

$$I_n^-(c) = \min\{m \in \mathbb{N} \mid f^i(W_m^-(c)) \subseteq W_0^-(f^i(c)), \forall i \leq n\}$$

Finally we define the pointwise Lyapunov exponents as

$$\lambda^+(c) = \liminf_{n \to \infty} \frac{I_n^+(c)}{n}$$

and

$$\lambda^-(c) = \liminf_{n \to \infty} \frac{I_n^-(c)}{n}.$$

Definition 3. *Let X be a set. A relation is a subset $R \subseteq X \times X$. We will use the standard notation aRb if $(a, b) \in R$. We will denote the complement of R as R^c, i.e. $R^c = (X \times X) \setminus R$.*

One way to simulate Turing machines in the CA setting, is to use the moving head model, or TMH for short, as introduced in [10] and by adding arrows, which separate different simulation areas from each other. We will be using a slight variation.

In the following definition we will describe a function induced from a given Turing machine. The function can then be used to define different types of local rules for CA. The construction is using the conveyor belt model, which has been used previously at least in [7], albeit the notations might differ.

Definition 4. *Let $\mathcal{M} = (Q, \Gamma, \delta)$ be a Turing machine. We will define an alphabet for the conveyor belt model. Elements from Q_2 will be called Turing machine heads and elements from T_2 will be called tape symbols. The set $\Delta = \{\rightarrow, \leftarrow\}$, consisting of direction symbols, is used for locating the Turing machine heads. The conveyor belt model uses two layers of tape, where the second one is reversed and the two tapes are connected at the ends of the simulation areas. We will define a relation, which allows us to define these simulation areas as simulation words, each consisting of at most one Turing machine head and where directions are forced to point to the unique Turing machine head. Let $\Gamma_2' = Q_2 \cup T_2$, where $Q_2 = \Gamma^2 \times Q \cup Q \times \Gamma^2$, $T_2 = \Gamma^2 \times \Delta$.*

Define a relation R_2 in a following way: Let $a \in \Gamma_2'$ and $b \in \Gamma_2'$, then

$$aR_2b \text{ if } \begin{cases} a \in \Gamma^2 \times \{\rightarrow\} \wedge b \in (\Gamma^2 \times \{\rightarrow\}) \cup Q_2 \\ \vee \quad a \in Q_2 \wedge b \in \Gamma^2 \times \{\leftarrow\} \\ \vee \quad a \in \Gamma^2 \times \{\leftarrow\} \wedge b \in \Gamma^2 \times \{\leftarrow\}. \end{cases}$$

Now we can define a set of simulation words:

$$\Sigma_{\mathcal{M},2} = \{w \in \Gamma_2'^\Omega \mid w_j R_2 w_{j+1}, \forall j\}.$$

In the following, in the case that the input word contains a Turing machine head, we will assume $uvwxy$ to be such a decomposition of the input word, that $w \in Q_2$ and that the following conditionals hold: If $|uv| > 0$, then $|v| = 1$. If $|xy| > 0$, then $|x| = 1$. This decomposition is then unique. In the cases when *the input word consists of only tape symbols the decomposition can be arbitrary. From the transition rule of the Turing machine, we can construct a mapping* $m_2 : \Sigma_{\mathcal{M},2} \to \Sigma_{\mathcal{M},2}$ *in the following way:*

$$m_2(uvwxy) = \begin{cases} uv'w'xy & \text{if } w = (q,a,a') \wedge v = (b,b',\to) \wedge \delta(q,a) = (r,c,\leftarrow), \\ & \text{where } v' = (r,b,b') \wedge w' = (c,a',\leftarrow), \\ w'xy & \text{if } uv = \epsilon \wedge, w = (q,a,a') \wedge \delta(q,a) = (r,c,\leftarrow), \\ & \text{where } w' = (c,a',r), \\ uv'w'xy & \text{if } w = (a,a',q) \wedge v = (b,b',\to) \wedge \delta(q,a') = (r,c',\to), \\ & \text{where } v' = (b,b',r) \wedge w' = (a,c',\leftarrow), \\ w'xy & \text{if } uv = \epsilon \wedge, w = (a,a',q) \wedge \delta(q,a') = (r,c',\to), \\ & \text{where } w' = (r,a,c'), \\ uvw'x'y & \text{if } w = (q,a,a') \wedge x = (b,b',\leftarrow) \wedge \delta(q,a) = (r,c,\to), \\ & \text{where } x' = (r,b,b') \wedge w' = (c,a',\to), \\ uvw' & \text{if } xy = \epsilon \wedge, w = (q,a,a') \wedge \delta(q,a) = (r,c,\to), \\ & \text{where } w' = (c,a',r), \\ uvw'x'y & \text{if } w = (a,a',q) \wedge x = (b,b',\to) \wedge \delta(q,a') = (r,c',\leftarrow), \\ & \text{where } x' = (b,b',r) \wedge w' = (a,c',\to), \\ uvw' & \text{if } xy = \epsilon \wedge, w = (a,a',q) \wedge \delta(q,a') = (r,c',\leftarrow), \\ & \text{where } w' = (r,a,c'), \\ uvwxy & \text{otherwise.} \end{cases}$$

Definition 5. *Let* $\mathcal{M} = (Q,\Gamma,\delta)$ *be a Turing machine. Using the notations introduced in Definition 4, we define a tracking function* $T : \Sigma_{\mathcal{M},2} \times \mathbb{N} \to \mathbb{Z}$, *where* $T(w,j) = k$ *if* $m_2^j(w)_k \in Q_2$ *and* $T(w,j) = 0$ *if* $w_i \notin Q_2$ *for each* i *in the inputs domain. We also define the number of indices visited by a Turing machine head in* j *steps, given some initial word, by a function* $V(w,j) : \Sigma_{\mathcal{M},2} \times \mathbb{N} \to \mathbb{N}$, *defined as* $V(w,j) = |\{T(w,j') \in \mathbb{Z} \mid j' \le j\}|$. *Finally we define a movement bound* $M : \mathbb{N} \to \mathbb{N}$ *as a function such that* $M(j) = max_{w \in \Sigma_{\mathcal{M},2}} V(w,j)$.

The sublinearity of the movement bound for aperiodic Turing machines is already proved in [8]. We will however make use of the following tighter bound.

Theorem 1. *[7] Let* $\mathcal{M} = (Q,\Gamma,\delta)$ *be Turing machine, and* M *its movement bound. If* $\mathcal{M}$ *is aperiodic, then* $M = \mathcal{O}(\frac{n}{\log n})$.

3   Lyapunov Exponents for Sensitive Cellular Automata

In this section we study the question whether or not the sum of the pointwise Lyapunov exponents of a given sensitive CA can take the value 0 or not. We use the notations of the previous sections without explicitly referring to them. In Theorem 2 we show how to construct a sensitive cellular automaton for a given aperiodic Turing machine, such that its left and right pointwise Lyapunov exponents are bounded from above by a sublinear function derived from the movement bound of the Turing machine.

Theorem 2. *There exists such a sensitive one-dimensional cellular automaton (Σ, N, f), that $\lambda^+(c) = \lambda^-(c) = 0$ for every configuration $c \in \Sigma^{\mathbb{Z}}$.*

Proof. Let $\mathcal{M} = (Q, \Gamma, \delta)$ be an aperiodic, complete Turing machine. We will alter $\mathcal{M}$ slightly to produce a new Turing machine $\mathcal{M}' = (Q', \Gamma, \delta')$, where $Q' = Q \times \{0, 1\}$ and $\delta'((q, x), a) = ((r, x), b, d)$, where $\delta(q, a) = (r, b, d)$. Essentially this modification gives us two copies of the original Turing machine and the computations of the new machine can be projected to the computations of the original machine. Using the new Turing machine, we can set our symbol set for the CA, which we are constructing, as $\Sigma = \Gamma_2' \cup \{>\}$. We will refer the symbol $>$ as the *eraser*. We will also use the notations $Q_2^i = \Gamma^2 \times Q \times \{i\} \cup Q \times \{i\} \times \Gamma^2$, where $i \in \{0, 1\}$ and $Q_2 = Q_2^0 \cup Q_2^1$. For each configuration $c \in \Sigma^{\mathbb{Z}}$, we define a set of locations for the Turing machine heads as

$$H_c = \{i \in \mathbb{Z} \mid c_i \in Q_2\}$$

and a set of locations for the erasers as

$$E_c = \{i \in \mathbb{Z} \mid c_i = >\}.$$

Next we define the *simulation bounds* as functions $l_c : H_c \to \mathbb{Z} \cup \{-\infty\}$ and $r_c : H_c \to \mathbb{Z} \cup \{\infty\}$ in the following way:

$$l_c(i) = \sup\{j \in \mathbb{Z} \mid j \leq i \text{ and } c_{j-1} R_2^c c_j\}$$

and

$$r_c(i) = \inf\{j \in \mathbb{Z} \mid i \leq j \text{ and } c_j R_2^c c_{j+1}\}.$$

From these bounds we can define the set of cells that are not part of any simulation area as

$$U_c = \mathbb{Z} \setminus \left(\bigcup_{i \in H_c} (l_c(i) - 1, r_c(i) + 1) \right).$$

Using the simulation bounds, we can define a function, which simulates all Turing machines in their respective simulation areas as $m : \Sigma^{\mathbb{Z}} \to \Sigma^{\mathbb{Z}}$, where

$$m(c)_{(l_c(i)-1, r_c(i)+1)} = m_2(c_{(l_c(i)-1, r_c(i)+1)}) \ \forall i \in H_c \text{ and}$$
$$m(c)_i = c_i \ \forall i \in U_c.$$

Clearly m is a cellular automaton since we can extract a radius-1 local rule from its definition.

Next we fix a state $a_0 \in \Gamma^2 \times \{\leftarrow\}$ and define a second cellular automaton $e : \Sigma^{\mathbb{Z}} \to \Sigma^{\mathbb{Z}}$, whose local rule is described in Table 1. The dynamics of e can be described in the following way: If a cell i, containing the eraser state $>$, sees a Turing machine head from the state set Q_2^1 at a cell $i - 1$, then the eraser state gets pushed to the next cell at $i + 1$. This happens regardless of the previous content of the cell $i + 1$. As a consequence, the simulation area in the left side increases by one cell. If there is a simulation area on the right side, then either its size is reduced by one or it is removed entirely. The simulation area gets removed if there is a Turing machine head at a cell $i + 1$ or $i + 2$. In such situation, the Turing machine head is replaced with a tape symbol a_0. Otherwise if a cell at state $>$ does not see a Turing machine head from the state set Q_2^1 to their immediate left, then it stays at its current state. When a Turing machine head from the state set Q_2^1 moves an eraser state, it changes to an equivalent symbol from the state set Q_2^0. If a Turing machine head from the state set Q_2^0 visits the left bound of the simulation area, which it belongs to, then if it does not get erased, it changes to an equivalent symbol from the state set Q_2^1. The idea is that the simulation areas can increase in their size arbitrarily far to the right, but only one cell at a time and in between the increments, the Turing machine head must visit the left bound of the simulation area.

Table 1. The definition of the local rule of the CA $e : \Sigma^{\mathbb{Z}} \to \Sigma^{\mathbb{Z}}$. Here a_0 is a fixed state from the set $\Gamma^2 \times \{\leftarrow\}$. The rule uses a neighbourhood $(-2, -1, 0, 1)$. Input is written on the first row and output on the second row. If the output is written, but the input is partially missing, it means that the missing cells do not affect the output. For the inputs that do not appear in the table, the local rule behaves as the identity mapping.

$q, q' \in Q_2, q_i = (q, i), x \in \Sigma$

$u \in \Sigma \setminus Q_2^1, u' \in \Sigma \setminus Q_2, v, v' \in \Sigma \setminus \{>\}, v'' \in \Gamma^2 \times \{\leftarrow\} \cup Q_2$

$q_1 > x\ u'$	$q_1 > x\ q'$	$v\ v'\ q_1 >$
$a_0 >\ u'$	$a_0 >\ a_0$	$q_0\ a_0$
$u > u'$	$u > q'$	$v\ v''\ q_0$
$>\ u'$	$>\ a_0$	q_1

We are ready to define our cellular automaton of interest as $f : \Sigma^{\mathbb{Z}} \to \Sigma^{\mathbb{Z}}$, where $f = m \circ e$. The behaviour of the CA is depicted in Fig. 1.

In Lemmas 1 and 2 we prove, that the CA we constructed has the desired properties and therefore the claim follows. □

Lemma 1. *The cellular automaton (Σ, N, f) constructed in Theorem 2 has the property that $\lambda^+(c) = \lambda^-(c) = 0$ for every configuration $c \in \Sigma^{\mathbb{Z}}$.*

Proof. We will begin the proof by introducing tracking functions for the eraser states, the simulation bounds and the Turing machine heads. The point of them is, that given an initial configuration and a cell containing a Turing machine head, an eraser or a simulation bound, we can tell to which cell said symbol has travelled to in time. In the output of each function, we will use the symbol $-$ to denote, that the symbol no longer exists, i.e. it has been destroyed by a symbol $>$. We will then show that a difference can only propagate inside each simulation area or by the movement of the simulation areas. In either case the movement is

Fig. 1. In this figure, we have depicted the behaviour of the CA constructed in Theorem 2. The black lines represent the left and right simulation bounds, the blue and cyan lines represent Turing machine heads from the sets Q_2^1 and Q_2^0, respectively, and the red lines represent the erasers. We also note, that in the figure, time increases from top to bottom. One can witness several types of behaviour in the two simulation areas. When the Turing machine head in the state from the set Q_2^1, of the left simulation area, visits the right boundary, then in the next time-step, the eraser moves one cell to the right, which also moves the left boundary of the second simulation area. In the same time step, the Turing machine head switches to some state in the set Q_2^0. Such Turing machine heads do not move the eraser states as witnessed when the cyan coloured line visits the right boundary. For the Turing machine to be allowed to move the eraser state again, it needs to switch back to an element from Q_2^1, which happens if and only if it visits the left boundary. The right simulation area does not have an eraser on the right side and hence its simulation area can never increase in size. In the middle of the image we can see that the Turing machine head on the right simulation area visits a cell within the distance of two, to a cell containing an eraser state and hence gets removed. This happens eventually in all simulation areas, in which at some time-step an eraser state can be seen in a cell within distance two to its left boundary. (Color figure online)

bounded from above by a sublinear function derived from the movement bound of the Turing machine.

First we will define the tracking function for the eraser states as $e_c : E_c \times \mathbb{N} \to \mathbb{Z} \cup \{-\}$, where

$$
e_c(i,j) = \begin{cases} i & \text{if } j = 0, \\ e_c(i, j-1) + 1 & \text{if } f^{j-1}(c)_{[e_c(i,j-1)-1, e_c(i,j-1)]} \in Q_2^1 >, \\ - & \text{if } f^{j-1}(c)_{[e_c(i,j-1)-2, e_c(i,j-1)-1]} \in Q_2^1 >, \\ e_c(i, j-1) & \text{otherwise.} \end{cases}
$$

Next we will define the tracking functions for the simulation bounds and for the Turing machine head, inductively with respect to $j \in \mathbb{N}$, as $l_c : H_c \times \mathbb{N} \to \mathbb{Z} \cup \{-\}$, $r_c : H_c \times \mathbb{N} \to \mathbb{Z} \cup \{-\}$ and $h_c : H_c \times \mathbb{N} \to \mathbb{Z} \cup \{-\}$, where

$$l_c(i,j) = \begin{cases} l_c(i) & \text{if } j = 0, \\ l_c(i,j-1)+1 & \text{if } f^{j-1}(c)_{[l_c(i,j-1)-2,l_c(i,j-1)+1]} \in Q_2^1 > T_2T_2, \\ l_c(i,j-1) & \text{if } f^{j-1}(c)_{[l_c(i,j-1)-2,l_c(i,j-1)-1]} \notin Q_2^1 >, \\ & \text{and } > \not\sqsubseteq f^{j-1}(c)_{[h_c(i,j-1)-2,h_c(i,j-1)-1]}, \\ - & \text{if } > \sqsubset f^{j-1}(c)_{[h_c(i,j-1)-2,h_c(i,j-1)-1]}, \end{cases}$$

$$r_c(i,j) = \begin{cases} r_c(i) & \text{if } j = 0, \\ r_c(i,j-1)+1 & \text{if } l_c(i,j) \neq - \\ & \text{and } f^{j-1}(c)_{[r_c(i,j-1),r_c(i,j-1)+1]} \in Q_2^1 >, \\ r_c(i,j-1) & \text{if } l_c(i,j) \neq - \\ & \text{and } f^{j-1}(c)_{[r_c(i,j-1),r_c(i,j-1)+1]} \notin Q_2^1 >, \\ - & \text{if } l_c(i,j) = -, \end{cases}$$

and

$$h_c(i,j) = \begin{cases} i & \text{if } j = 0, \\ k & \text{if } l_c(i,j) \leq k \leq r_c(i,j) \\ & \text{and } f^j(c)_k \in Q_2, \\ - & \text{if } l_c(i,j) = -. \end{cases}$$

We will show that for each $i' \in E_{f(c)}$ there exists unique $i \in E_c$, such that $e_c(i,1) = i'$. By the definition of f it follows immediately, that $c_{i'} = >$ or $c_{i'-1} = >$ and furthermore if only the latter holds, then necessarily $c_{i'-2} \in Q_2^1$. By the definition of e_c if $c_{[i'-2,i'-1]} \in Q_2^1 >$, then $i' = i+1$ and otherwise $i = i'$. Then furthermore by a straightforward induction, it holds that for each $n \in \mathbb{N}$ and $i' \in E_{f^n(c)}$ there exists unique $i \in E_c$, such that $e_c(i,n) = i'$.

Analogously we will show that for each $i' \in H_{f(c)}$ there exists unique $i \in H_c$, such that $h_c(i,1) = i'$, $l_c(i,1) = l_{f(c)}(i')$ and $r_c(i,1) = r_{f(c)}(i')$. From the definition of the CA m, it follows immediately that there exists such $i \in [i'-1, i'+1]$, that $i \in H_c$. Let us first assume, that such i is unique. Then by definition $l_c(i) = \sup\{j \in \mathbb{Z} \mid j \leq i \text{ and } c_{j-1}R_2^c c_j\}$. Clearly if $l_c(i) = -\infty$, then also $l_{f(c)}(i') = -\infty$. Let us then assume that $l_c(i) \in \mathbb{Z}$. From the definition of m and e it follows that $l_{f(c)}(i') \in [l_c, l_c+1]$ and furthermore $l_{f(c)}(i') = l_c+1$ if and only if $c_{[l_c-2,l_c-1]} \in Q_2^1 >$. But this is consistent with the definition of $l_c(i,1)$ and hence $l_c(i,1) = l_{f(c)}(i')$. Similarly we can show that $r_c(i,1) = r_{f(c)}(i')$. It is then apparent, that $h_c(i,1) = i'$ as cell i' is the only cell containing a Turing machine head in the interval $(l_c(i,1) - 1, r_c(i,1) + 1)$. If there exist multiple Turing machine heads in the interval $[i'-1, i'+1]$, then let us first assume that $i'-1 \in H_c$ and $i'+1 \in H_c$. Then if $i' \in H_c$ it follows that $l_c(i') = i' = r_c(i')$ and since $i'-1 \neq >$ and $i'+1 \neq >$, we have that $l_c(i',1) = i' = r_c(i',1)$ and hence the claim follows. If $i' \notin H_c$, then $i' \in T_2$, hence either we have that $r_c(i'-1) = i'$ and $l_c(i'+1) = i'+1$ or $l_c(i'+1) = i'$ and $r_c(i'-1) = i'-1$. We only prove the case of the former as the latter is analogous. Immediately it follows that $r_c(i'-1,1) = i' = r_{f(c)}(i')$ as $i'+1 \neq >$. The analysis that results in to showing that $l_c(i'-1,1) = l_{f(c)}(i')$ is similar to the case where there was only one Turing machine head in the interval $[i'-1, i'+1]$. Hence we have that $h_c(i,1) = i'$, where $i = i'-1$. The case when $i'-1 \in H_c$, $i' \in H_c$, but $i'+1 \notin H_c$ and the case when $i'-1 \notin H_c$, $i' \in H_c$, but $i'+1 \in H_c$ are proved similarly. Now again by a straightforward induction it can be proved that for each $n \in \mathbb{N}$ and $i' \in H_{f^n(c)}$ there exists unique $i \in H_c$, such that $l_c(i,n) = l_{f^n(c)}(i')$, $r_c(i,n) = r_{f^n(c)}(i')$ and $h_c(i,n) = i'$.

Denote by $S_c(i,j) = (l_c(i,j)-1, r_c(i,j)+1)$, $w_{i,j} = c_{S_c(i,j)}$ and $s_{i,j} = |w_{i,j}|$. Suppose that $i \in H_c$ and $j \in \mathbb{N}$ are such that $r_c(i,j+1) = r_c(i,j) + 1$. By definition of the tracking function, we have that $f^j(c)_{[r_c(i,j),r_c(i,j)+1]} \in Q_2^1 >$ and by the definition of the CA e, we have that $f^{j+1}(c)_{h_c(i,j+1)} \in Q_2^0$. We assume that there exists such $k \in \mathbb{N}$, that $r_c(i,j+1) < r_c(i,j+1+k)$. Then necessarily, from the aperiodicity of the Turing machine, we get that there exists a minimal such $k' \geq 1$, that $h_c(i,j+k') = l_c(i,j+k')$. From the definition of e, this means that $f^{j+k''}(c)_{h_c(i,j+k'')} \in Q_2^0$ for each $1 \leq k'' \leq k'$ and $f^{j+k'+1}(c)_{h_c(i,j+k'+1)} \in Q_2^1$. Notice that it also implicitly holds that $> \not\subset f^t(c)_{[l_c(i,t)-2,l_c(i,t)-1]}$ for each $t \leq j+k'$ as otherwise we would have $h_c(i,j+k') = -$. We denote by $M^{-1}(n) = \min\{t \in \mathbb{N} \mid M(t) \geq n\}$ for each $n \in \mathbb{N}$. By the movement bound of the Turing machine we have that $M^{-1}(s_{i,j}) \leq k' \leq p^{s_{i,j+1}}$, where $p = |\Sigma|$. Furthermore from the definition of k, we have that $M^{-1}(s_{i,j+1}) \leq k - k' \leq p^{s_{i,j+1}}$ and hence $2M^{-1}(s_{i,j}) \leq k \leq 2p^{s_{i,j+1}}$. It is easy to see that during these k steps a valid Turing machine computation is performed with the input word $w_{i,j+k}$. Finally let $z_j = s_{i,j} - s_{i,0}$ and assume that $r_c(i,j) = h_c(i,j)$. From the above considerations we get that $M^{-1}(s_{i,0} + z_j - 1) \leq j \leq 2 \sum\limits_{1 \leq k \leq z_j} p^{(s_{i,0}+k)} \leq p^{(s_{i,0}+2+z_j)}$. From the lower bound it follows that $|\{\alpha_{i,j} \in \mathbb{N} \mid j \leq n\}| \leq M(n)$, for each $n \in \mathbb{N}$ and $i \in H_c \cup E_c$, where α is any of the tracking functions for either the simulation bounds, the Turing machine heads or the erasers.

We are ready to prove the claim of the theorem. Let $c \in \Sigma^{\mathbb{Z}}$. For an infinite set of integers $n \in \mathbb{N}$, we want to find such values $m_n \in \mathbb{N}$, that if $c' \in W_{-m_n}^+(c)$ and there exists j_n, such that $f^{j_n}(c') \notin W_{-m_n}^+(f^{j_n}(c))$, then $j_n > n$. For each n, we can first assume that $m_n \geq M(n)$. We will analyse three cases: 1) None of the cells in the interval $[-m_n - 3, 0]$ are in the eraser state in either of the configurations, during the first n iterations. 2) There is an upper bound $k < n$, after which none of the cells in the interval $[-m_n - 3, 0]$ are in the eraser state in either of the configurations. 3) One of the configurations has a cell in the interval $[-m_n - 3, 0]$, which is at an eraser state at the nth iteration.

First let us assume that $> \not\subset f^j(c'')_{[-m_n-3,0]}$ holds for each $j \leq n$ and $c'' \in \{c, c'\}$. Then by the definition of the global rule e, we have that $e(f^j(c''))_i = f^j(c'')_i$ for each $j \leq n$, $i \in [-m_n, 1]$ and $c'' \in \{c, c'\}$. Hence if $j_n \leq n$, is such that $f^{j_n}(c') \notin W_{-m_n}^+(f^{j_n}(c))$, then the difference must be caused by applying the global rule m. By the definition of m, this means that $f^{j_n}(c'')_0 \in Q_2$ for either $c'' = c$ or $c' = c$. From the movement bound and the assumption that $m_n \geq M(n)$, it then follows that there exists such $i \in H_{c''}$, that $h_{c''}(i,j) \in [-m_n, m_n]$ for each $j \leq n$. Since $c' \in W_{-m_n}^+(c)$, then $i \in H_c \cap H_{c'}$ and hence locally within the cells in $[-m_n, m_n]$, the same Turing machine computation is simulated for the n steps and thus $j_n > n$.

Assume then that there exists such $j \leq n$ and $c'' \in \{c, c'\}$, that $> \sqsubset f^j(c'')_{[-m_n-3,0]}$. We further assume, that there exists minimal such $k < n$, that $> \not\sqsubset f^j(c'')_{[-m_n-3,0]}$ for each $c'' \in \{c, c'\}$ and $j \in \mathbb{N}$, such that $k < j \leq n$. Then due to definition of e, necessarily for either $c'' = c$ or $c'' = c'$ it holds that $f^k(c'')[-1, 0] \in Q_2^1 >$ and $> \not\sqsubset f^k(c'')_{[-m_n-3,1]}$. We can assume that this holds for $c'' = c$. Then, from the movement bound it follows, that there exists such $i \in H_c$, that $h_c(i, j) \in [-m_n - 1, -1]$ for each $j \leq k$. We clearly have that $i \in H_{c'}$. If $h_{c'}(i, j) = h_c(i, j)$ for each $j \leq n$, then a difference cannot propagate to the origin during the n steps as again the same computation would happen in both configurations. On the other hand the only way that $h_{c'}(i, j) \neq h_c(i, j)$ for some $j \leq n$ is if $h_{c'}(i, j) = -$. This is however impossible as it would require that $> \sqsubset c'_{[-m_n-3,i-1]}$, which would mean that $> \sqsubset f^{k+1}(c')_{[-m_n-3,0]}$, which is against the assumption. Therefore again if $j_n \in \mathbb{N}$, is such that $f^{j_n}(c') \notin W^+_{-m_n}(f^{j_n}(c))$, then from the above consideration, we have that $j_n \geq n$.

Finally, for the last case we assume that $> \sqsubset f^n(c)_{[-m_n-3,0]}$. Then from the movement bound M, it follows that there exists such $i_e \in E_c$, that $e_c(i_e, j) \in [-2M(n) - 3, 0]$ for each $j \leq n$. We can then assume that $m_n \geq 2M(n) + 3$ and hence $i_e \in E_{c'}$. If $e_c(i_e, j) = e_{c'}(i_e, j)$ for each $j \leq n$, then directly from the definition of the CA f, it follows that $f^j(c)_k = f^j(c')_k$, for each $j \leq n$ and $k \geq e_c(i_e, j)$ and hence in such case $j_n > n$. Therefore we consider the case where there exists such $j \leq n$, that $e_{c'}(i_e, j) \neq e_c(i_e, j)$. Suppose that for each pair $i \in H_c$ and $i' \in E_c$, such that $i < i' = r_c(i) + 1 < i_e$, it holds that either there exists minimal such $j_0 \leq n$, that $e_{c''}(i', j_0) - 2 \geq h_{c''}(i, j_0)$ and $e_c(i_e, j) = e_c(i_e, j_0)$ for each $j_0 < j \leq n$ or $e_{c'}(i', j) - 2 < h_{c''}(i, j)$ for each $j \leq n$, where $c'' \in \Sigma^{\mathbb{Z}}$ is such a configuration that $c''_{j'} = c_{j'}$ for each $j' > l_c(i) - 1$ and $c''_{j'} = a_0$ for each $j' < l_c(i)$. If we now assume that $m_n \geq 3M(n) + 4$, then any $i'' \in E_{c'}$, such that $i'' < -m_n$ cannot effect the value of $e_{c'}(i_e, j)$ for any $j \leq n$ and neither can any $i'' \in E_{c'} \cap [-m_n, i_e - 1]$ by our assumption regarding configurations c''. Hence if $e_c(i_e, j) \neq e_{c'}(i_e, j)$ and $j \leq n$, the difference is caused by a Turing machine head. But during the first n steps said Turing machine head can only visit cells $[-M(n) + i_e - 1, i_e + M(n)] \subseteq [-3M(n) - 4, M(n)]$. So again both configurations c and c' are simulating the exact same computation during the first n steps and thus $j_n > n$.

Let us assume that there exists such $k \in \mathbb{N}$ and indices $i_j \in H_c$, where $1 \leq j \leq k + 1$, that $i_j < i_{j+1}$ for each $j \leq k$. Let us denote as $c^j \in \Sigma^{\mathbb{Z}}$ such a configuration that $c^j_{j'} = c_{j'}$ for each $j' > l_c(i_j) - 1$ and $c^j_{j'} = a_0$ for each $j' < l_c(i_j)$. We will also assume that for each $j \leq k + 1$, we have that $e_{i_j} = r_c(i_j) + 1 \in E_c$ and we will further assume that there exists such an increasing finite sequence of times t_j, that $h_{c^j}(i_{j+1}, t_j) \in [e_{c^j}(e_{i_j}, t_j) + 1, e_{c^j}(e_{i_j}, t_j) + 2]$ and $e_{c^{j+1}}(e_{i_{j+1}}, t_{j+1}) > e_{c^{j+1}}(e_{i_{j+1}}, t_j)$ for each $j \leq k$. That is the leftmost simulation area in c^j, destroys the simulation area of the Turing machine head i_{j+1} at time-step t_j. In c however, this might not happen as there could be another simulation, which destroys the leftmost simulation area of c^j before time t_j. This could allow an existence for an alternating chain of such simulation areas, where simulation areas of i_j are destroyed for each even j in configuration c and and odd j in configuration c'. We want to find an upper bound $a(n)$ for the maximum distance $e_{c^k}(e_{i_k}, t_{i_k}) - e_{c^1}(e_{i_1}, t_{i_1})$, assuming that $t_k \le n$, as then we know how fast a difference can potentially propagate via such a chain of simulation areas. In such a case, suppose that we would have that $c'_{[i_e - a(n) - 2M(n) - 4, \infty)} = c_{[i_e - a(n) - 2M(n) - 4, \infty)}$, where $i_e = e_{i_{k+1}}$. Assume that there exist such $j_0 \in \mathbb{N}$, that $e_c(i_e, j_0) \neq e_{c'}(i_e, j_0)$, then if the difference is due to a chain that we have described above, it must be that in some of the simulation areas of such chain, a different computation is performed in the configurations c and c'. If $i_e - e_{c^k}(e_{i_k}, t_{i_k}) > M(n) + 2$, then we would have that $e_c(i_e, j) = e_{c'}(i_e, j)$ for each $j \le n$. If $i_e - e_{c^k}(e_{i_k}, t_{i_k}) \le M(n) + 2$, then $e_{c^1}(e_{i_1}, t_{i_1}) \ge i_e - 2 - M(n) - a(n)$, but then in all of the simulation areas the same computation is performed during n iterations and hence $e_c(i_e, j) = e_{c'}(i_e, j)$ for each $j \le n$.

Let us assume that for each $j \le k$, we have that $p^n \le t_j \le p^{n+1}$, where $p = |\Sigma|$ and $n \ge 5$. Let $b_j = e_{c^{j+1}}(e_{i_{j+1}}, t_{j+1}) - e_{c^j}(e_{i_j}, t_j)$ and $b_{j,t} = e_c(e_{i_{j+1}}, t) - e_c(e_{i_j}, t)$. Since $h_{c^j}(i_{j+1}, t_j) \in [e_{c^j}(e_{i_j}, t_j) + 1, e_{c^j}(e_{i_j}, t_j) + 2]$ and $e_{c^{j+1}}(e_{i_{j+1}}, t_{j+1}) > e_{c^{j+1}}(e_{i_{j+1}}, t_j)$ for each $j \le k$, there must exist such $j' \le t_{j+1} - t_j$, that $h_{c^{j+1}}(i_{j+1}, t_j + j') = e_{c^{j+1}}(e_{i_{j+1}}, t_{j+1}) - 1$ and therefore we have that $b_j - 2 \le M(t_{j+1} - t_j)$ for each $j \le k$.

By Theorem 1 there exists such $h : \mathbb{N} \to \mathbb{N}$, that $M(n) \le h(n) = C \frac{n}{\log(n)}$ for each $n \in \mathbb{N}$ and where $C > 0$. It is easy to see that there exists such a positive real number C', that h is concave in the domain $[C', \infty)$. We will split the times t_j into two sets A and B, such that $j \in A$ if $t_{j+1} - t_j \ge C'$ and $t_j \in B$ otherwise. We have that

$$
\begin{aligned}
\sum_{j=1}^{k} b_j &\le 2k + \sum_{j=1}^{k} M(t_{j+1} - t_j) \\
&\le 2k + \sum_{j=1}^{k} h(t_{j+1} - t_j) \\
&\le 2k + |B| h(C') + \sum_{t_j \in A} h(t_{j+1} - t_j) \\
&\le k(2 + h(C')) + |A| h\left(\frac{\sum_{t_j \in A} t_{j+1} - t_j}{|A|}\right) \\
&\le k(2 + h(C')) + |A| h\left(\frac{p^{n+1}}{|A|}\right) \\
&= k(2 + h(C')) + C \frac{p^{n+1}}{\log\left(\frac{p^{n+1}}{|A|}\right)} \\
&\le k(2 + h(C')) + C \frac{p^{n+1}}{\log\left(\frac{p^{n+1}}{k}\right)},
\end{aligned}
$$

where the fourth inequality follows from Jensen's inequality for concave functions. Hence the upper bound is maximized when k is maximized. Thus we want to find an upper bound for the value k. First for each $t < t_1$, we have that

$$\sum_{j=1}^{k} b_{j,t} = e_c(e_{i_{k+1}}, t) - e_c(e_{i_1}, t)$$
$$\leq e_c(e_{i_{k+1}}, t_{k+1}) - e_c(e_{i_1}, t)$$
$$= e_c(e_{i_{k+1}}, t_{k+1}) - e_c(e_{i_1}, t_1) + e_c(e_{i_1}, t_1) - e_c(e_{i_1}, t)$$
$$\leq e_c(e_{i_1}, t_1) - e_c(e_{i_1}, t) + \sum_{j=1}^{k} b_j$$
$$= \sum_{j=0}^{k} b_j,$$

where $b_0 = e_c(e_{i_1}, t_1) - e_c(e_{i_1}, t)$. From the movement bounds we proved earlier and since for each j we assumed that $t_j \geq p^n$, we have that $b_{j,p^{n-1}} > n - 3$ for each $j \leq k$. This follows from the fact that the Turing machine head i_j is not erased before p^n steps in the configuration c^{j-1} and p^{n-1} is enough time to have have had any Turing machine head visit $n - 3$ cells, even if the simulation area had started from a size 1. Therefore it follows that $\sum_{j=0}^{k} b_j \geq k(n - 3)$. The function M^{-1} that we introduced earlier is bounded from below by identity mapping. Therefore we have that

$$p^{n+1} \geq \sum_{j=0}^{k} M^{-1}(b_j)$$
$$= k(n - 3).$$

Therefore we have the upper bound $k \leq \frac{p^{n+1}}{n-3}$. Denoting $C'' = \max\{C, h(C') + 2\}$ and by combining our inequalities we have that

$$\sum_{j=0}^{k} b_j \leq k(2 + h(C')) + C\frac{p^{n+1}}{\log(\frac{p^{n+1}}{k})}$$
$$\leq C''\frac{p^{n+1}}{n-3} + \frac{C''p^{n+1}}{\log(n-3)}$$
$$\leq 2C''\frac{p^{n+1}}{\log(n-3)}.$$

Recall that t_j were assumed to be inside the interval $[p^n, p^{n+1}]$, where $n \geq 5$. For the times less than p^5, we get some constant upper bound C''' and hence taking union of intervals $[p^i, p^{i+1}]$, where $1 \leq i \leq n$, we get our upper bound

$$a(n) = C''' + \sum_{i=5}^{n} C''\frac{p^{i+1}}{\log(i)} \leq C''' + C''\frac{p^{n+2}}{\log(n+1)}.$$

Hence if we choose $m_n = 5M(p^{n+1}) + C''' + C''\frac{p^{n+2}}{\log(n+1)}$, we have that $e_c(i_e, j) = e_{c'}(i_e, j)$ for each $j \leq p^{n+1}$.

Combining all the three cases, we have shown that

$$\frac{I_{p^n}^{+}(c)}{p^n} \leq \frac{5M(p^n) + 8 + C''' + C''\frac{p^{n+1}}{\log(n)}}{p^n} = \frac{5}{\log(p^n)} + \frac{C''' + 8}{p^n} + \frac{C''p}{\log(n)},$$

which goes to 0 as n goes to infinity. As this holds for each $c \in \Sigma^{\mathbb{Z}}$ and $n \in \mathbb{N}$. Hence we have that $\lambda^+(c) = 0$ for each $c \in \Sigma^{\mathbb{Z}}$.

The fact that $\lambda^-(c) = 0$ holds for each $c \in \Sigma^{\mathbb{Z}}$ is much easier to see. First of all we have seen that the eraser states travel only to the right direction. Hence if there exists such $i \in \mathbb{N}$ that $c_i = \,>$, for some $i \geq 0$, it means that if $c' \in W_i^-(c)$, then $f^n(c') \in W_i^-(f^n(c))$, for each $n \in \mathbb{N}$. Hence any difference coming from right must propagate within a single simulation area. But then it follows from the movement bound that $I_n^-(c) \leq M(n)$ and hence $\lambda^-(c) = 0$ for each $c \in \Sigma^{\mathbb{Z}}$. $\square$

Lemma 2. *The cellular automaton (Σ, N, f) constructed in Theorem 2 is sensitive.*

Proof. Let $c \in \Sigma^{\mathbb{Z}}$ and suppose that $I = \{i \in \mathbb{N} \mid f^i(c)_0 = \,>\}$ is finite. Then there exists such $m \in \mathbb{N}$, that $f^n(c)_0 \neq \,>$ for each $n \geq m$. Let $k \leq -M(m) - 1$ and $c' \in W_k^+(c)$, such that $c'_{[k-1,k]} \in Q_2^1 >$ and $c'_i = a_0$ for each $i < k - 1$. We saw in the proof of Lemma 1, that $e_{c'}(k, p^{n+2}) - e_{c'}(k, 0) \geq n$ for each $n \in \mathbb{N}$ and hence there exists such $n \geq m$, that $e_{c'}(k, n) = 0$.

Let us then suppose that $I = \{i \in \mathbb{N} \mid f^i(c)_0 = \,>\}$ is infinite. Then for each $k < 0$, we choose $c' \in W_k^+(c)$, such that $c'_{[k-1,k]} \in Q_2^1 >$ and $c'_i = a_0$ for each $i < k - 1$. From the aperiodicity it again follows that there exists such $n \in \mathbb{N}$ that $> \not\sqsubseteq f^{n'}(c')_{(-\infty,0]}$ for each $n' > n$. $\square$

Acknowledgements. The author acknowledges the emmy.network foundation under the aegis of the Fondation de Luxembourg for its financial support.

References

1. Blondel, V.D., Cassaigne, J., Nichitiu, C.M.: On the presence of periodic configurations in Turing machines and in counter machines. Theor. Comput. Sci. **289**, 573–590 (2002)
2. Bressaud, X., Tisseur, P.: On a zero speed sensitive cellular automaton. Nonlinearity **20**(1), 1–19 (2006). https://doi.org/10.1088/0951-7715/20/1/002
3. Cassaigne, J., Ollinger, N., Torres, R.: A small minimal aperiodic reversible Turing machine. J. Comput. Syst. Sci. **84** (2014). https://doi.org/10.1016/j.jcss.2016.10.004
4. D'amico, M., Manzini, G., Margara, L.: On computing the entropy of cellular automata. In: Larsen, K.G., Skyum, S., Winskel, G. (eds.) ICALP 1998. LNCS, vol. 1443, pp. 470–481. Springer, Heidelberg (1998). https://doi.org/10.1007/BFb0055076
5. Finelli, M., Manzini, G., Margara, L.: Lyapunov exponents vs expansivity and sensitivity in cellular automata. In: Bandini, S., Mauri, G. (eds.) ACRI 1996, pp. 57–71. Springer, London (1997). https://doi.org/10.1007/978-1-4471-0941-9_6
6. Greiner, W.: Lyapunov exponents and chaos. In: Greiner, W. (ed.) Classical Mechanics, pp. 503–516. Springer, Heidelberg (2010). https://doi.org/10.1007/978-3-642-03434-3_26

7. Guillon, P., Salo, V.: Distortion in one-head machines and cellular automata. In: Dennunzio, A., Formenti, E., Manzoni, L., Porreca, A.E. (eds.) Cellular Automata and Discrete Complex Systems, pp. 120–138. Springer International Publishing, Cham (2017). https://doi.org/10.1007/978-3-319-58631-1_10

8. Jeandel, E.: Computability of the entropy of one-tape Turing machines. Leibniz International Proceedings in Informatics, LIPIcs 25 (2013). https://doi.org/10.4230/LIPIcs.STACS.2014.421

9. Kůrka, P.: Topological dynamics of cellular automata. In: Meyers, R.A. (ed.) Encyclopedia of Complexity and Systems Science, pp. 9246–9268. Springer, New York (2009). https://doi.org/10.1007/978-0-387-30440-3_556

10. Kůrka, P.: On topological dynamics of Turing machines. Theor. Comput. Sci. **174**(1), 203–216 (1997). https://doi.org/10.1016/S0304-3975(96)00025-4. http://www.sciencedirect.com/science/article/pii/S0304397596000254

11. Lyapunov, A.: General Problem of the Stability of Motion. Control Theory and Applications Series. Taylor & Francis (1992). https://books.google.fi/books?id=4tmAvU3_SCoC

12. Shereshevsky, M.A.: Lyapunov exponents for one-dimensional cellular automata. J. Nonlinear Sci. **2**(1), 1–8 (1992). https://doi.org/10.1007/BF02429850

13. Tisseur, P.: Cellular automata and Lyapunov exponents. Nonlinearity **13**(5), 1547–1560 (2000). https://doi.org/10.1088/0951-7715/13/5/308

14. Wolfram, S.: Universality and complexity in cellular automata. Phys. D Nonlinear Phenom. **10**(1), 1–35 (1984). https://doi.org/10.1016/0167-2789(84)90245-8. http://www.sciencedirect.com/science/article/pii/0167278984902458

15. Wolfram, S.: Twenty problems in the theory of cellular automata. Phys. Scr. **T9**, 170–183 (1985). https://doi.org/10.1088/0031-8949/1985/t9/029

Self-stabilizing Distributed Algorithms by Gellular Automata

Taiga Hongu[(✉)] and Masami Hagiya

The University of Tokyo, Tokyo, Japan
hongu314@g.ecc.u-tokyo.ac.jp, hagiya@is.s.u-tokyo.ac.jp

Abstract. Gellular automata are cellular automata with the properties of asynchrony, Boolean totality, and non-camouflage. In distributed computing, it is essential to determine whether problems can be solved by self-stable gellular automata. From any initial configuration, self-stable gellular automata converge to desired configurations, as self-stability implies the ability to recover from temporary malfunctions in transitions or states. In this paper, we show that three typical problems in distributed computing, namely, solving a maze, distance-2 coloring, and spanning tree construction, can be solved with self-stable gellular automata.

Keywords: Gellular automata · Solving a maze · Distance-2 coloring · Spanning tree construction · Self-Stability

1 Introduction

Many studies have been conducted to implement cellular automata using physical or chemical materials, such as [6,7,13]. These include recent efforts to implement cellular automata by reaction-diffusion systems in porous gels [4]. One motivation for implementing cellular automata using gels is to develop smart materials that can autonomously respond to external environments.

The term *gellular automata (GA)* was coined in [3], where the diffusion of DNA molecules is controlled by opening and closing holes between cells. Gellular automata were later formalized as cellular automata with the features of asynchrony, Boolean totality, and non-camouflage in [10,11], where two types of DNA molecules were assumed, one for states of cells and the other for signals transmitting states.

In the research along the latter direction, the computational universality of gellular automata was shown [10], and the computational power of gellular automata as distributed systems was investigated in [9]. Self-stability is a crucial factor in distributed computing. According to [1], self-stability is the ability of a system to converge to states with desired conditions from any initial state. If gellular automata are self-stable, they recover desired conditions even if temporary malfunctions occur in transitions or states. Smart materials are expected to have this property.

© IFIP International Federation for Information Processing 2020
Published by Springer Nature Switzerland AG 2020. All Rights Reserved
H. Zenil (Ed.): AUTOMATA 2020, LNCS 12286, pp. 86–98, 2020.
https://doi.org/10.1007/978-3-030-61588-8_7

In our previous study, we developed self-stable gellular automata that solved a maze [12] using a distributed algorithm similar to Lee's algorithm [5] under the restrictions that the number of states is finite and state transitions are asynchronous. However, this system takes time to detect undesired situations, such as loops.

In this paper, we reconsider the transition rules and target configurations of the gellular automata and present new transition rules that can solve a maze in a relatively short time. Moreover, we examine two other typical problems in distributed computing: distance-2 coloring and spanning tree construction. Like solving a maze, we confirm that these problems can be solved with self-stable gellular automata and explain how to design suitable systems for this purpose.

There are a number of studies on cellular automata solving maze problems such as [8], but we could not find self-stable ones except ours. Self-stable cellular automata for k-coloring are proposed by a very recent study [2], but typical distributed problems such as mazes and spanning trees are not dealt with. We conjecture that their definition of stability is derived from ours, but detailed comparison is left for future work.

The gellular automaton for solving a maze and others are demonstrated by the simulator available at https://cell-sim.firebaseapp.com/. Select "New Maze" in "Simulation Target."

2 Solving a Maze

2.1 Definitions

In this paper, a two-dimensional square lattice and von Neumann neighborhood are assumed. Each cell in the square lattice has a state from the following set.

$$\{W, B, S, T_0, T^*, T^\dagger, R\} \cup \{P_i', P_i'', P_i^*, P_i^\dagger \mid i = 0, 1, 2, .., n - 1\}$$

The states T_0, T^*, and $T^\dagger$ are denoted T. The states P_i', P_i'', P_i^*, and $P_i^\dagger$ are collectively denoted P_i. If i is arbitrary, P_i is simply denoted P. The parameter n is the number of states in P_i and is equal to 5 in this section.

The state W denotes a *wall* of a maze, which does not make any transitions. The state B denotes a *blank*, which may make a transition to P or R. The states S and T are the *starting point* and the *terminal point*, respectively, and they do not make any transitions. The state R indicates that it is reachable from the terminal point, and a path consisting of P stretches on cells in R.

The superscripts $'$, $''$, $*$ and $\dagger$ are used for detecting junctions by rules (9–21), explained below, and the subscripts i are used for directing paths.

Definition 1 (transition rule). *A transition rule consists of three components: the current state of a cell that makes a transition, a condition to be satisfied by the neighboring cells, and the next state that the cell will take.*

Definition 2 (asynchrony, Boolean totality, non-camouflage). *Cellular automata are asynchronous if cells make transitions asynchronously, that is, each cell may either make a transition by following a transition rule or do nothing at each step. Cellular automata are Boolean totalistic if the conditions of transition rules depend only on neighboring cells being in a particular state, not on the direction or number of cells. Cellular automata are non-camouflage if no conditions of transition rules contain the current state of the cell that makes a transition.*

A transition rule of asynchronous Boolean-totalistic non-camouflage cellular automata is defined as follows.

$$s_1 \left(t_1 \wedge \cdots \wedge t_m \wedge \neg t_{m+1} \wedge \cdots \wedge \neg t_{m+n} \right) \rightarrow s_2$$

In this rule, s_1 is the current state, $t_1 \wedge \cdots \wedge t_m \wedge \neg t_{m+1} \wedge \cdots \wedge \neg t_{m+n}$ is the condition, and s_2 is the next state. This means that a cell in state s_1, whose neighborhood contains cells in states $t_1, \ldots, t_n$ and does not contain cells in states $t_{m+1}, \ldots, t_{m+n}$, can make a transition to state s_2. By the non-camouflage property, s_1 does not appear among $t_1, \ldots, t_{m+n}$.

Definition 3 (configuration, run, step). *A configuration is a mapping from cells at lattice points in a square lattice to states, and a run is an infinite sequence of configurations, each of which, except for the first one, is obtained by applying the transition rules to the previous configuration. A transition step is the process of transforming from configuration C_1 to configuration C_2, which is obtained by having each cell in C_1 make a single transition or do nothing. Due to asynchrony and possibility that several rules can be applied to a state, a configuration sometimes has more than one next possible configuration. In this case, one of them is chosen non-deterministically.*

Definition 4 (passage, path, loop, junction). *A passage is a sequence of neighboring cells, each of which is in state B, R, or P. A maze is connected if there is a passage from the starting point S to the terminal point T in the maze.*

A path is a sequence of neighboring cells in states $\ldots, P_0, P_1, \ldots, P_{n-1}, P_0, \ldots$, where the indices are incremented in $(\mathbb{Z}/n\mathbb{Z})$.

If a path has both ends, that is, a head that is not adjacent to P_{i-1} and a tail that is not adjacent to P_{i+1}, we say that the path is maximal. If the head of a maximal path is adjacent to T and its tail is adjacent to S, the maximal path is called a solving path.

If a path has no ends, it is called a loop. In particular, if a loop has no junctions (described later), we call that loop pure.

We say that a path has a junction if a cell in state P_i in the path is adjacent to two or more different cells in P_{i-1} (or S if $i = 0$) or two or more in P_{i+1} (or T). Such a cell in state P_i is called a collision point, which is also called an entrance in the former case and an egress in the latter case.

Definition 5 (solution). *A solution of a maze is a configuration in which there is only one maximal path, and its head (tail) is adjacent to the starting point S*

(the terminal point T, respectively). If the maze is connected, there are solutions, and if it is not connected, there are no solutions (Fig.1).

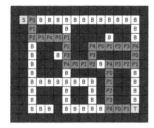

Fig. 1. An example of solutions of a maze (black cells denote W)

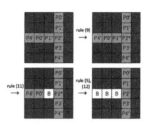

Fig. 2. Reduction of an entrance by rules (7–12)

Definition 6 (fair run). *A run R is fair if a certain configuration C appears in R infinitely often, and any configuration C' that can be obtained from C by a transition step also appears in R infinitely often.*

Throughout this paper, we assume non-deterministic models of computation. In probabilistic models such as Markov processes, probabilities of unfair runs are zero, i.e., runs are fair with probability 1.

Definition 7 (target configuration, self-stability). *Some configurations that are desirable (for a specific purpose) are defined as target configurations. Cellular automata are self-stable if in any fair run from any configuration, a target configuration appears in finite steps, and only target configurations appear after that.*

The above definition of self-stability is generally adopted in the field of distributed computing [1]. Even when a perturbation occurs in a target configuration, a new target configuration eventually appears if cellular automata are self-stable, because we can start a fair run from the resulting non-target configuration.

2.2   Procedure for Solving a Maze

2.2.1   Transition Rules

We introduce 21 transition rules of gellular automata for solving a maze.

(1)	$B\ (T_0)$	$\to R$		(12)	$P_i^*\ (\neg P_{i-1}'')$	$\to P_i'$
(2)	$B\ (R)$	$\to R$		(13)	$P_i\ (P_{i+1}' \wedge P_{i+1}'')$	$\to P_i^\dagger$
(3)	$R\ (S)$	$\to P_0'$		(14)	$P_i\ (T \wedge P_{i+1}'')$	$\to P_i^\dagger$
(4)	$R\ (P_i \wedge \neg P_{i+2})$	$\to P_{i+1}'$		(15)	$P_i''\ (P_{i-1}^\dagger)$	$\to B$
(5)	$P_i\ (\neg T \wedge \neg R \wedge \neg P_{i+1})$	$\to B$		(16)	$P_i^\dagger\ (\neg P_{i+1}'')$	$\to P_i'$
(6)	$P_i\ (\neg S \wedge \neg P_{i-1})$	$\to B$		(17)	$T_0\ (P_i)$	$\to T^*$
(7)	$P_i'\ ()$	$\to P_i''$		(18)	$T^*\ (P_i' \wedge P_j'')$	$\to T^\dagger$
(8)	$P_i''\ ()$	$\to P_i'$		(19)	$P_i''\ (T^\dagger)$	$\to B$
(9)	$P_i\ (P_{i-1}' \wedge P_{i-1}'')$	$\to P_i^*$		(20)	$T^\dagger\ (\neg P'')$	$\to T_0$
(10)	$P_0\ (S \wedge P_{n-1}'')$	$\to P_0^*$		(21)	$T^*\ (\neg P)$	$\to T_0$
(11)	$P_i''\ (P_{i+1}^*)$	$\to B$				

Each rule is actually a schema of rules and represents a number of concrete rules. For example, rule (4) represents $R\ (P_i' \wedge \neg P_{i+2}' \wedge \neg P_{i+2}'') \to P_{i+1}'$ and $R\ (P_i'' \wedge \neg P_{i+2}' \wedge \neg P_{i+2}'') \to P_{i+1}'$ for each i, because P_i' and P_i'' are collectively denoted by P_i.

If a cell in state B is adjacent to T_0 or R, rules (1–2) change its state to R. In this way, we can detect all reachable cells from the terminal point T. Once a cell in state B adjacent to the starting point S makes a transition to R, rules (3–4) generate a path from S and extend it while making as few loops as possible by preventing the path from joining to an existing path.

Rules (5–6) are intended to reduce dead ends of paths. If the head of a path is not adjacent to T and cannot stretch any more because there are no neighboring cells in state R, it changes back to state B. Similarly, if the tail of a path is not adjacent to S, it changes back to state B.

We reduce entrances with rules (7–12). First, cells in state P_i' or P_i'' switch their states from P_i' to P_i'' or P_i'' to P_i'. Next, a cell adjacent to both P_i' and P_i'' finds itself being an entrance and makes a transition to state P_i^*. Then, one (or more) of the paths joining at the entrance cell disappears gradually, and the entrance changes back to state P_i'.

Figure 2 shows the procedure for reducing entrances. We also reduce egresses with rules (13–16).

Rules (17–21) restrict the number of paths reaching the terminal point T to fewer than one. If the terminal point T_0 is adjacent to cells in state P, it makes a transition to state T^*, and no more cells in R are generated from it. As in the case of junctions, if the terminal point T is adjacent to several cells in P, one (or more) of the paths joining at T disappears gradually.

2.2.2   Self-stability of Solving a Maze

An initial configuration is a configuration that satisfies all of the following conditions:

(I-1) There is just one starting point S and one terminal point T, and these are not adjacent.

(I-2) The number of cells not in state W is finite.

A target configuration is a configuration that does not satisfy the above conditions for an initial configuration or that satisfies all of the following conditions:

(T-1) If the maze is connected, there is only one solving path from S to T^*.

(T-2) There are no maximal paths except solving paths.

(T-3) There are no cells in R adjacent to S, P, or B.

(T-4) If the maze is not connected, there is a cell in T_0 not adjacent to B or P.

(T-5) There are no junctions, that is, there are no cells in P_i adjacent to two or more cells in P_{i-1} (or S if $i = 0$), or two or more in P_{i+1} (or T).

(T-6) There are no cells in P_i^* or $P_i^\dagger$.

We now prove that these gellular automata are self-stable.

Theorem 1 (Self-stability of Solving a Maze). *Gellular automata with the above states, transition rules, and conditions of target configurations are self-stable.*

First, we show that from any initial configuration, a target configuration appears after a finite number of steps. Second, we show that once a target configuration appears, only target configurations appear afterward.

Lemma 1. *Assume that from any initial configuration, a target configuration can be obtained by some transition steps. Then a target configuration appears in any fair run.*

Proof. Assume that no target configuration appears in a fair run. As the cellular space is finite, the number of possible configurations is also finite. Therefore, there exists a configuration C that appears an infinite number of times in the run, and because of fairness, any configurations that can be obtained from C, including a target configuration, also appear in the run. This is a contradiction.

To prove the theorem, we first show that we can obtain a target configuration from any initial configuration by the following operations (i)–(iv) in order.

(i) We spread R by rules (1–2) until they can no longer be applied, then spread P by rules (3–4) until they can no longer be applied.

(ii) By applying rules (5–16), we remove all maximal paths except solving paths. Then there are only solving paths without junctions and pure loops. If there remain cells in P_i^* or $P_i^\dagger$, we get rid of them by applying rules (8,12,16).

(iii) If the maze is connected and there are solving paths, we move to (iv).

If the maze is connected but there are no solving paths, because the terminal point T is not adjacent to P, we change T to T_0 by applying rules (20–21). We then spread R from T_0 only on the passage that will be a solving path without junctions. When R is adjacent to P in a pure loop, we change all

R on the passage to P by applying rules (3–4) and remove the loop and the resulting path using rules (5–16). By repeating this process, a single solving path is obtained.

If there remain cells in P_i^* or $P_i^\dagger$, we get rid of them using rules (8,12,16). There should be no cells in R adjacent to B, S, and P because we spread R only on the passage of a solving path, and there should be no junctions.

If the maze is not connected, we also change T to T_0, as above. We then spread R to all cells reachable from T while removing pure loops by rules (3–4), (7–16). Then there should be no cells in R adjacent to B, S, and P and no junctions. Moreover, T_0 should not be adjacent to B, P.

(iv) If there are two or more solving paths, we keep one and remove the others by applying rules (17–21). Because there are no junctions in the paths, we can remove them by applying rule (5) until just one cell is adjacent to S. Finally, we change T to T^* by rule (17).

Figure 3 shows the operations (i)–(iv).

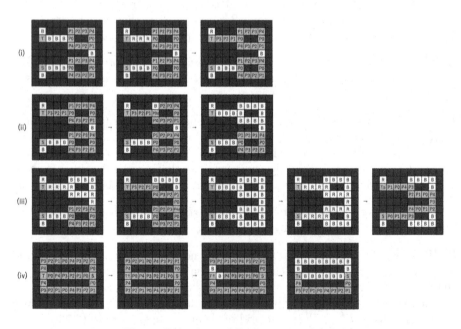

Fig. 3. Procedure of the operation (i–iv)

We now show that only target configurations appear after a target configuration is obtained. Table 1 shows the conditions satisfied after each transition step.

Table 1. Conditions of mazes satisfied after each operation (*init.* denotes initial configurations)

	(I)	(II)	(III)	(IV)	(V)	(VI)	(VII)	(VIII)
init.	x	x	x	x	x	x	x	x
(i)	o	o	x	x	o	x	x	x
(ii)	o	o	o	o	x	x	x	x
(iii)	o	o	o	o	o	o	x	x
(iv)	o	o	o	o	o	o	o	o

(I) There are no cells in R adjacent to S, P.
(II) There are no cells in B adjacent to R.
(III) There are no junctions and no cells in P_i^* or $P_i^\dagger$.
(IV) There are no maximal paths except solving paths.
(V) If the maze is unconnected, there is a cell in T_0 not adjacent to B, P.
(VI) If the maze is connected, there are solving paths.
(VII) If the maze is connected, each of the cells in S or T has just one neighboring cell in P.
(VIII) If the maze is connected, there is a cell in T^*.

After (iv), all of the above conditions (I–VIII) are satisfied. We can see that the conditions of the target configurations are satisfied. (T-1) holds because of (III), (VI), (VII), (VIII). (T-2), (T-3), (T-4), (T-5), and (T-6) hold because of (IV), (II), (V), (III), and (III). (In fact, if and only if all of the conditions (I–VIII) are satisfied, all of the conditions of target configurations (T-1–T-6) are satisfied.) Then only rules (7–8) can be applied to cells under target configurations, and they continue to satisfy (T-1–T-6). Therefore, after the first, only target configurations appear.

3   Distance-2 Coloring

3.1   Definitions

The space of cellular automata for solving the distance-2 coloring problem is the same as that for solving a maze. A state of a cell is either W, which represents a wall, or a pair $(c, conf)$ of a *color state* c and a *conflict state* $conf$. Cells whose state is a pair $(c, conf)$ is called *colored*.

A color state c is either c_i' or c_i'' ($i = 1, 2, \ldots, n$), and cells whose color state is c_i' or c_i'' are considered to have the same color i. They are sometimes collectively denoted by c_i or c, as in the case of automata for solving a maze. The parameter n is the number of colors used, which is 13 in this section. A conflict state $conf$ is a list of 0 or 1, such as $[0, 1, 0, \ldots, 1]$, whose length is n. The i-th element is 1 if there are two or more neighboring cells in the color i and is 0 otherwise. A cell in the color i may change its color if $conf[i]$ of any neighboring cell is 1 or it has a neighboring cell in the same color i.

Definition 8 (distance-2 coloring). *A colored cell is called unsafe if there is a neighboring cell in the same color as the cell or a pair of neighboring cells in the same color and safe otherwise. A configuration is called distance-2 colored if there are no unsafe cells.*

The color of any cell in a distance-2 colored configuration is different from those of the cells within a distance of two cells from it.

Figure 4 shows distance-2 coloring with five colors. Cells with different letters have different colors. Panel (a) shows a distance-2 colored configuration, but panel (b) does not because there are colored cells adjacent to two cells in R. (Note that cells W adjacent to more than two cells in the same color are allowed.)

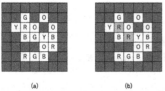

(a) (b)

Fig. 4. An example of distance-2 coloring of cells

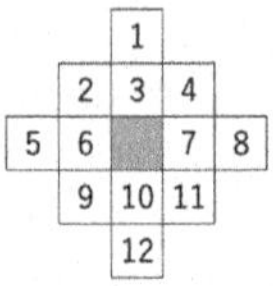

Fig. 5. 12-cells

3.2 Procedure for Distance-2 Coloring

In this section, we introduce the transition rules and the proof of self-stability of the automata for distance-2 coloring.

3.2.1 Transition Rules

The automata for distance-2 coloring have the following seven transition rules. The symbol $*$ expresses an arbitrary color state or conflict state. The symbol $conf|_{[i]=j}$ is a conflict state such that $conf[i] = j$, that is, $[*, \ldots, *, j, *, \ldots, *]$, where the i-th element is replaced by j.

$$
\begin{array}{lll}
(1) & (c'_i, conf)\,() & \rightarrow (c''_i, conf) \\
(2) & (c''_i, conf)\,() & \rightarrow (c'_i, conf) \\
(3) & (c_i, conf|_{[j]=0})\,((c'_j, *) \wedge (c''_j, *)) & \rightarrow (c_i, conf|_{[j]=1}) \\
(4) & (c_i, conf|_{[j]=1})\,((\neg c''_j, *)) & \rightarrow (c_i, conf|_{[j]=0}) \\
(5) & (c'_i, conf)\,((c''_i, *)) & \rightarrow (c'_j, conf) \\
(6) & (c''_i, conf)\,((c'_i, *)) & \rightarrow (c''_j, conf) \\
(7) & (c''_i, conf_1)\,((*, conf_2|_{[i]=1})) & \rightarrow (c'_j, conf_1)
\end{array}
$$

These transition rules work as follows.

- (1–2): They switch the color states of cells from c_i' to c_i'' or c_i'' to c_i' to enable cells to recognize whether there are two or more neighboring cells in the same color.
- (3–4): If a cell has two or more neighboring cells in the same color i, they change $conf[i]$ of the cell from 0 to 1. If not, they change it from 1 to 0.
- (5–6): If a cell is adjacent to cells in the same color, they change the color of the cell to an arbitrary one.
- (7): If a cell is in a color state c_i'' and there is a neighboring cell whose $conf[i]$ is 1, they change its color to an arbitrary one.

3.2.2   Self-stability of Distance-2 Coloring

An initial configuration is a configuration in which the number of cells not in state W is finite. A target configuration is a configuration that does not satisfy the above condition for initial configurations or that satisfies all of the following conditions:

(T-1) There are no colored cells whose colors are the same as one of their neighboring cells.

(T-2) There are no colored cells that are adjacent to two or more neighboring cells with the same color.

(T-3) There are no colored cells whose conflict states are not $[0, 0, \ldots, 0]$.

Now we show that these gellular automata are self-stable.

Theorem 2 (Self-Stability of Distance-2 Coloring). *Gellular automata with the above states, transition rules, and conditions of target configurations are self-stable.*

As in the case for solving a maze, we consider the following operations (i–iii).

(i) If there is a cell such that $conf[i] = 1$ for some i and there is at most one neighboring cell in color i, we change its $conf[i]$ from 1 to 0 by applying rule (4).

(ii) If a cell and one of its neighboring cells are in the same color, we change its color according to rules (5–6). Also, if two or more neighboring cells of a cell are in the same color i, we first make both c_i' and c_i'' appear in the neighboring cells by rules (1–2). We then change its $conf[i]$ to 1 by rule (3) and finally change c_i'' by rule (7). In both cases, we choose the color to which the cell changes, except the color of neighboring cells and that of the cells to which they are adjacent. As the number of colors we cannot choose is at most 12 (as in Fig. 5), which is less than the number of colors, 13, we can always choose one, and the number of unsafe cells decreases.

(iii) By repeating (i–ii), we can change all of the unsafe cells to safe ones and their conflict states to $[0, 0, \ldots, 0]$.

Through the above operations (i–iii), a target configuration is obtained. Then only rules (1–2) can be applied to cells in target configurations, which does not change conditions (T-1–T-3). Therefore, after the first, only target configurations appear.

4 Spanning Tree

4.1 Definitions

The space of cellular automata for spanning tree construction is the same as that for solving a maze. A state of a cell is either W, which represents a wall, or a pair (P, C), which should belong to a spanning tree. Here P is called a *tree state* and C is called a *color-conflict state*. A tree state P is one of the following set:

$$\{r_i, t_i[c_j], l_i[c_j] \mid i = 0, 1, \ldots, m - 1, \ j = 1, 2, \ldots, n\}$$

A cell whose tree state is r_i, $t_i[c_j]$, or $l_i[c_j]$ is called a *root*, an *inner node*, or a *leaf* of a spanning tree. The index i is called a *wave index*, and c_j is called a *parent color*. If i or j are arbitrary, r_i is denoted r, and $t_i[c_j]$ is denoted by t_i, $t[c_j]$, and t (and similarly for $l_i[c_j]$). A color-conflict state C is a pair of a *color state* and a *conflict state*, similar to the case of distance-2 coloring. The parameter m is the number of r_i, which is 6 in this section.

If a tree state of a cell is $t_i[c_j]$ or $l_i[c_j]$, it points to a neighboring cell whose color is j as its parent. In this manner, we can define a parent-child relation in the cellular space if the parent of each cell is uniquely determined. Figure 6 shows an example of the construction of a spanning tree.

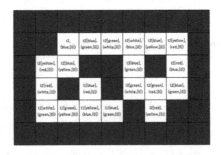

Fig. 6. An example of a spanning tree construction

4.2 Self-stability of Spanning Tree Construction

As in the case of the other two problems, we can construct a spanning tree with self-stable gellular automata. First, we construct the parent-child relation of cells by distance-2 coloring. If configurations are distance-2 colored, there are no cells with a pair of neighboring cells of the same color, so the parent of each cell is uniquely determined by designating the color of the parent. This enables us to construct a tree in which no cells have two or more parents. Next, we propagate a wave from a root to leaves and from leaves to a root. This enables us to detect a pure loop as cells to which the wave does not propagate. We then add the cells in the loop to the tree.

5   Conclusions

In this paper, we showed how to construct gellular automata that solve three problems: solving a maze, distance-2 coloring, and spanning tree construction. As self-stable gellular automata can recover from malfunctions of states and transitions, materials that contain them are able to form structures like blood vessels or neural networks that can repair themselves following external damage or environmental changes.

By adding and changing some states and transition rules, we can also design gellular automata for solving other problems. For instance, gellular automata that solve the Hamiltonian circuit problem can be constructed by modifying those for a maze. The actual construction of these gellular automata remains for future studies. We also plan to improve the automata by decreasing the number of states and transition rules and reducing the number of steps required for them to converge to a target configuration.

Acknowledgements. We thank Akira Yagawa for valuable discussions and implementing the simulator. We also thank the anonymous reviewers for improving the paper. This work was partially supported by Grant-in-Aid for challenging Exploratory Research 17K19961.

References

1. Dolev, S.: Self-Stabilization. MIT Press, Cambridge (2000)
2. Fatés, N., Marcovici, I., Taati, S.: Cellular automata for the self-stabilisation of colourings and tilings. In: Filiot, E., Jungers, R., Potapov, I. (eds.) RP 2019. LNCS, vol. 11674, pp. 121–136. Springer, Cham (2019). https://doi.org/10.1007/978-3-030-30806-3_10
3. Hagiya, M., et al.: On DNA-based gellular automata. In: Ibarra, O.H., Kari, L., Kopecki, S. (eds.) UCNC 2014. LNCS, vol. 8553, pp. 177–189. Springer, Cham (2014). https://doi.org/10.1007/978-3-319-08123-6_15
4. Hosoya, T., Kawamata, I., Nomura, S.I.M., Murata, S.: Pattern formation on discrete gel matrix based on DNA computing. New Gener. Comput. **37**(1), 97–111 (2019). https://doi.org/10.1007/s00354-018-0047-1
5. Lee, C.Y.: An algorithm for path connections and its applications. IRE Trans. Electron. Comput. **EC–10**(3), 346–365 (1961)
6. Peper, F., Lee, J., Adachi, S., Isokawa, T.: Cellular nanocomputers: a focused review. Int. J. Nanotechnol. Mol. Comput. (IJNMC) **1**(1), 33–49 (2009)

7. Scalise, D., Schulman, R.: Emulating cellular automata in chemical reaction-diffusion networks. Nat. Comput. **15**(2), 197–214 (2016). https://doi.org/10.1007/s11047-015-9503-8

8. Tsompanas, M.-A.I., Sirakoulis, G.C., Adamatzky, A.: Cellular automata models simulating slime mould computing. In: Adamatzky, A. (ed.) Advances in Physarum Machines. ECC, vol. 21, pp. 563–594. Springer, Cham (2016). https://doi.org/10.1007/978-3-319-26662-6_27

9. Yamashita, T., Hagiya, M.: Simulating population protocols by gellular automata. In: 57th Annual Conference of the Society of Instrument and Control Engineers of Japan (SICE), pp. 1579–1585. IEEE (2018)

10. Yamashita, T., Isokawa, T., Peper, F., Kawamata, I., Hagiya, M.: Turing-completeness of asynchronous non-camouflage cellular automata. In: Dennunzio, A., Formenti, E., Manzoni, L., Porreca, A.E. (eds.) AUTOMATA 2017. LNCS, vol. 10248, pp. 187–199. Springer, Cham (2017). https://doi.org/10.1007/978-3-319-58631-1_15

11. Yamashita, T., Isokawa, T., Peper, F., Kawamata, I., Hagiya, M.: Turing-completeness of asynchronous non-camouflage cellular automata. Inf. Comput. **274**, 104539 (2020)

12. Yamashita, T., Yagawa, A., Hagiya, M.: Self-stabilizing gellular automata. In: McQuillan, I., Seki, S. (eds.) UCNC 2019. LNCS, vol. 11493, pp. 272–285. Springer, Cham (2019). https://doi.org/10.1007/978-3-030-19311-9_21

13. Yin, P., Sahu, S., Turberfield, A.J., Reif, J.H.: Design of autonomous DNA cellular automata. In: Carbone, A., Pierce, N.A. (eds.) DNA 2005. LNCS, vol. 3892, pp. 399–416. Springer, Heidelberg (2006). https://doi.org/10.1007/11753681_32

A Characterization of Amenable Groups by Besicovitch Pseudodistances

Silvio Capobianco[1(✉)] and Pierre Guillon[2]

[1] Department of Software Science, Tallinn University of Technology, Tallinn, Estonia
`silvio@cs.ioc.ee, silvio.capobianco@taltech.ee`
[2] CNRS, Aix-Marseille Université, Institut de Mathématiques de Marseille, Marseille, France
`pguillon@math.cnrs.fr`

Abstract. The Besicovitch pseudodistance defined in [BFK99] for one-dimensional configurations is invariant by translations. We generalize the definition to arbitrary countable groups and study how properties of the pseudodistance, including invariance by translations, are determined by those of the sequence of finite sets used to define it. In particular, we recover that if the Besicovitch pseudodistance comes from a nondecreasing exhaustive Følner sequence, then every shift is an isometry. For non-Følner sequences we prove that some shifts are not isometries, and the Besicovitch pseudodistance with respect to some subsequence even makes them non-continuous.

Keywords: Besicovitch distance · Følner sequences · Submeasures · Amenability · Non-Compact space · Symbolic dynamics

1 Introduction

The Besicovitch pseudodistance was proposed by Blanchard, Formenti and Kůrka in [BFK99] as an "antidote" to sensitivity of the shift map in the prodiscrete (Cantor) topology of the space of 1D configurations over a finite alphabet. The idea is to take a window on the integer line, which gets larger and larger, and compute the probability that in a point under the window, chosen uniformly at random, two configurations will take different values. The upper limit of this sequence of probabilities behaves like a distance, except for taking value zero only on pairs of equal configurations: this defines an equivalence relation, and

This research was supported by the Estonian Ministry of Education and Research institutional research grant no. IUT33-13.

The original version of this chapter was revised: the fictitious author has been removed. The correction to this chapter is available at https://doi.org/10.1007/978-3-030-61588-8_12

the resulting quotient space is a metric space on which the shift is an isometry, or equivalently, the distance is shift-invariant.

The original choice of windows is $X_n = [-n : n]$, the set of integers from $-n$ to n included. This notion can be easily extended to arbitrary dimension $d \geq 1$, taking a sequence of hypercubic windows. If we allow arbitrary shapes, the notion of Besicovitch space can be extended to configurations over arbitrary groups; in this case, however, the properties of the group and the choice of the windows can affect the distance being or not being shift-invariant. An example of a Besicovitch pseudodistance which is not shift-invariant is given in [Cap09], where it is also proved that, if a countable group is *amenable* (cf. [CGK13] and [CSC10, Chapter 4]), then the Besicovitch distance with respect to any nondecreasing exhaustive *Følner sequence* is shift-invariant. The class of amenable groups is of great interest and importance in group theory, symbolic dynamics, and cellular automata theory.

In this paper, we explore the relation between the properties of Besicovitch pseudodistances over configuration spaces with countable base group and those of the sequence of finite sets used to define it. We introduce a notion of *synchronous Følner equivalence* between sequences, and a related order relation where one sequence comes before another sequence if it is synchronously Følner-equivalent to a subsequence of the latter. This notion, on the one hand, generalizes that of Følner sequences, and on the other hand, allows us to compare the Besicovitch distances and submeasures associated to different sequences. In particular, we prove that an increasing sequence of finite sets is Følner if and only if every shift is an isometry for the corresponding Besicovitch distance: this provides the converse of [Cap09, Theorem 3.5]. Finally, we give conditions for absolute continuity and Lipschitz continuity of Besicovitch submeasures with respect to each other.

2   Background

We use the notation $X \Subset Y$ to mean that X is a finite subset of Y. We denote the *symmetric difference* of two sets X and Y as $X \Delta Y$. We write $a_n \sim_{n \to \infty} b_n$ if $\lim_{n \to \infty} a_n / b_n = 1$ and $a_n = o_{n \to \infty} b_n$ if $\lim_{n \to \infty} a_n / b_n = 0$. For $\alpha \in \mathbb{R}$ we put $\lfloor \alpha \rfloor = \max\{m \in \mathbb{Z} \mid m \leq \alpha\}$.

2.1   Submeasures

The following definition is classical (see for instance [Sab06]).

Definition 1. *A submeasure over a set G is a map $\mu : 2^G \to \mathbb{R} \sqcup \{+\infty\}$ such that:*

1. $\mu(\emptyset) = 0$;
2. $\mu(W) < \infty$ *if W is finite*;
3. $\mu(V \cup W) \leq \mu(V) + \mu(W)$ *for every $V, W \subset G$.*

If G and A are two sets, the *difference set* of two functions $x, y : G \to A$ is the set $\Delta(x, y) = \{i \in G \mid x(i) \neq y(i)\}$. Any submeasure over G gives rise to an associated pseudodistance over A^G:

$$d_\mu(x, y) = \mu(\Delta(x, y)) \ \forall x, y \in A^G \ .$$

Remark 1. The topological space corresponding to such a pseudodistance is homogeneous in the following sense: the balls around every two points y and z are isometric. Indeed, identify A with the additive group $\mathbb{Z}/|A|\mathbb{Z}$. Then for every $y, z \in A^G$ the map $\psi_{y,z} : A^G \to A^G$ defined by $\psi_{y,z}(x)(i) = x(i) - y(i) + z(i)$ for every $x \in A^G$ and $i \in G$ is an isometry between any ball around y and the corresponding one around z.

We say that submeasure μ is *absolutely continuous* (resp. α-Lipschitz, for some $\alpha > 0$) with respect to submeasure ν if $\nu(W) = 0 \implies \mu(W) = 0$ (resp. $\mu(W) \leq \alpha\nu(W)$) for any $W \subset G$.

Remark 2. Let $\varepsilon, \delta > 0$, μ, ν two submeasures on G, and $z \in A^G$. The following are equivalent.

1. For every set $W \subset G$, $\mu(W) \geq \varepsilon \implies \nu(W) \geq \delta$.
2. For every $x, y \in A^G$, $d_\mu(x, y) \geq \varepsilon \implies d_\nu(x, y) \geq \delta$.
3. For every $x \in A^G$, $d_\mu(x, z) \geq \varepsilon \implies d_\nu(x, z) \geq \delta$.

Consequently, the identity map, from space A^G endowed with d_ν onto space A^G endowed with d_μ, is continuous (resp. α-Lipschitz) if and only if μ is absolutely continuous (resp. α-Lipschitz) with respect to ν. In that case the identity is even absolutely continuous.

2.2   Shifts and Translations

If A is an alphabet, G is a group, and $g \in G$, the *shift* by g is the function $\sigma^g : A^G \to A^G$ defined by $\sigma^g(x)(i) = x(g^{-1}i)$, for every $x \in A^G$ and $i \in G$. A map ψ from A^G to itself is *shift-invariant* if $\psi\sigma^g = \sigma^g\psi$ for every $g \in G$. Note that $\Delta(\sigma^g(x), \sigma^g(y)) = g\Delta(x, y)$ for every $x, y \in A^G$ and $g \in G$.

Since the maps $\psi_{y,z}$ from Remark 1 are shift-invariant, one can see that the shift is continuous, Lipschitz, etc in every x if and only if it is in one x.

Given $g \in G$, let $g\mu(X) = \mu(g^{-1}X)$ for every $X \subset G$. Then $d_\mu(\sigma^g(x), \sigma^g(y)) = d_{g^{-1}\mu}(x, y)$, that is, the shift by g, within space A^G endowed with d_μ, is topologically the same as the identity map, from A^G endowed with d_μ onto space A^G endowed with $d_{g^{-1}\mu}$. Remark 1 can then be rephrased into the following.

Remark 3. If G is a group, $g \in G$, and A^G is endowed with d_μ, then σ^g is continuous (resp. α-Lipschitz) if and only if $g^{-1}\mu$ is absolutely continuous (resp. α-Lipschitz) with respect to μ. In that case, the shift by g is even absolutely continuous.

2.3   Besicovitch Submeasure and Pseudodistance

Among classical examples of submeasures are the ones that induce the Cantor topology, the shift-invariant Besicovitch pseudodistance, the Weyl pseudodistance (see [HM17, Def 4.1.1])... We will focus on the Besicovitch topology. Let X and Y be nonempty sets and let (X_n) be a nondecreasing sequence of finite subsets of X. We may or may not require that (X_n) be *exhaustive*, that is, $\bigcup_n X_n = X$.

Let us denote $\mathfrak{P}(W|V) = \frac{|W \cap V|}{|V|}$ (by convention, this is $+\infty$ if $V = \emptyset$).

The *Besicovitch submeasure* $\mu_{(X_n)} : 2^X \to [0,1]$ is defined by:

$$\mu_{(X_n)}(W) = \limsup_n \mathfrak{P}(W|X_n) .$$

The *Besicovitch pseudodistance* is $d_{(X_n)} = d_{\mu_{(X_n)}}$.

For example, if $X = \mathbb{N}$, $Y = \{0,1\}$, $X_n = [0:n-1]$, $x(i) = 0$ for every $i \in \mathbb{N}$ and $y \in \{0,1\}^{\mathbb{N}}$ is the characteristic function of the prime numbers, then $d_{(X_n)}(x,y) = 0$. The topology of the quotient space is very different from the prodiscrete topology.

We will now concentrate on the case of nondecreasing sequences (X_n).

3   Følner Equivalence and Besicovitch Submeasures

3.1   Føner Equivalence

Let (X_n) and (Y_n) be nondecreasing sequences of finite subsets of G. We say that they are *synchronously Følner-equivalent* if

$$\lim_{n \to \infty} \frac{|X_n \Delta Y_n|}{|X_n|} = 0 .$$

Proposition 1. *Consider nondecreasing sequences (X_n) and (Y_n). The following are equivalent.*

1. (X_n) and (Y_n) are synchronously Følner-equivalent.
2. $|X_n \cap Y_n| \sim_{n \to \infty} |X_n| \sim_{n \to \infty} |Y|_n$.
3. $|X_n| \sim_{n \to \infty} |Y_n|$ and $|X_n \setminus Y_n| = o_{n \to \infty}(|X_n|)$.

Corollary 1. *The synchronous Følner equivalence is an equivalence relation.*

The proofs are left to the reader (see [CGN] for details).

We also denote $(X_n) \preceq (Y_n)$ if (X_n) is synchronously Følner-equivalent to a subsequence (Y_{m_n}). Equivalently,

$$\lim_{n \to \infty} \min_{m \in \mathbb{N}} \frac{|X_n \Delta Y_m|}{|X_n|} = 0 .$$

To be convinced of the equivalence, note that the minimum is reached by some m_n for each $n \in \mathbb{N}$, because (Y_m) is nondecreasing and X_n is finite. Thanks to symmetry of synchronous equivalence, we also have that $(X_n) \preceq (Y_n)$ if and only if $\lim_{n \to \infty} \min_{m \in \mathbb{N}} \frac{|X_n \Delta Y_m|}{|Y_m|} = 0$. We say that they are *Følner-equivalent*, and write $(X_n) \sim (Y_n)$, if both $(X_n) \preceq (Y_n)$ and $(Y_n) \preceq (X_n)$. This is the case if they are synchronously Følner equivalent, but the converse is false. As counterexamples, one can consider twice the same sequence, but with repetitions on both sides that are longer and longer, and not synchronized. If one wants to obtain strictly increasing sequences, repetitions can be replaced by very slowly increasing sequences (point by point).

Remark 4. It is easy to see that $\preceq$ is a preorder relation. In turn, Følner-equivalence, being defined as the equivalence corresponding to the preorder $\preceq$, is an equivalence relation.

Proposition 2. *Assume that* $|X_n| \sim_{n \to \infty} |Y_n|$. *Then* (X_n) *and* (Y_n) *are synchronously Følner-equivalent if and only if* $(X_n) \preceq (Y_n)$.

Proof. Assume $(X_n) \preceq (Y_n)$ (the converse implication is trivial). Let $n, m \in \mathbb{N}$. If $m \leq n$, then $|X_n \setminus Y_n| \leq |X_n \setminus Y_m|$ and $|Y_n \setminus X_n| \leq |Y_n \setminus Y_m| + |Y_m \setminus X_n|$ since (Y_n) is nondecreasing. Summing up, $|X_n \Delta Y_n| \leq |X_n \Delta Y_m| + |Y_n \setminus Y_m|$. Symmetrically, if $n \leq m$, $|X_n \Delta Y_n| \leq |X_n \Delta Y_m| + |Y_m \setminus Y_n|$. Overall for every $m \in \mathbb{N}$, we get $|X_n \Delta Y_n| \leq |X_n \Delta Y_m| + ||Y_m| - |Y_n||$. If we apply this with (m_n) the subsequence from the definition of $\preceq$, which is such that $(X_n) \sim (Y_{m_n})$, we have $|X_n \Delta Y_{m_n}| = o_{n \to \infty}(|X_n|)$, and by Proposition 1 (applied to (X_n) and (Y_{m_n})), $|Y_{m_n}| \sim_{n \to \infty} |X_n| \sim_{n \to \infty} |Y_n|$. Summing up, we deduce that $|X_n \Delta Y_n| = o_{n \to \infty}(|X_n|)$. $\qquad \square$

3.2 Comparing Besicovitch Submeasures

A basic tool in our set constructions will be the following elementary remark.

Remark 5. If (X_n) is nondecreasing and exhaustive, then for every finite set W and every $\varepsilon > 0$, there exists $n_{(X_n)}(W, \varepsilon)$ such that for every $n \geq n_{(X_n)}(W, \varepsilon)$, $\mathfrak{P}(W \mid X_n) < \varepsilon$ and $W \subset X_n$.

We deduce the following, which will be useful in our constructions.

Lemma 1. *Let* (X_n) *be a nondecreasing exhaustive sequence of an infinite group* G. *Let* $W = \bigcup_{i \in \mathbb{N}} W_i$ *where* $\emptyset \neq W_i \Subset G$ *for each* $i \in \mathbb{N}$, *such that, for every* $n \in \mathbb{N}$, *there are at most finitely many* i's *such that* $W_i \cap X_n \neq \emptyset$ *(this is the case, for example, if the* W_i's *are pairwise disjoint); in that case* $j_n = \max_{W_j \cap X_n \neq \emptyset} j$ *is well-defined for every* n. *Then:*

1.
$$\mu_{(X_n)}(W) \geq \limsup_{i \to \infty} \max_{m \in \mathbb{N}} \mathfrak{P}(W_i \mid X_m) .$$

2. *If there is a sequence* (ε_n) *converging to 0 such that* $n_{(X_n)}(\bigcup_{i < j_n} W_i, \varepsilon_n) \leq n$ *for every* $n \in \mathbb{N}$, *then:*
$$\mu_{(X_n)}(W) = \limsup_{i \to \infty} \max_{m \in \mathbb{N}} \mathfrak{P}(W_i \mid X_m) .$$

3. *In general, there exists a nondecreasing integer sequence* $\mathbf{l}$ *such that, denoting* $W_{\mathbf{l}} = \bigcup_{i \in \mathbb{N}} W_{l_i}$:

$$\mu_{(X_n)}(W_{\mathbf{l}}) = \lim_{i \to \infty} \max_{m \in \mathbb{N}} \mathfrak{P}\left(W_{l_i}\,|\,X_m\right) \ .$$

Proof

1. Let $(m_i) \in \mathbb{N}^{\mathbb{N}}$ be such that $\mathfrak{P}\left(W_i\,|\,X_{m_i}\right) = \max_{m \in \mathbb{N}} \mathfrak{P}\left(W_i\,|\,X_m\right)$. We know that this sequence goes to infinity (even though it may not be nondecreasing), because only finitely many W_i's intersect each X_m, but they all intersect at least one. Hence, $\mu_{(X_n)}(W) \geq \limsup_{i \to \infty} \mathfrak{P}\left(W\,|\,X_{m_i}\right)$. We get the desired inequality by noting that $W_i \subset W$.
2. Point 1 already gives one inequality. For the converse:

$$\mu_{(X_n)}(W) = \limsup_{n \to \infty} \mathfrak{P}\left(\bigcup_{i < j_n} W_i \cup W_{j_n} \cup \bigcup_{i > j_n} W_i \,\Big|\, X_n\right)$$

$$\leq \limsup_{n \to \infty} \left(\mathfrak{P}\left(\bigcup_{i < j_n} W_i \,\Big|\, X_n\right) + \mathfrak{P}\left(W_{j_n}\,|\,X_n\right) + \mathfrak{P}\left(\bigcup_{i > j_n} W_i \,\Big|\, X_n\right)\right)$$

$$\leq \limsup_{n \to \infty} \left(\varepsilon_n + \max_{m \in \mathbb{N}} \mathfrak{P}\left(W_{j_n}\,|\,X_m\right) + 0\right)$$

$$\leq \limsup_{n \to \infty} \varepsilon_n + \limsup_{n \to \infty} \max_{m \in \mathbb{N}} \mathfrak{P}\left(W_{j_n}\,|\,X_m\right)$$

$$\leq 0 + \limsup_{i \to \infty} \max_{m \in \mathbb{N}} \mathfrak{P}\left(W_i\,|\,X_m\right) \ .$$

The last inequality comes from the fact that the sequence (j_n) is nondecreasing (because (X_n) is nondecreasing), and not upper-bounded (because the W_i's are nonempty), so it goes to infinity.

3. Let us define some sequence $\mathbf{l}$ by recurrence, from any seed $l_0 \in \mathbb{N}$. Assume that l_n is defined, and write $k_n = n_{(X_n)}(\bigcup_{j \leq n} W_{l_j})$. Choose any l_{n+1} such that for every $m \geq l_{n+1}$, W_m does not intersect $X_{k_n - 1}$ (this is possible by assumption). If $j_n = \max_{W_{l_j} \cap X_n \neq \emptyset} j$, then $n_{(X_n)}(\bigcup_{j < j_n} W_{l_j}) = k_{j_n - 1}$. By definition, $W_{l_{j_n}}$ does not intersect $X_{k_{j_n - 1} - 1}$. Since $W_{l_{j_n}}$ intersects X_n, we can deduce that $n > k_{j_n - 1} - 1$. This means that (W_{l_i}) satisfies the hypothesis of Point 2.

   Replacing the lim sup by a lim can be achieved by taking a subsequence. $\qquad\square$

Lemma 2. *Let* $\varepsilon, \delta > 0$, *and* (X_n), (Y_n) *be nondecreasing and exhaustive. The following are equivalent.*

1. *For every* $W \subset G$, *if* $\mu_{(Y_n)}(W) \geq \varepsilon$, *then* $\mu_{(X_n)}(W) \geq \delta$.
2. $\liminf_{n \in \mathbb{N}} \max_{m \in \mathbb{N}} \dfrac{\varepsilon\,|Y_n| - |Y_n \setminus X_m|}{|X_m|} \geq \delta$.

If m_n *realizes the maximum for each* $n \in \mathbb{N}$, *and if* $\varepsilon < 1$, *then these properties imply that*

$$\frac{\delta}{\varepsilon} \leq \liminf_{n \in \mathbb{N}} \frac{|Y_n|}{|X_{m_n}|} \leq \limsup_{n \in \mathbb{N}} \frac{|Y_n|}{|X_{m_n}|} \leq \frac{1 - \delta}{1 - \varepsilon} \ .$$

In particular, the properties imply that $\delta \leq \varepsilon$.

Proof. Let us start by proving the final inequalities. Suppose $\liminf_{n\in\mathbb{N}} \frac{\varepsilon|Y_n|-|Y_n\setminus X_{m_n}|}{|X_{m_n}|} \geq \delta$. Then on the one hand, it is clear that $\liminf_{n\in\mathbb{N}} \frac{\varepsilon|Y_n|}{|X_{m_n}|}$ is even bigger, which gives the first inequality. On the other hand, since $|Y_n \setminus X_{m_n}| \geq |Y_n|-|X_{m_n}|$, we can see that $\liminf_{n\in\mathbb{N}}(\varepsilon-1)\frac{Y_n}{X_{m_n}}+1 \geq$ $\liminf_{n\in\mathbb{N}} \frac{\varepsilon|Y_n|-|Y_n\setminus X_{m_n}|}{|X_{m_n}|} \geq \delta$, which gives that $\limsup_{n\in\mathbb{N}} \frac{|Y_n|}{|X_{m_n}|} \leq \frac{1-\delta}{1-\varepsilon}$, provided that $\varepsilon < 1$.

$2\Rightarrow 1$ If property 2 is satisfied and $\mu_{(Y_n)}(W) \geq \varepsilon$, then:

$$
\begin{aligned}
\mu_{(X_n)}(W) &\geq \limsup_{n\to\infty} \mathfrak{P}\left(W \cap Y_n \mid X_{m_n}\right) \\
&\geq \limsup_{n\to\infty} \frac{|W \cap Y_n| - |Y_n \setminus X_{m_n}|}{|X_{m_n}|} \\
&= \limsup_{n\to\infty} \left(\frac{\varepsilon|Y_n| - |Y_n \setminus X_{m_n}|}{|X_{m_n}|} + \frac{|W \cap Y_n| - \varepsilon|Y_n|}{|Y_n|}\frac{|Y_n|}{|X_{m_n}|} \right) \\
&\geq \liminf_{n\to\infty} \frac{\varepsilon|Y_n| - |Y_n \setminus X_{m_n}|}{|X_{m_n}|} \\
&\quad + \left(\limsup_{n\to\infty} \frac{|W \cap Y_n|}{|Y_n|} - \varepsilon\right)\liminf_{n\in\mathbb{N}} \frac{|Y_n|}{|X_{m_n}|} \\
&\geq \delta + 0\frac{\delta}{\varepsilon} \text{ by the two premises and the first inequalities.}
\end{aligned}
$$

$1\Rightarrow 2$ Assume that $\liminf_{i\to\infty} \frac{\varepsilon|Y_i|-|Y_i\setminus X_{k_i}|}{|X_{k_i}|} < \delta$. Let us build a set W that contradicts Point 1.

For each $n \in \mathbb{N}$, there exists $k_n = \min\{k \mid |Y_n \setminus X_k| \leq \varepsilon|Y_n|\}$, because for large k, $Y_n \setminus X_k = \emptyset$ (because (X_k) is exhaustive and Y_n is finite). By noting that $(Y_n \cap X_{k_n}) \setminus X_{k_n-1} = (Y_n \setminus X_{k_n-1}) \setminus (Y_n \setminus X_{k_n})$ (by convention X_{-1} is empty), we can write that $|(Y_n \cap X_{k_n}) \setminus X_{k_n-1}| = |Y_n \setminus X_{k_n-1}| - |Y_n \setminus X_{k_n}|$, which is bigger than $\varepsilon|Y_n| - |Y_n \setminus X_{k_n}|$, by minimality of k_n. Hence $(Y_n \cap X_{k_n}) \setminus X_{k_n-1}$ admits a subset Z_n of cardinality $|Z_n| = \lfloor \varepsilon|Y_n| \rfloor - |Y_n \setminus X_{k_n}|$. Define $W_n = (Y_n \setminus X_{k_n}) \bigsqcup Z_n$. Note that $W_n \subset Y_n$, and that $\varepsilon - \frac{1}{|Y_n|} < \mathfrak{P}(W_n|Y_n) \leq \varepsilon$.

The W_i satisfy the hypotheses of Lemma 1, so that Point 3 gives $\mathbf{l} \in \mathbb{N}^{\mathbb{N}}$, with $\mu_{(X_n)}(W_{\mathbf{l}}) = \lim_{i\to\infty} \max_{m\in\mathbb{N}} \mathfrak{P}(W_{l_i} \mid X_m)$. By construction, we have:

$$
\begin{aligned}
\mathfrak{P}(W_i \mid X_m) &= \mathfrak{P}(Y_i \setminus X_{k_i} \mid X_m) + \mathfrak{P}(Z_i \mid X_m) \\
&= \frac{|Y_i \cap X_m \setminus X_{k_i}| + |Z_i \cap X_m|}{|X_m|}.
\end{aligned}
$$

If $m < k_i$, then $X_m \subseteq X_{k_i}$, and $Z_i \cap X_m \subseteq Z_i \cap X_{k_i-1} = \emptyset$, so that this quantity is 0. On the contrary, if $m \geq k_i$, then $Z_i \subseteq X_{k_i} \subseteq X_m$, and $Y_i \cap X_m \setminus X_{k_i} = (Y_i \setminus X_{k_i}) \setminus (Y_i \setminus X_m)$, so that:

$$\mathfrak{P}\left(W_i|\,X_m\right) = \frac{|Y_i \cap X_m \setminus X_{k_i}| + |Z_i \cap X_m|}{|X_m|}$$

$$= \frac{|Y_i \cap X_m \setminus X_{k_i}| + |Z_i|}{|X_m|}$$

$$= \frac{|Y_i \setminus X_{k_i}| - |Y_i \setminus X_m| + \lfloor \varepsilon\,|Y_i| \rfloor - |Y_i \setminus X_{k_i}|}{|X_m|}$$

$$\leq \max_{m \in \mathbb{N}} \frac{|\lfloor \varepsilon\,|Y_i| \rfloor| - |Y_i \setminus X_m|}{|X_m|}$$

$$< \delta \text{ by hypothesis.}$$

Taking the limit, we get that $\mu_{(X_n)}(W_1) < \delta$.

On the other hand, applying now Point 1 of Lemma 1 to sequence (Y_n):

$$\mu_{(Y_n)}(W_1) \geq \lim_{i \in \mathbb{N}} \max_{m \in \mathbb{N}} \mathfrak{P}\left(W_{l_i}|\,Y_m\right) \geq \mathfrak{P}\left(W_{l_i}|\,Y_{l_i}\right) = \varepsilon. \qquad \square$$

The previous lemma now allows to characterize the main properties of interest for comparing two Besicovitch submeasures.

Theorem 1. *Let* (X_n) *and* (Y_n) *be nondecreasing and exhaustive.*

1. $\mu_{(Y_n)}$ *is* λ-*Lipschitz with respect to* $\mu_{(X_n)}$, *where* $\lambda > 0$, *if and only if*

$$\forall \varepsilon > 0, \liminf_{n \to \infty} \max_{m \in \mathbb{N}} \frac{|Y_n| - \frac{1}{\varepsilon}|Y_n \setminus X_m|}{|X_m|} \geq \frac{1}{\lambda}.$$

2. $\mu_{(Y_n)}$ *is absolutely continuous with respect to* $\mu_{(X_n)}$ *if and only if it is Lipschitz.*
3. $\mu_{(Y_n)} \leq \mu_{(X_n)}$ *if and only if* $(Y_n) \preceq (X_n)$.
4. $\mu_{(Y_n)} = \mu_{(X_n)}$ *if and only if* $(Y_n) \sim (X_n)$.

One can even see from the proof that $(Y_n) \preceq (X_n)$ if and only if there exists $\varepsilon \in]0, 1[$ such that $\forall W \subset G, \mu_{(X_n)}(W) < \varepsilon \implies \mu_{(Y_n)}(W) < \varepsilon$.

Proof

1. Just note that the λ-Lipschitz property of $\mu_{(Y_n)}$ is equivalent to the properties in Lemma 2, for every δ and $\varepsilon = \lambda\delta$, and hence to:

$$\liminf_{n \in \mathbb{N}} \max_{m \in \mathbb{N}} \frac{|Y_n| - \frac{1}{\varepsilon}|Y_n \setminus X_m|}{|X_m|} \geq \frac{1}{\lambda}.$$

2. From Lemma 2, $\mu_{(Y_n)}$ is absolutely continuous with respect to $\mu_{(X_n)}$ if and only if

$$\forall \varepsilon > 0, \liminf_{n \to \infty} \max_{m \in \mathbb{N}} \frac{|Y_n| - \frac{1}{\varepsilon}|Y_n \setminus X_m|}{|X_m|} > 0.$$

From Point 1, this is equivalent to the existence of some λ such that $\mu_{(Y_n)}$ is λ-Lipschitz with respect to $\mu_{(X_n)}$.

3. Let $(m_n) \in \mathbb{N}^{\mathbb{N}}$ satisfy $\lim_{n \to \infty} \frac{|Y_n \Delta X_{m_n}|}{|Y_n|} = 0$. Then

$$\lim_{n \in \mathbb{N}} \frac{|Y_n| - \frac{1}{\varepsilon}|Y_n \setminus X_{m_n}|}{|X_{m_n}|} = \lim_{n \in \mathbb{N}} \frac{|Y_n|}{|X_{m_n}|} \left(1 - \frac{1}{\varepsilon} \lim_{n \in \mathbb{N}} \frac{|Y_n \setminus X_{m_n}|}{|Y_n|} \right) = 1 \ .$$

We can conclude by Point 1.
Conversely, suppose that

$$\liminf_{n \in \mathbb{N}} \frac{|Y_n| - \frac{1}{\varepsilon}|Y_n \setminus X_{m_n}|}{|X_{m_n}|} \geq 1 \ .$$

By the last inequalities in Lemma 2, we know that $\lim_{n \in \mathbb{N}} \frac{|Y_n|}{|X_{m_n}|} = 1$. Moreover,

$$\lim_{n \to \infty} \frac{|Y_n \setminus X_{m_n}|}{|X_{m_n}|} \leq \lim_{n \to \infty} \frac{\varepsilon |Y_n|}{|X_{m_n}|} - \varepsilon \liminf_{n \in \mathbb{N}} \frac{|Y_n| - \frac{1}{\varepsilon}|Y_n \setminus X_{m_n}|}{|X_{m_n}|} \quad = \varepsilon - \varepsilon = 0 \ .$$

By Point 3 of Proposition 1, we obtain that $(Y_n) \preceq (X_n)$.
4. This is direct from the definitions and the Point 3. $\qquad\square$

The following is direct from Theorem 1 and Remark 2.

Corollary 2. *If (X_n) and (Y_n) are nondecreasing and exhaustive, then $(Y_n) \preceq (X_n)$ (resp. $(Y_n) \sim (X_n)$) if and only if the identity map from A^G endowed with $d_{(X_n)}$ onto A^G endowed with $d_{(Y_n)}$ is 1-Lipschitz (resp. an isometry).*

Here are particular classes of sequences, where the proposition can be applied.

Corollary 3. *Let (X_n) and (Y_n) be nondecreasing and exhaustive.*

1. *If there exist $\lambda > 0$ and a sequence (m_n) such that $\liminf_{n \to \infty} \mathfrak{P}(X_n | Y_{m_n}) \geq \frac{1}{\lambda}$ and $X_n \subset Y_{m_n}$, then $\mu_{(X_n)}$ is λ-Lipschitz with respect to $\mu_{(Y_n)}$.*
2. *If for cofinitely many $n \in \mathbb{N}$, $Y_n \subset X_{n+1}$ and $\liminf_{n \to \infty} \mathfrak{P}(X_n | X_{n+1}) \geq \lambda$, then $\mu_{(X_n)}$ is λ-Lipschitz with respect to $\mu_{(Y_n)}$.*
3. *On the other hand, if $|X_n| \sim_{n \to \infty} |Y_n|$ but (X_n) and (Y_n) are not (synchronously) Følner-equivalent , and $n_{(Y_m)}(X_n, \varepsilon_n) = n+1$ for some real sequence (ε_n) converging to 0, then $\mu_{(X_n)}$ is not absolutely continuous with respect to $\mu_{(Y_n)}$.*

Proof

1. For every $\varepsilon > 0$,

$$\liminf_{n \to \infty} \max_{m \in \mathbb{N}} \frac{|X_n| - \frac{1}{\varepsilon}|X_n \setminus Y_m|}{|Y_m|} \geq \liminf_{n \to \infty} \frac{|X_n| - \frac{1}{\varepsilon}|X_n \setminus Y_{m_n}|}{|Y_{m_n}|} = \liminf_{n \to \infty} \frac{|X_n|}{|Y_{m_n}|} \geq \frac{1}{\lambda} \ .$$

2. Apply Point 1 with $m_n = \min \{ m \in \mathbb{N} | X_n \subset Y_m \}$; the hypothesis is that m_n is ultimately $n + 1$.

3. Suppose $|X_n| \sim_{n\to\infty} |Y_n|$ and (X_n) and (Y_n) are not synchronously Følner-equivalent. By Proposition 2, $(X_n) \not\preceq (Y_n)$, that is, $\varepsilon = \limsup_{n\to\infty} \frac{|X_n \setminus Y_n|}{|Y_n|} > 0$.
We can write $\liminf_{n\to\infty} \frac{|X_n| - \frac{1}{\varepsilon}|X_n \setminus Y_n|}{|Y_n|} = 0$.
By the second assumption, for every $m > n$, $X_n \setminus Y_m = \emptyset$ and $\frac{|X_n|}{|Y_m|} \leq \varepsilon_n$.
We get:

$$\max_{m\in\mathbb{N}} \frac{|X_n| - \frac{1}{\varepsilon}|X_n \setminus Y_m|}{|Y_m|} \leq \max\left(\frac{|X_n| - \frac{1}{\varepsilon}|X_n \setminus Y_n|}{|Y_n|}, \varepsilon_n\right).$$

Putting things together, $\liminf_{n\to\infty} \max_{m\in\mathbb{N}} \frac{|X_n| - \frac{1}{\varepsilon}|X_n \setminus Y_m|}{|Y_m|}$ is 0. We conclude by Point 2 of Theorem 1. $\qquad\square$

Corollary 4. *Let (X_n) and (Y_n) be nondecreasing and exhaustive. Assume that $|X_n| \sim_{n\to\infty} |Y_n|$. Then the following are equivalent.*

1. *(X_n) and (Y_n) are synchronously Følner-equivalent.*
2. *$\mu_{(Y_{l_n})} = \mu_{(X_{l_n})}$, for every increasing sequence $(l_n) \in \mathbb{N}^\mathbb{N}$.*
3. *$\mu_{(Y_{l_n})}$ is absolutely continuous with respect to $\mu_{(X_{l_n})}$, for every increasing sequence (l_n).*

Proof
$1 \Longrightarrow 2$ If (X_n) and (Y_n) are synchronously Følner equivalent, then so are (X_{l_n}) and (Y_{l_n}) for every increasing $(l_n) \in \mathbb{N}^\mathbb{N}$. We conclude thanks to Theorem 1.
$2 \Longrightarrow 3$ This is obvious.
$\not 1 \Longrightarrow \not 3$ If (X_n) and (Y_n) are not synchronously Følner-equivalent, then there exists an infinite set $I \subset \mathbb{N}$ and a real number $\alpha > 0$ such that $\forall n \in I, \frac{|X_n \Delta Y_n|}{|X_n|} \geq \alpha$. This implies that for every increasing sequence $(l_n) \in I^\mathbb{N}$, (X_{l_n}) and (Y_{l_n}) are not synchronously Følner-equivalent. We can take an increasing sequence $(l_n) \in I^\mathbb{N}$ such that $n_{(Y_m)}(X_{l_n}, \varepsilon_{l_n}) = l_{n+1}$, for some real sequence (ε_n) converging to 0. Then (X_{l_n}) and (Y_{l_n}) satisfy the assumptions for Point 3 of Corollary 3. $\quad\square$

3.3   Shift

If G is a group and $(X_n) \sim (gX_n)$, then we say that (X_n) is *(left) g-Følner*; (X_n) is right g-Følner if (X_n^{-1}) is left g^{-1}-Følner. Since $|X_n| = |gX_n|$, Proposition 2 says that it is enough to require $(X_n) \preceq (gX_n)$, and in this case, (X_n) and (gX_n) are even synchronously Følner-equivalent.

A *(left) Følner sequence* for a countable group G is a g-Følner sequence for every $g \in G$. A countable group is *amenable* if and only if it admits a Følner sequence: see [CSC10, Chapter 4] also for many equivalent definitions.

The following is a rephrasing of Corollary 2.

Corollary 5. *Let G be a countable group and let (X_n) be a nondecreasing exhaustive sequence.*

1. *(X_n) is g-Følner if and only if $\mu_{(X_n)} = \mu_{(g^{-1}X_n)}$ if and only if the shift by g is an isometry.*

2. (X_n) is Følner if and only if every shift is an isometry.
3. If G is finitely generated (see below) then it is amenable if and only if there exists a nondecreasing exhaustive sequence (X_n) of finite subsets of G such that every shift is an isometry.

Note that one implication of Point 3 was already stated in [Cap09, Theorem 3.5], but the proof contains a confusion between left and right Følner.

A group G is *finitely generated* (briefly, f.g.) if $E \Subset G$ exists such that for every $g \in G$ there exists $e_1, \ldots, e_n \in E \cup E^{-1}$ such that $e_1 \cdots e_n = g$. Remarkably (cf. [Pet, Lemma 5.3]) if a f.g. group is amenable, then it has a nondecreasing exhaustive Følner sequence. In addition, if the size of the balls grows polynomially with the radius, then they form a Følner sequence, so Point 3 of Corollary 5 generalizes [HM17, Cor 4.1.4].

Corollary 6. *Let G be a finitely generated group.*

1. *If (X_n) is the sequence of balls with respect to some generating set of cardinality α, then every shift is α-Lipschitz.*
2. *If $g \in G$, a nondecreasing exhaustive sequence is g-Følner if and only if all of its subsequences yield a Besicovitch pseudodistance for which the shift by g is continuous.*
3. *G is amenable if and only if it admits a nondecreasing exhaustive sequence of finite subsets of which all subsequences yield a Besicovitch distance for which every shift is continuous.*

The first point generalizes [HM17, Prop 4.1.3]. Note that it still applies in non-amenable groups, but the shifts are no longer isometries, and there is a subsequence of balls with respect to which the Besicovitch pseudodistance makes them non-continuous.

Proof

1. If E is the generating set and E_n the corresponding radius-n ball, then $E_0 = \{e\}$ where e is the identity of G and $E_{n+1} = (E \cup E^{-1}) \cdot E_n$, so $|E_n| \leq (2\,|E| + 1)^n$. We can apply Point 2 of Corollary 3.
2. This comes from Corollary 4.
3. This comes from Point 2. □

There are nondecreasing non-Følner sequences for which the shift is Lipschitz (but not an isometry) in $\mathbb{Z}^d$. Here's an example: $X_n = (\llbracket -n, n \rrbracket \cup 2\,\rrbracket -n, n\llbracket)^d$. Indeed, for every n, $1 + X_n \subset X_{2n}$ and $\frac{|X_{2n}|}{|X_n|} = \frac{(8n-1)^d}{(4n-1)^d}$, which converges to 2^d when n goes to infinity. We conclude by Point 1 of Corollary 3, with $m_n = 2n$ and $\alpha = 2^d$. But the shift is not an isometry because the sequence is not Følner: $\mu((2\mathbb{Z})^d) = 2^d/3^d > \mu((2\mathbb{Z} + 1)^d) = 1/3^d$.

"Dually" to shifts, we can define the *propagation* $\pi^g : A^G \to A^G$ by $\pi^g(x)(i) = x(ig)$. A *block map* (see [LM95] for $G = \mathbb{Z}$) is, in essence, a composition of a radius-0 function with a product of propagations. The same characterizations are true for propagations as for shift maps, to which we can derive the following:

Corollary 7. *A nondecreasing exhaustive sequence (X_n) of finite subsets of a f.g. group G is right Følner if and only if for every increasing sequence $(l_n) \in \mathbb{N}^{\mathbb{N}}$, every block map with neighborhood size k is k-Lipschitz for $d_{(X_{l_n})}$.*

4   Conclusions

We have presented a way to compare Besicovitch submeasures (in terms of absolute continuity, Lipschitz continuity, equality) thanks to the sequences of finite sets which describe them. In a shift space (with respect to a finitely generated group) endowed with the Besicovitch topology, we have derived conditions on the defining sequence for the shift maps to be continuous, Lipschitz or isometries. As part of this, we gave another characterization of f.g. amenable groups.

Future work will involve the study of other topological and dynamical properties (cf. [CGN]) or extension to configuration spaces on possibly uncountable groups. The latter would require the use of the more general notions of *directed set* and of *net*, and although the definition of Besicovitch pseudodistance and submeasure would be immediate to extend, the techniques used to prove the main lemmas could need a major revision.

References

[BFK99] Blanchard, F., Formenti, E., Kůrka, P.: Cellular automata in the Cantor, Besicovitch and Weyl spaces. Complex Syst. **11**, 107–123 (1999)

[Cap09] Capobianco, S.: Surjunctivity for cellular automata in Besicovitch spaces. J. Cell. Automata **4**, 89–98 (2009)

[CGK13] Capobianco, S., Guillon, P., Kari, J.: Surjective cellular automata far from the Garden of Eden. Discret. Math. Theor. Comput. Sci. **15**, 41–60 (2013)

[CGN] Capobianco, S., Guillon, P., Noûs, C.: Besicovitch pseudodistances with respect to non-Følner sequences. Preprint, ⟨hal-02566187⟩ (2020)

[CSC10] Ceccherini-Silberstein, T., Coornaert, M.: Cellular Automata and Groups. Springer, Heidelberg (2010). https://doi.org/10.1007/978-3-642-14034-1

[HM17] Hadeler, K.P., Müller, J.: Cellular Automata : Analysis and Applications. Springer, Heidelberg (2017). https://doi.org/10.1007/978-3-642-14034-1

[LM95] Lind, D., Marcus, B.: An Introduction to Symbolic Dynamics and Coding. Cambridge University Press, Cambridge (1995)

[Pet] Pete, G.: Probability and geometry on groups. Lecture Notes (2019). http://math.bme.hu/~gabor/PGG.pdf. Accessed 19 May 2019

[Sab06] Sablik, M.: Étude de l'action conjointe d'un automate cellulaire et du décalage: une approche topologique et ergodique. Ph.D. Thesis, Université de Provence, July 2006

Four Heads are Better than Three

Ville Salo[(✉)] [iD]

University of Turku, Turku, Finland
vosalo@utu.fi

Abstract. We construct recursively-presented finitely-generated torsion groups which have bounded torsion and whose word problem is conjunctive equivalent (in particular positive and Turing equivalent) to a given recursively enumerable set. These groups can be interpreted as groups of finite state machines or as subgroups of topological full groups, on effective subshifts over other torsion groups. We define a recursion-theoretic property of a set of natural numbers, called impredictability. It roughly states that a Turing machine can enumerate numbers such that every Turing machine occasionally incorrectly guesses (by either halting or not) whether they are in the set, even given an oracle for a prefix of the set. We prove that impredictable recursively enumerable sets exist. Combining these constructions and slightly adapting a result of [Salo and Törmä, 2017], we obtain that four-headed group-walking finite-state automata can define strictly more subshifts than three-headed automata on a group containing a copy of the integers, confirming a conjecture of [Salo and Törmä, 2017]. These are the first examples of groups where four heads are better than three, and they show the maximal height of a finite head hierarchy is indeed four.

Keywords: Torsion groups · Finite-state automata · Subshifts · Recursion theory

1 Introduction

In this paper, we combine construction techniques from group theory and recursion theory to verify a conjecture the author and Törmä made in [15] about group-walking automata. The a priori motivation was this conjecture, but the constructions and definitions we give may be of independent interest.

1.1 The Results

Theorem 1. *Let A be Σ_1^0. Then there exists a recursively presented torsion group with bounded torsion, whose word problem is Turing equivalent to A.*

Research supported by Academy of Finland grant 2608073211.

The exact types of reduction are that A many-one reduces to the word problem, and the word problem conjunctively reduces to A.

Our recursion-theoretic contributions are of a somewhat technical nature (though not particularly difficult). We define a possibly new notion called ϕ-impredictability (Definition 1), which roughly states that a Turing machine can enumerate numbers such that every Turing machine occasionally incorrectly guesses (by either halting or not) whether they are in the set, even given an oracle for a prefix of the set.

Theorem 2. *For every total recursive function ϕ, there exists a ϕ-impredictable Σ_1^0 set.*

We now state our main "navigation-theoretic" contribution. In [15], for a f.g. (finitely-generated) group G and $n \in N$, the class of G-subshifts defined by group-walking finite-state machines with n heads is denoted by $\mathcal{S}(G, n)$. See [15] or Sect. 5 for the definitions. The following is a slight adaptation of a result of [15].

Lemma 1. *If G has bounded torsion and has ϕ-impredictable word problem for fast-enough growing ϕ, then $\mathcal{S}(G \times \mathbb{Z}, 3) \subsetneq \mathcal{S}(G \times \mathbb{Z}, 4)$.*

For example $\phi = \exp \circ \exp \circ \exp \circ \exp \circ \exp$ is fast enough. By putting the above results together, we obtain that four heads are better than three, as claimed in the title.

Theorem 3. *There exists a finitely-generated recursively-presented group G containing a copy of the integers, such that $\mathcal{S}(G, 3) \subsetneq \mathcal{S}(G, 4)$.*

See Sect. 1.3 for some context for this result, and a new conjecture.

1.2   Some Relevant Existing Work

The main group-construction result (recursively presented groups with bounded torsion and with a word problem of a prescribed difficulty) uses the idea from [3,13] of groups of finite-state machines. It also uses existing torsion groups as a black-box, in particular it is an application of the deep theory that arose from the Burnside problem [1].

The idea of hiding information into the word problem is of course not a new idea in combinatorial group theory, but we are not aware of it appearing previously in the context of torsion groups. The Dehn monsters from [11], recursively presented groups where no infinite set of distinct elements can be enumerated, seem strongly related. (Our construction cannot be used to produce such groups due to using another group as a black box, but it is possible that their construction can be adapted to produce our result.)

Topological full groups (already on $\mathbb{Z}$) are a well-known source of interesting examples of groups [6,9,10], and our groups can also be interpreted as subgroups of topological full groups of subshifts on torsion groups. In a symbolic dynamics context, [7] (independently) uses a similar construction to prove that the automorphism groups of multidimensional SFTs can have undecidable word problem.

Dan Turetsky showed in the MathOverflow answer [12] that the halting problem is not ϕ-impredictable for some total recursive ϕ, and that there exists a Σ_1^0 set which is simultaneously ϕ-impredictable for all total recursive ϕ. The latter result of course implies Theorem 2.

1.3   Head Hierarchies

For context, we state what is now known about the head hierarchies, and state a bold conjecture. See Definition 3 for the definitions.

Theorem 4. *For an infinite finitely-generated group G, denote by $h(G) \in \mathbb{N}_{>0} \cup \{\infty\}$ the supremum of n such that $\mathcal{S}(G, n-1) \subsetneq \mathcal{S}(G, n)$. Then*

$$\{3, 4, \infty\} \subset \mathcal{H} = \{h(G) \mid G \text{ an infinite f.g. group}\} \subset \{2, 3, 4, \infty\}.$$

Our contribution is the 4 on the left, which is notable because the maximal finite height is now known.

Proof (Proof sketch). The fact $4 \in \mathcal{H}$ follows from Theorem 3. The fact $h \in \mathcal{H} \cap \mathbb{N} \implies h \leq 4$ is proved in [15], and the facts $3 \in \mathcal{H}$ and $\infty \in \mathcal{H}$ are proved in [15] and [14] respectively. The fact $1 \notin \mathcal{H}$ is seen as follows: In [14] it is shown that $\mathcal{S}(\mathbb{Z}, 1) \subsetneq \mathcal{S}(\mathbb{Z}, 2)$ and the proof easily generalizes to virtually $\mathbb{Z}$ groups. On the other hand it is easy to see that the sunny-side-up $X_{\leq 1}$ separates one from four heads, i.e. $X_{\leq 1} \in \mathcal{S}(G, 4) \setminus \mathcal{S}(G, 1)$, for all f.g. infinite groups G which are not virtually $\mathbb{Z}$, which can be proved using methods of [15] and [14].   □

We conjecture that four heads are needed if and only if the word problem is undecidable:

Conjecture 1. Let G be a finitely-generated infinite group which is not torsion. Then

– if $\mathbb{Z} \leq G$ and G has decidable word problem, then $h(G) = 3$,
– if $\mathbb{Z} \leq G$ and G has undecidable word problem, then $h(G) = 4$.

The upper bounds are known, and $h(G) = \infty$ is known for torsion groups [15]. The first item is the join of conjectures in [15] and [14]. It is known that the sunny-side-up subshift $X_{\leq 1}$ does not prove $h(\mathbb{Z}) = h(\mathbb{Z}^2) = 3$, as on these groups two heads suffice for it. We do not know any other non-torsion groups where the sunny-side-up requires fewer heads than the above conjecture would suggest.

Settling this conjecture in the positive would not be the end of the story. A more refined invariant than $h(G)$ would be to ask what the precise set of n such that $\mathcal{S}(G, n-1) \subsetneq \mathcal{S}(G, n)$ is. In particular this is of interest when G is a torsion group; [15] only gives an affine function $f(n) \sim 3n$ such that $\mathcal{S}(G, n) \subsetneq \mathcal{S}(G, f(n))$.

These results are of course about just one way to associate subshift classes to n-headed automata. We believe the results are relatively robust to changes in the definition, but some details are critical. It is in particular open what happens when G is a torsion group and the heads are allowed to communicate over distances, i.e. if they have a shared state.

2   Preliminaries

For two functions f, g write $f = O(g)$ (resp. $f = \Omega(g)$) if for some choice of $a > 0$, $f(n) \le ag(n)$ (resp. $f(n) \ge ag(n)$) for large enough n. Write $f = \Theta(g)$ if $f = O(g)$ and $f = \Omega(g)$. Write $f \sim g$ for $f(n)/g(n) \to 1$. For $a, b \in \mathbb{N}$ write $a \mid b$ for "a divides b".

We assume some familiarity with computability/recursion theory, but we state some (not necessarily standard) conventions. We identify partial computable functions with Turing machines, and also their Gödel numbers. Let $\mathcal{T} \subset \mathbb{N}$ be the set of codings of Turing machines which halt on every input, and write $\mathcal{P} = \mathbb{N}$ for all partial recursive functions. "Recursive" means the same as "computable" and refers to the existence of a Turing machine, which always halts unless the function is explicitly stated to be partial. If χ is a Turing machine, we write $\chi(p)\!\downarrow$ if χ halts on input p. A partial (not necessarily computable) function from A to B is denoted $g : A \nrightarrow B$.

Let us recall some basic definitions of reductions. A set A *many-one reduces* to a set B if there is $\phi \in \mathcal{T}$ such that $n \in A \iff \phi(n) \in B$. For the following three reductions, we give quantitative versions, so we have a handle on the rate at which reduction happens. The definitions are stated in terms of characteristic sequences, but correspond to their usual meaning.

We say B *weakly truth table reduces*, or *wtt-reduces*, to A if there exists $g \in \mathcal{P}$ and nondecreasing $\beta \in \mathcal{T}$ with $\beta(n) \to \infty$ such that when applied to words as $g : \{0,1\}^* \nrightarrow \{0,1\}^*$, if $x \in \{0,1\}^{\mathbb{N}}$ is the characteristic function of A and y that of B, we have that $g(w)$ is defined on prefixes of y, and

$$w \prec y \implies (g(w) \prec x \wedge |g(w)| \ge \beta(|w|)).$$

We call β the *rate* of the reduction.

We say B *positively reduces* to A if it wtt-reduces to A, for some $\beta \in \mathcal{T}$, with the following additional properties for g: $g \in \mathcal{T}$, $|g(w)| = \beta(|w|)$ for all w, and g is *monotone* in the sense that $u \le v \implies g(u) \le g(v)$, where $\le$ is letterwise comparison. If further $g(u)_i$ only depends on whether $u \ge w_{i,|u|}$ for some $w_{i,|u|}$ computable from $i, |u|$, then B *conjunctively reduces* to A.

We say B *Turing reduces* to A if there is an A-oracle machine that can determine membership in B. Clearly many-one reducibility implies conjunctive reducibility implies positive reducibility implies weak truth table reducibility implies Turing reducibility.

We assume some familiarity with group theory, but state some conventions. Our groups are discrete and mostly finitely-generated. Finitely-generated groups come with a finite generating set, which we usually do not mention. The identity of a group G is denoted by e_G (or just e). For words $u, v \in S^*$ where S is the generating set, write $u \approx_G v$ (or just $u \approx v$ if G is clear from context) when u and v represent (evaluate to) the same element of G. For $g, h \in G$, write $[g, h] = g^{-1}h^{-1}gh$ for the *commutator* of g and h.

The *word problem* of a group G is the following subset $W \subset \mathbb{N}$: Let S be the fixed symmetric generating set, and order elements of S^* (finite words over S) first by length and then lexicographically. Include $n \in W$ if the nth word evaluates to the identity of G. Slight inconvenience is caused by linearizing the word problem this way, but on the other hand sticking to subsets of $\mathbb{N}$ slightly simplifies the discussion in Sect. 3. We denote the word problem of G as $\mathrm{WP}(G) \subset \mathbb{N}$.

If a countable group G acts on a compact zero-dimensional space X, the corresponding *topological full group* is the smallest group of homeomorphisms $g : X \to X$ which contains every homeomorphism g with the following property: there exists a clopen partition $(P_i)_{i=1}^k$ of X and $g_i \in G$ such that for $\forall i \in \{1, .., k\} : \forall x \in P_i : gx = g_i x$. It turns out that the group contains precisely such homeomorphisms, i.e. they are closed under composition. One may think of $((P_i)_i, (g_i)_i)$ as a local rule for g.

A group is *torsion* if all elements have finite order, i.e. G does not contain a copy of the integers. The *torsion function* of a torsion group is $T_G : \mathbb{N} \to \mathbb{N}$ defined by

$$T_G(n) = \sup\{\mathrm{ord}(g) \mid g \in G, |g| \le n\}$$

where $\mathrm{ord}(g) = |\langle g \rangle|$ and $|g|$ is the word norm with respect to the implicit generating set. A group is of *bounded torsion* if $T_G(n) = O(1)$.

In [8] Ivanov shows that the *free Burnside group*

$$B(2, 2^{48}) = \langle a, b \mid \forall w \in \{a, b, a^{-1}, b^{-1}\}^* : w^{2^{48}} \approx e \rangle$$

is infinite and has decidable word problem ([8, Theorem A]), and we obtain

Lemma 2. *There exists a finitely-generated torsion group with bounded torsion and decidable word problem.*

The decision algorithm is given in [8, Lemma 21.1]. For a survey on the Burnside problem see [1]. Theorem 3 could be proved using any torsion group with recursive torsion function (e.g. the Grigorchuk group), with minor modifications, as explained after the proof of Theorem 3. Our technical construction results (in particular Theorem 6) are stated and proved without assuming the existence of infinite f.g. groups of bounded torsion, though obviously to obtain Theorem 1 the existence of one is necessary (since it states the existence of one).

We assume some familiarity with symbolic dynamics on groups (see [2] for more information), but state some conventions. If G is a group, and Σ a finite set, Σ^G with the product topology and the G-action $gx_h = x_{g^{-1}h}$ is called the *full shift*, and the actions $(g, x) \mapsto gx$ are called *shifts*. A *subshift* is a topologically closed subset X satisfying $GX = X$. A particularly important subshift is the *sunny-side-up* subshift $X_{\le 1} = \{x \in \{0, 1\}^G \mid \sum_{g \in G} x_g \le 1\}$. Equivalently a subshift is defined by a family of *forbidden patterns*, i.e. a (possibly infinite) family of clopen sets that the *orbit* Gx of x may not intersect. If G has decidable word problem then $X \subset \Sigma^G$ is *effective* if there exists a Turing machine that enumerates a family of forbidden patterns which defines the subshift. A *cellular automaton* on a subshift is a continuous shift-commuting self-map of it.

3   Impredictability

Definition 1. *For a function ϕ, a set $A \subset \mathbb{N}$ is ϕ-impredictable if*

$$\exists \psi \in \mathcal{T} : \forall \chi \in \mathcal{P} : \exists^\infty p : \psi(p) \in A \iff \chi(p, A \upharpoonright \phi(p)) \downarrow .$$

To unravel this definition a bit, we want to have a Turing machine ψ which always halts and gives us positions $\psi(p)$ on the number line $\mathbb{N}$ so that, for any Turing machine χ, $\psi(p) \in \mathbb{N}$ is just the halting information about χ for infinitely many inputs p, even if χ is allowed oracle access to the first $\phi(p)$ bits of A. Since χ is quantified universally, this definition is one way to formalize the idea that it is hard to predict whether $\psi(p) \in A$ even given access to the first $\phi(p)$ bits of A.

Lemma 3. *Let $\phi', \phi \in \mathcal{T}$ and $\phi'(n) \geq \phi(n)$ for all large enough n. Then every ϕ'-impredictable set is ϕ-impredictable, with the same choice of ψ.*

Proof. Let $\phi, \phi' \in \mathcal{T}$ and suppose A is ϕ'-impredictable. We need to show ϕ-impredictability where $\phi(n) \leq \phi'(n)$ for all large enough n. Clearly changing finitely many initial values does not change ϕ-impredictability, so we may assume $\phi \leq \phi'$. Let $\psi \in \mathcal{T}$ be given by ϕ'-impredictability, so

$$\forall \chi \in \mathcal{P} : \exists^\infty p : \psi(p) \in A \iff \chi(p, A \upharpoonright \phi'(p)) \downarrow$$

In particular, we can restrict to $\hat{\chi} \in \mathcal{P}$ which given (p, w) first cuts off all but at most the first $\phi(p) \leq \phi'(p)$ symbols of w, and then apply χ. This restriction is

$$\forall \hat{\chi} \in \mathcal{P} : \exists^\infty p : \psi(p) \in A \iff \chi(p, A \upharpoonright \phi(p)) \downarrow,$$

which is just the definition of ϕ-impredictability.   □

Theorem 5. *For every $\phi \in \mathcal{T}$, there exists a ϕ-impredictable Σ^0_1 set.*

Proof. We construct an increasing total computable function ψ, and A will be contained in its image. We want to have

$$\psi(p) \in A \iff \chi(p, A \upharpoonright \phi(p)) \downarrow$$

infinitely many times for all χ. The way we construct A is we go through $n \in \mathbb{N}$ and set either $n \notin A$, or set up the rule $n \in A \iff \xi_n \downarrow$ for some Turing machine ξ_n whose behavior we describe (informally). We refer to those $n \in \mathbb{N}$ already considered as *determined*.

List all partial functions χ in an infinite-to-one way, i.e. we consider functions χ successively, so that each χ appears infinitely many times. When considering χ, we want to determine new values in A so as to make sure that

$$\psi(p) \in A \iff \chi(p, A \upharpoonright \phi(p)) \downarrow$$

for at least one new $p \in \mathbb{N}$. Suppose we have already determined the first m values of A, i.e. the word $w \in \{0,1\}^m$ such that the characteristic sequence of A will begin with the word w is already determined, and that we have not determined whether $n \in A$ for any $n \geq m$. The idea is that while we do not know what the word w actually is, there are only 2^m possible choices, and we simply try all of them to get the equivalence above to hold for one new p. To achieve this we will determine whether $n \in A$ for some interval of choices $n \in [m, M']$.

Enumerate the words of $\{0,1\}^m$ as $w_0, w_1, ..., w_{2^m-1}$. Now, let $p_0 < p_1 < ... < p_{2^m-1}$ be minimal such that $\phi(p_i) \geq m$ for all i. Let $M = \max_j \phi(p_j)$ Set $n \notin A$ for all $n \in [m, M]$. As $\psi(p_i)$ for $i \in [0, 2^m - 1]$ pick any distinct values greater than M, and determine $\psi(p_i) \in A \iff \chi(p_i, w_i \cdot 0^{\phi(p_i)-m}) \downarrow$. If $w = w_i$, then for $p = p_i$ we have

$$\psi(p) \in A \iff \chi(p_i, w_i \cdot 0^{\phi(p_i)-m}) \downarrow \iff \chi(p, A \upharpoonright \phi(p)) \downarrow,$$

because the characteristic sequence of A indeed begins with the word $w_i \cdot 0^{\phi(p_i)-m}$. Thus, we have obtained a new value $p = p_i$ at which the statement is satisfied for χ.

For all n that are yet undetermined, but some larger number is determined, we determine $n \notin A$, so that we determine the values in some new interval $[m, M']$. We can then inductively continue to the next value of χ. This process determines all values of A, and by construction A is a recursively enumerable set which is ϕ-impredictable. □

Lemma 4. *Let $A, B \subset \mathbb{N}$ and suppose A many-one reduces to B, and B wtt-reduces to A with rate β. If A is ϕ-impredictable, then B is $(\beta \circ \phi)$-impredictable.*

Proof. Let $\phi' = \beta \circ \phi$. Let $f : \mathbb{N} \to \mathbb{N}$ be the many-one reduction from A to B, and $g : \{0,1\}^* \to \{0,1\}^*$ the wtt-reduction from B to A with rate β. Since A is ϕ-impredictable there exists $\psi : \mathbb{N} \to \mathbb{N}$ such that

$$\forall \chi \in \mathcal{P} : \exists^\infty p : \psi(p) \in A \iff \chi(p, A \upharpoonright \phi(p)) \downarrow.$$

Setting $\psi' = f \circ \psi$, we have, by the definition of f, that

$$\forall \chi \in \mathcal{P} : \exists^\infty p : \psi'(p) \in B \iff \chi(p, A \upharpoonright \phi(p)) \downarrow.$$

For $\chi \in \mathcal{P}$ define $\hat\chi \in \mathcal{P}$ as follows: Given (p, w), compute $g(w) = u$ and then evaluate $\chi(p, u \upharpoonright \phi'(p))$, so that

$$\hat\chi(p, A \upharpoonright \phi(p)) \downarrow \iff \chi(p, g(A \upharpoonright \phi(p)) \upharpoonright \phi'(p)) \downarrow,$$

where we observe that $g(A \upharpoonright \phi(p)) \upharpoonright \phi'(p) = B \upharpoonright \phi'(p)$ (in particular g indeed halts with an output so the formula makes sense).

Specializing the first quantifier, we have

$$\forall \hat{\chi} \in \mathcal{P} : \exists^\infty p : \psi'(p) \in B \iff \hat{\chi}(p, A \upharpoonright \phi(p))\downarrow,$$

equivalently

$$\forall \chi \in \mathcal{P} : \exists^\infty p : \psi'(p) \in B \iff \chi(p, B \upharpoonright \phi'(p)),$$

so ψ' proves that B is ϕ'-impredictable, as desired. $\qquad\square$

We show that impredictability implies uncomputability.

Proposition 1. *If A is Π_1^0, then A is not ϕ-impredictable for any $\phi \in \mathcal{T}$.*

Proof. Suppose for a contradiction that A is Π_1^0 and is ϕ-impredictable with $\phi \in \mathcal{T}$. Let $\psi \in \mathcal{P}$ be such that

$$\forall \chi \in \mathcal{P} : \exists^\infty p : \psi(p) \in A \iff \chi(p, A \upharpoonright \phi(p))\downarrow.$$

In particular, this applies to the following χ: given (p, w), we ignore w and if $\psi(p) \notin A$, then $\chi(p, w)\downarrow$, and otherwise $\chi(p, w)\uparrow$. This well-defines $\chi \in P$ since A is Π_1^0, and for all $p \in \mathbb{N}$ we have

$$\psi(p) \in A \iff \chi(p, A \upharpoonright \phi(p))\uparrow,$$

a contradiction. $\qquad\square$

4   Impredictable Torsion Groups

Definition 2. *We define a group $K(G, A, H)$ which depends on a choice of a finitely-generated groups G, H (and choices of generating sets for them, kept implicit), and a set $A \subset \mathbb{N}$. First define a subshift on G by*

$$X_A = \{x \in \{0,1\}^G \mid \sum_{g \in G} x_g \leq 2, \text{ and } \sum_{k \in \{g,h\}} x_k = 2 \implies d(g,h) \notin A\}$$

where $d : G \times G \to \mathbb{N}$ is the (left-invariant) word metric. To each $g \in G$ associate the bijection

$$\hat{g}(x, h') = (g \cdot x, h'), \quad \hat{g} : X_A \times H \to X_A \times H$$

i.e. the usual shift action in the first component, and to each $b \in \{0,1\}$ and $h \in H$ associate the bijection

$$h_b(x, h') = (x, h^{1-|x_{e_G}-b|} \cdot h'), \quad h_b : X_A \times H \to X_A \times H$$

where $h^{1-|x_{e_G}-b|}$ evaluates to e_H if $x_{e_G} = b$, and to h otherwise. Define

$$K(G, A, H) = \langle \{\hat{g}, h_b \mid g \in G, h \in H, b \in \{0,1\}\} \rangle \leq \mathrm{Sym}(X_A \times H)$$

Obviously $K = K(G, A, H)$ is finitely-generated, and the implicit generators we use for K are the ones from the definition, with $\hat{g}$ taken only for g in the generating set of G, and h_b only for h in the generating set of H.

Remark 1. This group can be interpreted as a group of finite-state machines in the sense of [3] (with obvious nonabelian generalization) when H is finite, by simulating the actions of $\hat{g}$ by translations of the head, having $|H|$ states, and changing the state by the left-regular action of H (if in the correct clopen set) when h_b is applied. Again if H is finite, K can also be interpreted as a subgroup of the topological full group of the $G \times H$-subshift $X_A \times H$ under the action $(g, h) \cdot (x, h') = (gx, hh')$, by having $\hat{g}$ act by (g, e_H) and having h_B act by either (e_G, h) or (e_G, e_H) depending on x_{e_G}.

We now prove some important technical properties of these groups, leading up to the proof that they give examples of bounded torsion groups with impredictable word problem.

Lemma 5. *If $A' \subset A$, the defining action of $K(G, A, H)$ can be seen as a restriction of the action of $K(G, A', H)$ in a natural way, thus $K(G, A, H)$ is a quotient group of $K(G, A', H)$.*

Proof. Map generators to generators in the obvious way. The group $K(G, A', H)$ acts on $X_{A'} \times H \supset X_A \times H$ and the restriction of the action to $X_A \times H$ is precisely that of $K(G, A, H)$. Thus, all identities of $K(G, A', H)$ are identities also in $K(G, A, H)$. □

In particular, the defining action of $K(G, A, H)$ is always a restriction of $K(G, \emptyset, H)$.

Lemma 6. *For any G, A, H, there exists a split epimorphism $K(G, A, H) \to G$.*

Proof. We have $X_{\leq 1} = X_{\mathbb{N}} \subset X_A$, so the $\hat{g}$-translations act nontrivially on the X_A component as the action on $X_{\leq 1}$ is the one-point compactification of the left-regular action of G on itself. Observe also that the X_A-component is not modified by any of the maps h_b, so the action of K_A on this component factors is just the shift action $G \curvearrowright X_A$. This gives a homomorphism $\gamma : K(G, A, H) \to G$, and the map $g \mapsto \hat{g}$ is a section for it. □

We refer to γ as the *natural epimorphism*.

Lemma 7. *If $\mathrm{WP}(G)$ is decidable and A is Σ_1^0, then X_A is an effective subshift.*

Proof. Since we can list elements of A, and can compute the distance between given group elements, we can forbid all finite patterns where two 1s appear at g, h with $d(g, h) \in A$. □

Lemma 8. *If G has decidable word problem and H is recursively presented, then the following statements hold.*

– If H has decidable word problem, then the word problem of $K(G, A, H)$ conjunctively reduces to A with exponential rate.
– If A is Σ_1^0 then $K(G, A, H)$ is recursively presented.

Proof. Let $K = K(G, A, H)$ and let S be the finite generating set of K. We begin with the proof of the latter item. We need to find a semi-algorithm that, given $w \in S^*$, halts if and only if w represents the identity. For this, first consider the natural epimorphism image $\gamma(w) \in G$. Because G is in particular recursively presented, we can first verify that $\gamma(w) = e_G$ (if not, then also $w \neq e_K$, and the computation diverges as desired).

Assuming $\gamma(w) = e_G$, we next check that w acts trivially on all elements of $X_A \times H$. We define an action of the free group on generators S on pairs $(P, h) \in \mathcal{L}(X_\emptyset) \times H$ by

$$\hat{g}(P, h') = (g \cdot P, h'),$$

(where $\operatorname{dom}(gP) = g\operatorname{dom}(P)$ and $gP_k = P_{g^{-1}k}$), and for $b \in \{0, 1\}$ and $h \in H$ we map

$$h_b(P, h') = (P, h^{1 - |P_{e_G} - b|} h'),$$

when $e_G \in \operatorname{dom}(P)$, and $h_b(P, h') = (P, h')$ otherwise.

If $|w| \leq n$ and $\gamma(w) = e_G$, clearly $w \approx e_K$ if and only if the action of w fixes all $P \times h$ where $P \in \mathcal{L}_n(X_A), h \in H$. Naturally, if $\mathcal{P} \supset \mathcal{L}_n(X_A)$ and the action fixes (P, h) for all $P \in \mathcal{P}, h \in H$, then a fortiori $w \approx e_K$. We can verify this for a particular (P, h) by using the fact H is recursively presented. By the previous lemma, X_A is effective, so we can enumerate upper approximations to $\mathcal{L}_n(X_A)$ which eventually converge. In other words, we eventually obtain the set $\mathcal{L}_n(X_A)$, and it $w \approx e_K$, then at this point (at the latest) we can conclude that w indeed acts trivially and halts.

The proof of the first item is similar. To see that there is a wtt-reduction with exponential rate, observe that if we know the first n values of A, then we can determine the legal contents of all G-patterns with domain $B_n(G)$ in X_A, and using this, and the decidable word problem of H, we can determine whether $w \approx e_K$ for any word with $|w| \leq n$. Since we list elements of groups in lexicographic order, the resulting rate β is exponential, as there are exponentially many words w with $|w| \leq n$.

To see that this is a conjunctive reduction, we observe that the reduction function $g : \{0, 1\}^* \to \{0, 1\}^*$ (computing initial segments of the word problem from initial segments of A) of the previous paragraph can be written uniformly for all sets A so it is total computable, and that we should set $g(u)_i = 1$ if and only if the ith group element acts trivially on the set of patterns not containing elements of A. It can be checked by a terminating computation whether the group element acts nontrivially on some pattern containing only one 1. Our query on A should check that whenever the element acts nontrivially on a pattern with two 1s, then A contains the distance between the 1s of the pattern. This corresponds to checking $u \geq w_{|u|, i}$ where $w_{|u|, i}$ lists these finitely many bad distances.   □

Lemma 9. *Suppose G has decidable word problem and H is not abelian. Then A many-one reduces to the word problem of $K(G, A, H)$.*

Proof. For $n \geq 1$, let g_n be any effective list of elements of G satisfying $|g_n| = n$ (using the fact G has decidable word problem), and consider $g'_n = [h'_1, h_1^{g_n}]$ where $[h', h] \neq e_H$ (using that H is not abelian) and the action of $h_1^{g_n} = g_n h_1 g_n^{-1}$ is

$$h_1^{g_n}(x, h') = (x, h^{1-|x_{g_n}-b|} \cdot h')$$

We have $g'_n \approx e_K$ if and only if $n \in A$. Namely, if $n \notin A$ then g'_n acts nontrivially on (x, e_H) where $x \in X_A$ is the unique configuration satisfying $x_{e_G} = x_{g_n} = 1$, while if $n \in A$ then for all $x \in X_A$ either $x_{e_G} = 0$ or $x_{g_n} = 0$, and in either case a direct computation shows $g'_n(x, h) = (x, h)$ for all $h \in H$.   □

Lemma 10. *For any torsion groups G, H, we have $T_{K(G,A,H)} = O(T_G T_H)$.*

Proof. Let $K = K(G, A, H)$. If $w \in K$ with $|w| \leq n$, then $\gamma(w) \in G$ with $|\gamma(w)| = m \leq n$. Let $k = T_G(m)$ (note that $k \mid T_G(n)$), so $\gamma(w^k) = \gamma(w)^k = e_G$. If w^k has order ℓ for all w, then $w^{\ell k} = (w^k)^\ell = e_K$, and thus $T_K(n) \leq \ell T_G(m)$, and we have shown $T_K = O(T_G T_H)$ as claimed.

So suppose that $\gamma(w) = e_G$, and consider the action on $(x, h) \in X_A \times H$. The action of w shifts x around, and based on its contents multiplies h from the right by elements of H. For any fixed $x \in X_A$, $\gamma(w) = e_G$ implies that there exists $h_x \in H$ with $|h_x| \leq |w|$, such that $w \cdot (x, h) = (x, h_x h)$ for all $h \in H$. Since h_x has order at most $T_H(|h'|)$, and $T_H(|h'|) \mid T_H(|w|)$, we have $w^{T_H(|w|)} \cdot (x, h) = (x, h_x^{T_H(|w|)} h) = (x, h)$, concluding the proof.   □

Theorem 6. *Let $A \subset \mathbb{N}$ be Σ_1^0. For any f.g. torsion group G with decidable word problem there exists a recursively presented torsion group K with $T_K = \Theta(T_G)$, such that the word problem of K conjunctively reduces to A with exponential rate and A many-one reduces to the word problem of K.*

Proof. By the previous lemmas, if $K = K(G, A, H)$ for finitely-generated groups G and H which have decidable word problems, and H is nonabelian with bounded torsion, then

- K is recursively presented (Lemma 8),
- $T_K \geq T_G$ because $G \leq K$ and by the choice of generators (Lemma 6),
- $T_K \leq T_G T_H = O(T_G)$ (Lemma 10),
- WP(K) conjunctively reduces to A with exponential rate (Lemma 8),
- A many-one reduces to WP(K) (Lemma 9).   □

In the previous theorem, the implicit constants for Θ can be taken to be 1 (for the lower bound) and 6 (for the upper bound, by setting $H = S_3$). Of course, if G has bounded torsion, so does K.

Theorem 7. *Let ϕ be a total recursive function. Then there exists a recursively presented torsion group with bounded torsion, whose word problem is ϕ-impredictable.*

Proof. Let A be a ϕ-impredictable Σ_1^0 set (Theorem 5) and apply the previous theorem to obtain a recursively presented torsion group K with bounded torsion, such that the word problem of K conjunctively reduces to A with exponential rate β and A many-one reduces to the word problem of K. Then in particular the word problem of K wtt-reduces to A with exponential rate β. By Lemma 4, the word problem of K is $(\beta \circ \phi)$-impredictable. In particular, it is ϕ-impredictable by Lemma 3.   □

5   Application: Four Heads are Better than Three

We first define group-walking automata and the subshifts they recognize. By π_i we mean the projection to the ith coordinate of a finite Cartesian product. For $Q_i \not\ni 0$ a finite set write $X_{Q_i}^1$ for the subshift on a group G clear from context containing those $x \in (Q_i \cup \{0\})^G$ satisfying $|\{g \in G \mid x_g \neq 0\}| \leq 1$.

Definition 3. *Let Σ be a finite alphabet. A k-headed group-walking automaton on the full shift Σ^G is a tuple $\mathcal{A} = (\prod_{i=1}^k Q_i, f, I, F, S)$, where $Q_1, Q_2, \ldots, Q_k$ are state sets not containing the symbol 0, I and F are finite clopen subsets of the product subshift $Y = \prod_{i=1}^k X_{Q_i}^1$, and $f : \Sigma^G \times Y \to \Sigma^G \times Y$ is a cellular automaton satisfying $\pi_1 \circ f = \pi_1$ and*

$$\pi_i(\pi_2(f(x,y))) = 0^G \iff \pi_i(y) = 0^G$$

for all $x \in \Sigma^G$, $y \in Y$ and $i \in \{1, \ldots, k\}$.
For a k-headed automaton $\mathcal{A}$ as above, we denote by $\mathcal{S}(\mathcal{A}) \subset \Sigma^G$ the subshift

$$\{x \in \Sigma^G \mid \forall g, h \in G, y \in I, n \in \mathbb{N} : h \cdot \pi_2(f^n(g \cdot x, y)) \notin F\}.$$

For $k \geq 1$, we denote by $\mathcal{S}(G, k)$ the class of all subshifts $\mathcal{S}(\mathcal{A})$ for k-headed automata $\mathcal{A}$, and $\mathcal{S}(G, 0)$ is the class of all G-SFTs. We also write $\mathcal{S}(G) = \bigcup_{k \in \mathbb{N}} \mathcal{S}(G, k)$.

This definition may seem cryptic on a first reading. Its details are unraveled in [15] (see [14] for a discussion of possible variants). Our interpretation of $X \in \mathcal{S}(G, k)$ is that a k-headed group-walking automaton can define X, for a particular (in our opinion natural) way of defining subshifts by such automata.

Key points are that interpreting the ith track of Y as giving the position or a head and its current state, f is a local rule that tells how the heads move on configurations, and the assumptions imply that all heads are always present, are initialized in (roughly) the same position (described by I), have to join together to reject a configuration (described by F), and cannot communicate over distances (because f is a cellular automaton).

The following observation is essentially Proposition 2 in [15], though here we "complement" the separating subshift, because the result of [15] cannot be used with recursively presented groups.

Lemma 11. *Let G be a finitely-generated torsion group, let $T(n) = \max(n, T_G(n))$, and suppose that there exists a superexponential function $\zeta : \mathbb{N} \to \mathbb{N}$ such that the word problem of G is $(\zeta \circ \zeta \circ T \circ \zeta \circ T \circ \zeta)$-impredictable. Then*

$$\mathcal{S}(G \times \mathbb{Z}, 3) \subsetneq \mathcal{S}(G \times \mathbb{Z}, 4).$$

We sketch the proof from [15], for our complemented definitions.

Proof (Proof sketch). Let ζ be superexponential and recursive, let G be such that the word problem of G is ϕ-impredictable for $\phi = \zeta \circ \zeta \circ T \circ \zeta \circ T \circ \zeta$, and let ψ be the corresponding function, so

$$\forall \chi \in \mathcal{P} : \exists^\infty p : \psi(p) \sim e_G \iff \chi(p, G \upharpoonright \phi(p)) \!\downarrow .$$

For each $p \in \mathbb{N}$, let $x^p \in \{0,1\}^{G \times \mathbb{Z}}$ be the configuration where $x^p_{(g,n)} = 1$ if and only if $n \equiv 0 \bmod p$. Define $B = \{p \in \mathbb{N} \mid \psi(p) \sim e_G\}$, and let $Y_B \subset \{0,1\}^{G \times \mathbb{Z}}$ be the smallest subshift containing the configurations x^p with $p \in B$, i.e. the forbidden patterns are (encodings of) the complement of the word problem of G (together with the recursive set of patterns ensuring $Y_B \subset Y_\emptyset$). We clearly have $x^p \in Y_B \iff p \in B \iff \psi(p) \sim e_G$.

The crucial observation in [15] was that for any fixed three-headed automaton $\mathcal{A}$, the function $(\zeta \circ T \circ \zeta \circ T \circ \zeta)(p)$ eventually bounds how far the G-projections of the heads can be from each other during valid runs on a configuration x^p, which means that we can construct a Turing machine that, given access to an oracle for the initial segment $G \upharpoonright \phi(p)$ of the word problem (we add an extra ζ since we linearize the word problem), we can simulate all runs of $\mathcal{A}$ on the configurations x^p (observe that there are essentially only p different starting positions that need to be considered), halting if and only if one of them halts (i.e. the finite clopen set F is entered and the configuration is forbidden).

Suppose for a contradiction that $\mathcal{A}$ is a three-headed automaton that defines Y_B. Letting χ be the Turing machine described above which simulates $\mathcal{A}$, we have for all large enough p that

$$\chi(p, G \upharpoonright \phi(p)) \!\downarrow \iff x^p \notin Y_B$$

but by the definition of ψ there exist arbitrarily large p such that

$$\psi(p) \sim e_G \iff \chi(p, G \upharpoonright \phi(p)) \!\downarrow \iff x^p \notin Y_B \iff \psi(p) \not\sim e_G,$$

a contradiction.

On the other hand $Y_B \in \mathcal{S}(G \times \mathbb{Z}, 4)$ since it is intrinsically Π^0_1 in the sense of [15], by a similar proof as in [15], observing that using an oracle for the word problem of G we can easily forbid all x^p with $p \notin B$. $\square$

Four heads are now seen to be better than three:

Proof. (Proof of Theorem 3). By Theorem 7, there exists a group G which has bounded torsion and has $\exp \circ \exp \circ \exp \circ \exp \circ \exp$-impredictable word problem. Such a group is $(\zeta \circ \zeta \circ T \circ \zeta \circ T \circ \zeta)$-impredictable for some superexponential function ζ, where $T(n) = n$, and thus the previous lemma implies $\mathcal{S}(G \times \mathbb{Z}, 3) \subsetneq \mathcal{S}(G \times \mathbb{Z}, 4)$. $\square$

Remark 2. For maximal "automaticity"[1], or to avoid using f.g. bounded torsion groups (whose infiniteness is rather difficult to verify for mortals), one can replace the use of bounded torsion groups by any torsion group with recursive torsion function. For example using the Grigorchuk group as G in the construction of K (then $T_K(n) \leq O(n^3)$ by [5, Theorem VIII.70]), and using Theorem 6 directly, the previous proof goes through with the same exponential tower. Automata groups in the sense of [4] cannot have bounded torsion by Zelmanov's theorem [5,16,17].

References

1. Adian, S.I.: The Burnside problem and related topics. Russ. Math. Surv. **65**(5), 805–855 (2011)
2. Aubrun, N., Barbieri, S., Sablik, M.: A notion of effectiveness for subshifts on finitely generated groups. Theoret. Comput. Sci. **661**(Supplement C), 35–55 (2017)
3. Barbieri, S., Kari, J., Salo, V.: The group of reversible turing machines. In: Cook, M., Neary, T. (eds.) AUTOMATA 2016. LNCS, vol. 9664, pp. 49–62. Springer, Cham (2016). https://doi.org/10.1007/978-3-319-39300-1_5
4. Bartholdi, L., Silva, P.V.: Groups defined by automata. arXiv preprint arXiv:1012.1531 (2010)
5. de La Harpe, P.: Topics in Geometric Group Theory. University of Chicago Press, Chicago (2000)
6. Grigorchuk, R.I., Medynets, K.: On algebraic properties of topological full groups. Sb. Math. **205**(6), 843–861 (2014)
7. Guillon, P., Jeandel, E., Kari, J., Vanier, P.: Undecidable word problem in subshift automorphism groups. CoRR, abs/1808.09194 (2018)
8. Ivanov, S.V.: The free Burnside groups of sufficiently large exponents. Int. J. Algebra Comput. **4**(01n02), 1–308 (1994)
9. Juschenko, K., Monod, N.: Cantor systems, piecewise translations and simple amenable groups. arXiv e-prints (2012)
10. Matui, H.: Some remarks on topological full groups of cantor minimal systems. Int. J. Math. **17**(02), 231–251 (2006)
11. Myasnikov, A., Osin, D.: Algorithmically finite groups. J. Pure Appl. Algebra **215**(11), 2789–2796 (2011)
12. Salo, V.: Impredictable subsets of $\mathbb{N}$. MathOverflow (version: 2020-3-11). https://mathoverflow.net/questions/354526/
13. Salo, V., Schraudner, M.: Automorphism groups of subshifts through group extensions. Preprint
14. Salo, V., Törmä, I.: Plane-walking automata. In: Isokawa, T., Imai, K., Matsui, N., Peper, F., Umeo, H. (eds.) AUTOMATA 2014. LNCS, vol. 8996, pp. 135–148. Springer, Cham (2015). https://doi.org/10.1007/978-3-319-18812-6_11
15. Salo, V., Törmä, I.: Independent finite automata on Cayley graphs. Nat. Comput. **16**(3), 411–426 (2017). https://doi.org/10.1007/s11047-017-9613-6

---

[1] Using the Grigorchuk group or another torsion automata group, the statement of our main result is somewhat amusing, in that it states that a group of finite-state **automata** acting on a subshift on an **automata** group admits subshifts definable by group-walking **automata** with four heads but not three.

16. Zel'manov, E.I.: A solution of the restricted Burnside problem for 2-groups. Matematicheskii Sb. **182**(4), 568–592 (1991)
17. Zel'manov, E.I.: Solution of the restricted Burnside problem for groups of odd exponent. Math. USSR Izv. **36**(1), 41 (1991)

Complexity of Generic Limit Sets
of Cellular Automata

Ilkka Törmä[(✉)]

Department of Mathematics and Statistics, University of Turku, Turku, Finland
iatorm@utu.fi

Abstract. The generic limit set of a topological dynamical system is the smallest closed subset of the phase space that has a comeager realm of attraction. It intuitively captures the asymptotic dynamics of almost all initial conditions. It was defined by Milnor and studied in the context of cellular automata, whose generic limit sets are subshifts, by Djenaoui and Guillon. In this article we study the structural and computational restrictions that apply to generic limit sets of cellular automata. As our main result, we show that the language of a generic limit set can be at most Σ_3^0-hard, and lower in various special cases. We also prove a structural restriction on generic limit sets with a global period.

Keywords: Cellular automata · Limit set · Generic limit set · Topological dynamics

1 Introduction

One-dimensional cellular automata (CA for short) are discrete dynamical systems that act on the set $A^{\mathbb{Z}}$ of bi-infinite sequences by a local rule that is applied synchronously at every coordinate. They can be used to model physical and biological phenomena, as well as massively parallel computation.

The limit set of a topological dynamical system (X, T) consists of those points that can be seen arbitrarily late in its evolution. Limit sets of cellular automata have been studied by various authors from the computational (e.g. [2,4,6]) and structural (e.g. [1,8]) points of view. In [9], Milnor defined the likely and generic limit sets of a dynamical system. The likely limit set associated to an invariant probability measure μ on X is the smallest closed subset $C \subset X$ such that for μ-almost every $x \in X$, all limit points of $(T^n(x))_{n \in \mathbb{N}}$ are in C. The generic variant is a purely topological notion that replaces "for μ-almost every $x \in X$" with "for every x in a comeager subset of X". As far as we know, generic limit sets have been studied relatively little in dynamical systems theory.

In [5], Djenaoui and Guillon studied the generic limit sets of dynamical systems in general and *directed cellular automata* (arbitrary paths in spacetime

Research supported by Academy of Finland grant 295095.

H. Zenil (Ed.): AUTOMATA 2020, LNCS 12286, pp. 126–138, 2020.
https://doi.org/10.1007/978-3-030-61588-8_10

diagrams of CA) in particular. They related dynamical properties of a given CA to the structure of its generic limit set in different directions and its relation to the set of equicontinuity points and the limit set. For example, they proved that the generic limit set of an almost equicontinuous CA is exactly the closure of the asymptotic set of its equicontinuity points. They also provide a combinatorial characterization of the generic limit set of a CA, which allows us to study its descriptional and structural complexity and carry out complex constructions. This point of view was not present in [5], where relatively simple examples of generic limit sets were provided to highlight the main classification results.

As our main result, we prove that the language of a generic limit set of a CA is always Σ_3^0, and present an example which is complete for this class. If the generic limit set is minimal, then this bound cannot be attained, since its language is Σ_2^0. We also prove that the dynamics of the CA on its generic limit set must be nontrivial in complex instances: if the CA is eventually periodic or strictly one-sided on the generic limit set, its language is Σ_1^0 or Π_2^0, respectively, and if the restriction is a shift map, then the generic limit set is chain-transitive. These restrictions are proved by constructing "semi-blocking words" that restrict the flow of information. Finally, we present a structural restriction for generic limit sets: if they consist of a finite number of two-way chain components for the shift map, then they cannot have a global period.

2 Definitions

Let X be a topological space. A subset of X is comeager if it contains an intersection of countably many dense open sets.

A dynamical system is a pair (X, f) where X is a compact metric space and $f : X \to X$ is a continuous function. We say (X, f) has trivial dynamics if $f = \mathrm{id}_X$. The limit set of f is $\Omega_f = \bigcap_{t \in \mathbb{N}} f^t(X)$. For $x \in X$, we define $\omega(x)$ as the set of limit points of the forward orbit $(f^t(x))_{t \in \mathbb{N}}$, and $\omega(Y) = \bigcup_{y \in Y} \omega(y)$ for $Y \subset X$. The realm (of attraction) of a subset $Y \subset X$ is $\mathfrak{D}(Y) = \{x \in X \mid \omega(x) \subset Y\}$. The generic limit set of f, denoted $\tilde{\omega}(f)$, is the intersection of all closed subsets $C \subset X$ such that $\mathfrak{D}(C)$ is comeager; then $\tilde{\omega}(f)$ itself has a comeager realm.

We consider one-dimensional cellular automata over a finite alphabet A. The full shift $A^{\mathbb{Z}}$ is a compact metric space with the distance function $d(x, y) = \inf\{2^{-n} \mid x_{[-n,n]} = y_{[-n,n]}\}$, and the left shift map $\sigma : A^{\mathbb{Z}} \to A^{\mathbb{Z}}$, defined by $\sigma(x)_i = x_{i+1}$, is a homeomorphism. The cylinder sets $[w]_i = \{x \in A^{\mathbb{Z}} \mid x_{[i,i+|w|]} = w\}$ for $w \in A^*$ and $i \in \mathbb{Z}$ form a prebasis for the topology, and the clopen sets, which are the finite unions of cylinders, form a basis. We denote $[w] = [w]_0$. A subshift is a closed and σ-invariant set $X \subset A^{\mathbb{Z}}$. Every subshift is defined by a set $F \subset A^*$ of forbidden words as $X = A^{\mathbb{Z}} \setminus \bigcup_{w \in F} \bigcup_{i \in \mathbb{Z}} [w]_i$, and if F can be chosen finite, then X is a shift of finite type (SFT). The language of X is defined as $\mathcal{L}(X) = \{w \in A^* \mid [w] \cap X \neq \emptyset\}$, and we denote $\mathcal{L}_n(X) = \mathcal{L}(X) \cap A^n$. The order-$n$ SFT approximation of X is the SFT $\mathcal{S}_n(X) \subset A^{\mathbb{Z}}$ defined by the forbidden patterns $A^n \setminus \mathcal{L}_n(X)$. We say X is transitive if for all $u, v \in \mathcal{L}(X)$

there exists $w \in A^*$ with $uwv \in \mathcal{L}(X)$, and mixing if the length of w can be chosen freely as long as it is large enough (depending on u and v). We say X is chain transitive if each $\mathcal{S}_n(X)$ is transitive. We say X is minimal if it does not properly contain another subshift; this is equivalent to the condition that for every $w \in \mathcal{L}(X)$ there exists $n \in \mathbb{N}$ such that w occurs in each word of $\mathcal{L}_n(X)$.

A morphism between dynamical systems (X, f) and (Y, g) is a continuous function $h : X \to Y$ with $h \circ f = g \circ h$. If h is surjective, (Y, g) is a factor of (X, f). A cellular automaton is a morphism $f : (A^{\mathbb{Z}}, \sigma) \to (A^{\mathbb{Z}}, \sigma)$. Equivalently, it is a function given by a local rule $F : A^{2r+1} \to A$ for some radius $r \in \mathbb{N}$ as $f(x)_i = F(x_{[i-r,i+r]})$. The pair $(A^{\mathbb{Z}}, f)$ is a dynamical system. Generic limit sets were defined by Milnor in [9] for general dynamical systems, and were first considered in the context of cellular automata in [5].

In this article, a Turing machine consists of a finite state set Q with an initial state q_0 and a final state q_f, a tape alphabet Γ that is used on a one-way infinite tape together with a special blank symbol $\perp \notin \Gamma$, and a transition rule δ that allows the machine to move on the tape and modify the tape cells and its internal state based on its current state and the contents of the tape cell it is on. Turing machines can decide any computable language and compute any computable function in the standard way.

We give an overview of the arithmetical hierarchy. A computable predicate over $\mathbb{N}$ is Π_0^0 and Σ_0^0. If ϕ is a Π_n^0 predicate, then $\exists k_1 \cdots \exists k_m \phi$ is a Σ_{n+1}^0 formula, and conversely, if ϕ is Σ_n^0, then $\forall k_1 \cdots \forall k_m \phi$ is Π_{n+1}^0. Subsets of $\mathbb{N}$ defined by these formulas are given the same classifications, and we extend them to all sets that are in a computable bijection with $\mathbb{N}$. For these sets, we define $\Delta_n^0 = \Pi_n^0 \cap \Sigma_n^0$. The computable sets form Δ_1^0 and the computably enumerable sets form Σ_1^0. A subshift is given the same classification as its language.

3 Auxiliary Results

We begin with auxiliary results on generic limit sets of cellular automata that are used in several proofs.

Lemma 1 (Proposition 4.11 in [5]). *Let f be a CA. Then $\tilde{\omega}(f)$ is a nonempty f-invariant subshift.*

The following result gives a combinatorial characterization for generic limit sets of cellular automata.

Lemma 2 (Corollary of Remark 4.4 in [5]). *Let f be a CA on $A^{\mathbb{Z}}$. A word $s \in A^*$ occurs in $\tilde{\omega}(f)$ if and only if there exists a word $v \in A^*$ and $i \in \mathbb{Z}$ such that for all $u, w \in A^*$ there exist infinitely many $t \in \mathbb{N}$ with $f^t([uvw]_{i-|u|}) \cap [s] \neq \emptyset$.*

We say that the word v *enables* s for f.

Lemma 3. *Let f be a CA on $A^{\mathbb{Z}}$, let $n \in \mathbb{N}$, and let $[v]_i \subset A^{\mathbb{Z}}$ be a cylinder set. Then there exists a cylinder set $[w]_j \subset [v]_i$ and $T \in \mathbb{N}$ such that for all $t \geq T$ we have $f^t([w]_j) \subset [\mathcal{L}_n(\tilde{\omega}(f))]$.*

Words w with the above property are called $\tilde{\omega}(f)$-*forcing*, since they force the word $f^t(x)_{[0,n)}$ to be valid in $\tilde{\omega}(f)$ whenever w occurs in x at position j. The result intuitively states that any word can be extended into a $\tilde{\omega}(f)$-forcing word.

Proof. Denote $A^n \setminus \mathcal{L}_n(\tilde{\omega}(f)) = \{u_1, \ldots, u_k\}$. Since u_1 does not occur in $\tilde{\omega}(f)$, Lemma 2 applied to $[v]_i$ implies that there exist words $a_1, b_1 \in A^*$ and $T_1 \in \mathbb{N}$ such that $f^t([a_1 v b_1]_{i-|a_1|}) \cap [u_1] = \emptyset$ for all $t \geq T_1$. For u_2 we find words $a_2, b_2 \in A^*$ and $T_2 \in \mathbb{N}$ such that $f^t([a_2 a_1 v b_1 b_2]_{i-|a_2 a_1|}) \cap [u_2] = \emptyset$ for all $t \geq T_2$. Continuing like this, we obtain a word $w = a_k \cdots a_1 v b_1 \cdots b_k$, a position $j = i - |a_k \cdots a_1|$ and a number $T = \max(T_1, \ldots, T_k)$ that have the desired property.

Example 1 (Example 5.12 in [5]). Consider the minimum CA $f : \{0,1\}^{\mathbb{Z}} \to \{0,1\}^{\mathbb{Z}}$ defined by $f(x)_i = \min(x_i, x_{i+1})$. We claim that $\tilde{\omega}(f) = \{^{\infty}0^{\infty}\}$. Proving this directly from the definition is not difficult, but let us illustrate the use of Lemma 2. First, every word 0^n for $n \in \mathbb{N}$ is enabled by itself: for all $u, v \in \{0,1\}^*$ and $t \in \mathbb{N}$ we have $f^t([u0^n v]_{-|u|}) \subset [0^n]$. On the other hand, suppose $s \in \mathcal{L}(\tilde{\omega}(f))$, so that some cylinder set $[w]_j$ enables s. Choose $u = v = 0^{|j|+1}$. Then every $x \in [uwv]_{j-|u|}$ satisfies $x_{-|j|-1} = 0$, so that $f^{|j|+1+|s|}(x)_{[0,|s|)} = 0^{|s|}$. Since a cell can never change its state from 0 to 1, we have $s = 0^{|s|}$. Hence the language of $\tilde{\omega}(f)$ is 0^*, and the claim is proved.

4   Complexity of Generic Limit Sets

From the combinatorial characterization we can determine the maximal computational complexity of the language of the generic limit set.

Theorem 1. *The language of the generic limit set of any CA is Σ_3^0. For any Σ_3^0 set P, there exists a cellular automaton f such that P is many-one reducible to $\mathcal{L}(\tilde{\omega}(f))$.*

Proof. The condition given by Lemma 2 is Σ_3^0.

For the second claim, since P is a Σ_3^0 set, there is a computable predicate ψ such that $P = \{w \in A^* \mid \exists m \, \forall m' \, \exists k \, \psi(w, m, m', k)\}$. Let M be a Turing machine with state set Q, initial state $q_0 \in Q$, two final states $q_f^1, q_f^2 \in Q$, a read-only tape with alphabet $\Gamma_A = A \cup \{\#, \$\}$ and a read-write tape with some tape alphabet Γ with special symbol $1 \in \Gamma$. Both tapes are infinite to the right, and M has only one head that sees the same position of both tapes. When initialized in state q_0, the machine checks that the read-only tape begins with $\#w\#\$^m\#$ for some $w \in A^*$ and $m \geq 0$, and the read-write tape begins with $1^{3n+5}\bot$ for some $n \geq 0$, halting in state q_f^1 if this is not the case. Then it enumerates n pairs $(m', k) \in \mathbb{N}^2$, starting from $(0,0)$ and moving from (m', k) to $(m'+1, 0)$ if $\psi(w, m, m', k)$ holds, and to $(m', k+1)$ otherwise. If the process ends with $k > 0$, then M halts in state q_f^1. Otherwise it writes 0s to the $|w|+2$ leftmost cells of the read-write tape, goes to the leftmost cell and halts in state q_f^2. Then

$w \in P$ if and only if for some $m \in \mathbb{N}$, the machine halts in state q_f^2 for infinitely many choices of n; denote this condition by $M(w, m, n)$.

Denote $\Sigma_M = (Q \cup \{\leftarrow, \rightarrow\}) \times \Gamma$ and $\Sigma_0 = \{B, E, S_1, S_2, S_2', S_3, \vdash\}$. We construct a radius-3 CA f on the alphabet $\Sigma = (\Sigma_M \cup \Sigma_0) \times \Gamma_A$ to whose generic limit set P reduces. We write elements of $\Sigma_M \times \Gamma_A$ as triples $(q, g, a) \in (Q \cup \{\leftarrow, \rightarrow\}) \times \Gamma \times \Gamma_A$. The first track of f contains elements of Σ_M, which are used to simulate computations of M, and Σ_0, which perform a geometric process that initialized such simulations. The element B forms a *background* on which the *signals* E, S_1, S_2, S_2' and S_3 travel. The last track of Σ is never modified by f, and it serves as the read-only tape of M in the simulation. We think of f as a non-uniform CA over $\Sigma_M \cup \Sigma_0$ whose local function at each coordinate $i \in \mathbb{Z}$ depends on the element $s \in \Gamma_A$ at i. The automaton f is defined by the following constraints:

- The signal E always travels to the right at speed 2. For $k = 1, 2, 3$, as long as the signal S_k or S_k' has Bs to its right, it travels to the right at speed k. The signals E, S_1 and S_2 produce Bs in their wake, while S_3 produces $(\leftarrow, 1)$-states and S_2' produces $(\leftarrow, \perp)$-states.
- When the signals S_2 and S_1 collide, they produce the four-cell pattern $\vdash(q_0, 1)(\leftarrow, 1)S_3$, where S_3 lies at the point of their collision. When S_3 and S_2 collide, they are replaced by an S_2'.
- In an interval of the form

$$\vdash(\rightarrow, g_0)\ldots(\rightarrow, g_{m-1})(q, g_m)(\leftarrow, g_{m+1})\ldots(\leftarrow, g_{m+n})$$

that is either unbounded or terminated on its right by S_3 or S_2', f simulates a computation of M using q as the head, the Γ-track as the read-write tape and the Γ_A-track as the read-only tape. If $q = q_f^i$ is a final state, it is replaced by E instead.
- Any pattern not mentioned above produces E-states.

In particular, the signals S_1 and S_2 are never created, so they always originate from the initial configuration. The signal S_3 and all Turing machine heads originate either from the initial configuration or a collision of S_2 and S_1, and S_2' originates from the initial configuration or a collision of S_3 and S_2. An E-signal, once created, cannot be destroyed.

For a word $w \in A^+$, define $\hat{w} = (q_f^2 \leftarrow^{|w|+1}, 0^{|w|+2}, \#w\#)$. We claim that $w \in P$ if and only if $\hat{w} \in \mathcal{L}(\tilde{\omega}(f))$. The proof is visualized in Fig. 1.

Suppose first that $w \in P$, so that there exists $m \in \mathbb{N}$ such that $M(w, m, n)$ holds for infinitely many n. We claim that the word $\tilde{w} = (E^{|w|+m+3}, \#w\#\$^m\#)$ enables $\hat{w}$, so let $u, v \in \Sigma^*$ be arbitrary. We construct a configuration $x \in [u\tilde{w}v]_{-|u|}$, which corresponds to the horizontal line of Fig. 1, as follows. To the right of v we put $(E, \#)^\infty$, and to the left of u we put only $\#$-symbols on the second track. Let $n > |u| + 4$ be such that $M(w, m, n)$ holds. On the first track of $x_{[-n+2, -n+4]}$, put $S_1 S_2 E$; on x_{-2n+2} put S_2; on all remaining cells put B. The E-signals will destroy everything in their path and replace them with B-cells, so we can ignore the contents of the first track of $x_{[-|u|, \infty)}$. The S_1-signal and the

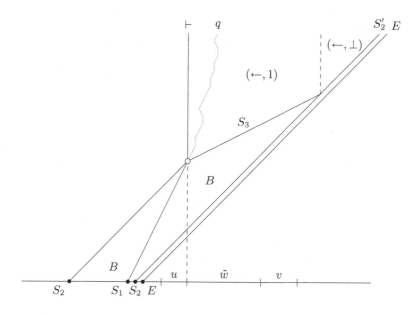

Fig. 1. Proof of Theorem 1, not drawn to scale. Time increases upward.

leftmost S_2-signal will collide at coordinate 2 of $f^n(x)$ (the white circle in Fig. 1), resulting in the pattern $\vdash(q_0, 1)(\leftarrow, 1)S_3$ at coordinate -1 and Bs to its left. The simulated computation of M begins at this time step. The resulting S_3-signal collides with the rightmost S_2-signal at coordinate $3n+5$ of $f^{2n+1}(x)$, producing $(\leftarrow, 1)$-states until that point and transforming into a S_2' that produces $(\leftarrow, \bot)$-states. This means M has $1^{3n+5}\bot$ on its the read-write tape at the beginning of the computation, and $\#w\#\$^m\#$ on the read-only tape. Hence it eventually writes $0^{|w|+2}$ to the tape and halts in state q_f^2 at some time step $t \in \mathbb{N}$. Then $f^t(x) \in [\hat{w}]$, and we have showed that $\tilde{w}$ enables $\hat{w}$, so $\hat{w} \in \mathcal{L}(\tilde{\omega}(f))$ by Lemma 2.

Suppose then $\hat{w} \in \mathcal{L}(\tilde{\omega}(f))$, so that $\hat{w}$ is enabled by some word $w' \in \Sigma^*$ at coordinate $i \in \mathbb{Z}$. We may assume $i \le 0$ and $|w'| \ge i + |w| + 2$ by extending w' if needed. Let $k \ge 0$ and choose $u = (E, \#)^k$ and $v = (E, \#)$. In a configuration x that contains $uw'v$, any Turing machine head to the right of u is eventually erased by the E-symbols. Those within w' are erased after $|w'|$ steps, and those to the right of w' are erased before they reach the origin. Thus, if $f^t(x) \in [\hat{w}]$ for some $t > |w'|$, then the q_f^2 in this configuration is the head of a Turing machine produced at the origin by a collision of some S_2-signal and S_1-signal at some earlier time $t' < t$ (again the white circle in Fig. 1). After a finite computation, M can halt in state q_f^2 only at the left end of the tape, so the collision happens at coordinate 2 and $t' > |w'|$. Since the signals S_2 and S_1 cannot be created, they originate at coordinates $-2t'-2$ and $-t'-2$ of x. Since the Turing machine eventually halts in state q_f^2, after being initialized it will read $1^{3n+5}\bot$ on its read-write tape and $\#w\#\$^m\#$ on the read-only tape for some $m, n \in \mathbb{N}$ with $M(w, m, n)$. Since the read-only tape cannot be modified by f, w' already contains the word $\#w\#$ on its second track, and since v has $\#$ on its second track, w' must contain $\#w\#\$^m\#^p$ for some $p \geq 0$. Hence m is independent of k.

The signal S_3 produced at the same collision as q_0 continues to the right at speed 3, producing $(\leftarrow, 1)$-states until it is destroyed. To its right we have B-states produced by the initial E-signals in u, followed by those E-signals. Since the Turing machine reads $1^{3n+5}\perp$ on its tape, the S_3-signal is destroyed after $n+1$ steps, at time $t'+n+1$, either by encountering an invalid pattern or by collision with an E-signal or S_2-signal. In the first two cases, after the removal of S_3 the segment of $(\leftarrow, 1)$-states produced by it is now bordered by an E-state, which is an invalid pattern and results in new E-states by the last rule of f. These E-states will eventually destroy the entire computation segment before the Turing machine can halt. Hence S_3 must collide with an S_2-signal at coordinate $3n+5$ at time $t'+n+1$. This signal originates at position $-2t'+n+3$ in x, which must be to the right of the S_1-signal at coordinate $-t'-2$ that produces S_3, since these signals do not collide. Hence $n > t' - 5 > k + |w'| - 5$, so n grows arbitrarily large with k. We have shown $w \in P$.

If we know more about the structure of $\tilde{\omega}(f)$ and the dynamics of f on it, we can improve the computability bound.

Proposition 1. *Let f be a CA. If $\tilde{\omega}(f)$ is a minimal subshift, then its language is Σ_2^0.*

Proof. Denote $X = \tilde{\omega}(f)$ and let $w \in \mathcal{L}(X)$. Since X is minimal, there exists $n \in \mathbb{N}$ such that w occurs in each word of $\mathcal{L}_n(X)$. Let $[v]_j$ be an X-forcing cylinder set that satisfies $f^t([v]_j) \subset [\mathcal{L}_n(X)]$ for all large enough t, as given by Lemma 3. For these t, the set $f^t([v]_j)$ intersects $[w]_i$ for some $0 \leq i \leq n - |w|$. On the other hand, if $w \notin \mathcal{L}(X)$ then such a word v does not exist, since each word can be extended into one that eventually forbids w. This means that $w \in \mathcal{L}(X)$ is equivalent to the Σ_2^0 condition that there exist $v \in A^*$, $j \in \mathbb{Z}$, $n \in \mathbb{N}$ and $T \in \mathbb{N}$ such that for all $t \geq T$ we have $f^t([v]_j) \cap \bigcup_{i=0}^{n-|w|} [w]_i \neq \emptyset$. $\square$

Proposition 2. *Let f be a CA and suppose that its restriction to $\tilde{\omega}(f)$ is equicontinuous. Then $\tilde{\omega}(f)$ has a Σ_1^0 language.*

Proof. Denote $X = \tilde{\omega}(f)$. An equicontinuous CA on any subshift is eventually periodic (this was shown in [7] for the full shift, and the general case is not much more difficult), so that there exist $k \geq 0, p \geq 1$ with $f^{k+p}|_X = f^k|_X$. Let $r \in \mathbb{N}$ be a common radius of f and f^p, and let $[w]_j \subset A^{\mathbb{Z}}$ and $T \in \mathbb{N}$ be given by Lemma 3, so that $f^t([w]_j) \subset [\mathcal{L}_{3r}(X)]$ for all $t \geq T$. By extending w if necessary, we may assume $j \leq 0$, $|w| = 3r + 2h$ and $f^t(x)_{[r,2r)} = f^t(x')_{[r,2r)}$ for all $x, x' \in [w]_j$ and $t \in [T, T+k+p)$, where $h = |j|$. Since f has radius r and is eventually periodic on X, we then have $v_t := f^t(x)_{[r,2r)} = f^t(x')_{[r,2r)}$ for all $t \geq T$, and the sequence of words $(v_t)_{t \geq T+k}$ is p-periodic.

Let $n \geq 0$ and $u \in A^{2n}$. For $t \geq T$ we have $f^t([wuw]_{-|w|-n}) \subset [v_t]_{-2r-h-n} \cap [v_t]_{n+h+r}$, so that no information can be transmitted over the v_t-words. For

$x \in [wuw]_{-|w|-n}$ the sequence of words $s = (f^t(x)_{[-2r-h-n,n+h+2r)})_{t \geq T}$ only depends on its values at $t \in [T, T + k + p)$, and eventually contains only words of $\mathcal{L}(X)$ since we may extend the central pattern of x into one that is X-forcing. Thus s is eventually p-periodic. Since each word s_{t+1} is determined by s_t using the local rule of f, the eventually periodic part is reached when a repetition occurs. The prefixes and suffixes of length r of each word s_t already form p-periodic sequences (since they are equal to v_t), so this happens after at most $p|A|^{2(r+h+n)}$ steps.

Let $v \in A^*$ be arbitrary. By Lemma 2, $v \in \mathcal{L}(X)$ if and only if there is a cylinder set $[v']_i$ with $f^t([u'v'w']_{i-|u'|}) \cap [v] \neq \emptyset$ for all $u', w' \in A^*$ and infinitely many t. By extending v' if necessary, we may assume $[v']_i = [wuw]_{-|w|-n}$ for some $n \geq |v|$ and $u \in A^{2n}$. Then v occurs infinitely often in words of the eventually periodic sequence s. We have shown that $v \in \mathcal{L}(X)$ if and only if there exist $n \geq |v|$ and $u \in A^{2n}$ with $f^t([wuw]_{-|w|-n}) \cap [v] \neq \emptyset$ for some $t \in [T, T + p|A|^{2(r+h+n)} + k + p)$, where w, T and h are fixed. Hence X has a Σ_1^0 language.

Proposition 3. *If a CA f is the identity on $\tilde{\omega}(f)$, then $\tilde{\omega}(f)$ is a mixing subshift.*

Proof. Let $v_1, v_2 \in \mathcal{L}(X)$ be arbitrary, and let $[w_1]_{i_1}, [w_2]_{i_2}$ be two cylinder sets that enable them and are X-forcing in the sense that $f^t([w_j]_{i_j}) \subset [\mathcal{L}_{n+2r}]_{-r}$ for all $t \geq T$. We may assume, by extending the w_j and increasing T if necessary, that $f^T(x)_{[0,n)} = v_j$ for all $x \in [w_j]_{i_j}$, and then $f^t([w_j]_{i_j}) \subset [v_j]$ for all $t \geq T$. For all large enough N the intersection $[w_1]_{j_1} \cap [w_2]_{j_2+N}$ is nonempty, and hence contains an X-forcing cylinder $[u]_k$ with $f^t([u]_k) \subset [\mathcal{L}_{N+|v_2|}(X)]$ for all large enough t. This implies that $v_1 A^{N-|v_2|} v_2$ intersects $\mathcal{L}(X)$ for all large enough N, i.e. X is mixing.

We say that a CA $f : X \to X$ on a subshift $X \subset A^{\mathbb{Z}}$ is *eventually oblique* if f^n has a neighborhood that is contained in $(-\infty, -1]$ or $[1, \infty)$ for some (equivalently, all large enough) $n \in \mathbb{N}$. All shift maps except the identity are eventually oblique.

Proposition 4. *Let f be a CA and suppose that its restriction to $\tilde{\omega}(f)$ is eventually oblique. Then $\tilde{\omega}(f)$ has a Π_2^0 language.*

Proof. Denote $X = \tilde{\omega}(f)$ and let $w \in A^*$. We claim that $w \in \mathcal{L}(X)$ if and only if the empty word enables w for f, which is a Π_2^0 condition. By Lemma 2 it suffices to prove the forward direction, and the idea of the proof is the following. Since w occurs in X, it is enabled by some cylinder set, which we can extend into one that eventually forces a long segment to contain patterns of X. On this segment, information can flow only from right to left under iteration of f. We use another X-forcing cylinder to block all information flow from the enabling word to the right-hand side of this segment before it is formed. Then the contents of the segment are independent of the word that originally enabled w, so we can swap it for any other word. The argument is visualized in Fig. 2.

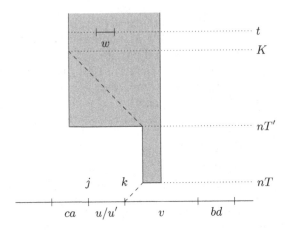

Fig. 2. Proof of Proposition 4, not drawn to scale. Time increases upward. In the shaded region, information flows only from right to left. The configurations $f^s(x)$ and $f^s(y)$ agree on the part that is right of the dashed line.

We assume without loss of generality that some f^n has $[1, r]$ as a neighborhood on X, where $r \in \mathbb{N}$ is a common radius for each f^h on $A^{\mathbb{Z}}$ for $0 \leq h \leq n$. Lemma 3 gives us a cylinder set $[v]_i \subset A^{\mathbb{Z}}$ and $T \in \mathbb{N}$ with $f^t([v]_i) \subset [\mathcal{L}_{3r}(X)]$ for all $t \geq nT$. By extending v if necessary, we may assume $-|v| \leq i \leq -rnT$.

Assume $w \in \mathcal{L}(X)$, so that there exists a cylinder set $[u]_j \subset A^{\mathbb{Z}}$ that enables it for f. For the empty word to enable w, it suffices to show that for an arbitrary cylinder set $[u']_{j'}$ there exist infinitely many $t \in \mathbb{N}$ with $f^t([u']_{j'}) \cap [w] \neq \emptyset$. By extending u and/or u' if necessary, we may assume $j = j'$ and $|u| = |u'| \geq |j|$, and denote $k = j + |u|$. Consider the cylinder set $[uv]_j$. By Lemma 3, there exists a cylinder set $[auvb]_{j-|a|}$ with $f^t([auvb]_{j-|a|}) \subset [\mathcal{L}_{3r+k-i}(X)]_{-2r}$ for all large enough $t \in \mathbb{N}$. For the same reason, there exists another cylinder set $[cau'vbd]_{j-|ca|}$ with $f^t([cau'vbd]_{j-|ca|}) \subset [\mathcal{L}_{3r+k-i}(X)]_{-2r}$ for all large enough $t \in \mathbb{N}$. Let $T' \geq T$ be such that nT' is a common bound for these conditions. Denote $K = nT' + n|uvbd| - j$, and let $t \geq K$ be such that $f^t(x) \in [w]$ for some $x \in [cauvbd]_{j-|ca|}$. There are infinitely many such t since u enables w for f. Let $y \in [cau'vbd]_{j-|ca|}$ be the configuration obtained by replacing the u in x by u'.

We claim $f^t(y) \in [w]$. Note first that $f^{hn}(x)_{[k+sr,\infty)} = f^{hn}(y)_{[k+sr,\infty)}$ for all $h \leq T$ since this holds for $h = 0$ and r is a radius for f^n. This is represented in Fig. 2 by the lower dashed line. Since $x, y \in [v]_k$, for all $s \geq nT$ we have $f^s(x), f^s(y) \in [\mathcal{L}_{3r}(X)]_{k-i}$. From $i \leq -rnT$ it follows that $k - i \geq k + rnT$, so that $f^{nT}(x)$ and $f^{nT}(y)$ agree on $[k - i, \infty)$. Since f^n has $[-r, r]$ as a neighborhood on $A^{\mathbb{Z}}$ and $[1, r]$ as a neighborhood on X, for each $j \in [k-i+r, k-i+2r]$ the value of $f^{s+n}(z)_\ell$ for $z \in \{x, y\}$ depends only on $f^s(z)_{[\ell+1, \ell+r]}$. Thus if $f^s(x)$ and $f^s(y)$ agree on $[k - i + r, \infty)$ for some $s \geq nT$, then so do $f^{s+n}(x)$ and $f^{s+n}(y)$. By induction, we obtain $f^{ns}(x)_{[k-i+r,\infty)} = f^{ns}(y)_{[k-i+r,\infty)}$ for all $s \geq T$.

Denote $g(s) = \max(-r, k - i + r - s)$. Then $f^{n(T'+s)}(x)$ and $f^{n(T'+s)}(y)$ agree on $[g(s), \infty)$ for all $s \geq 0$. This is represented in Fig. 2 by the upper dashed line. For $s = 0$ this is true by the previous paragraph, so suppose it holds for some $s \geq 0$. Since $x \in [auvb]_{j-|a|}$ and $y \in [cau'vbd]_{j-|ca|}$, we have $f^{n(T'+s)}(x), f^{n(T'+s)}(y) \in [\mathcal{L}_{3r+k-i}(X)]_{-2r}$. As in the previous paragraph, the value of $f^{n(T'+s+1)}(z)_{\ell}$ for $\ell \in [g(s)-1, k-i]$ and $z \in \{x, y\}$ depends only on $f^{n(T'+s)}(z)_{[\ell+1,\ell+r]}$. The claim follows by induction.

Writing $t = ns + h$ for $0 \leq h < n$, the configurations $f^t(x)$ and $f^t(y)$ agree on $[g(s)+r, \infty) = [0, \infty)$ since r is a radius for f^h. In particular $f^t(y) \in [w]$, so that $f^t([u']_j) \cap [w] \neq \emptyset$.

Proposition 5. *If the restriction of a CA f to $\tilde{\omega}(f)$ is a shift map, then $\tilde{\omega}(f)$ is a chain transitive subshift.*

Proof. Suppose $f|_X = \sigma^n|_X$ for some $n \in \mathbb{Z}$. By symmetry we may assume $n > 0$. Let $v_1, v_2 \in \mathcal{L}(X)$ be two words of equal length m, and let $N \geq m$ be arbitrary. We claim that there exist $M > 0$ and words $u_0, \ldots, u_M \in \mathcal{L}_{N+n}(X)$ such that v_1 is a prefix of u_0, v_2 is a prefix of u_M and the length-N suffix of each u_i is a prefix of u_{i+1}, which implies the chain transitivity of X. For this, let $[w]_j$ be an X-forcing cylinder with $f^t([w]_j) \subset [\mathcal{L}_{2r+N+n}(X)]_{-r}$ for all large enough t. By the proof of Proposition 4, $[w]_j$ enables both v_1 and v_2, so there exist $x \in [w]_j$ and $T \leq t_1 < t_2$ with $f^{t_i}(x)_{[0,m)} = v_i$ for $i = 1, 2$. Choose $M = t_2 - t_1$ and $u_k = f^{t_1+k}(x)_{[0,N+n)}$. Since r is a radius for f, these words have the required properties.

Using these results, we can prove that some individual subshifts cannot occur as generic limit sets.

Example 2. There is no CA $f : A^{\mathbb{Z}} \to A^{\mathbb{Z}}$ whose generic limit set is the orbit closure of $^{\infty}01^{\infty}$. Suppose for a contradiction that there is one. Since $X = \tilde{\omega}(f)$ is invariant under f, we have $f(^{\infty}01^{\infty}) = \sigma^n(^{\infty}01^{\infty})$ for some $n \in \mathbb{Z}$, and then $f|_X = \sigma^n|_X$. If $n = 0$, then Proposition 3 implies that X is mixing, and if $n \neq 0$, then Proposition 5 implies that X is chain transitive, but it is neither.

By the results of [10], all cellular automata on Sturmian shifts are restrictions of shift maps. Propositions 2 and 4 imply that the language of a Sturmian generic limit set is Π_2^0, and Proposition 1 (or the folklore result that every minimal Π_n^0 subshift is Σ_n^0) implies that it is Σ_2^0. Hence we obtain the following.

Corollary 1. *If a Sturmian shift is the generic limit set of a CA, then its language is Δ_2^0.*

5 Periodic Factors

In some situations, a nontrivial finite factor forbids a subshift from being realized as a generic limit set.

Definition 1. *Let $X \subset A^{\mathbb{Z}}$ be a subshift. The* chain relation of width n *is the relation on $\mathcal{L}_n(X)$ defined by $u \sim_n v$ if there exists $x \in X$ with $x_{[0,n)} = u$ and $x_{[k,k+n)} = v$ for some $k \geq 0$. The symmetric and transitive closure of $\sim_n$ is the* $\sigma^{\pm}$-chain relation of width n. *If each $\sim_n$ is equal to $\mathcal{L}_n(X)^2$, we say X is $\sigma^{\pm}$-chain transitive. A* $\sigma^{\pm}$-chain component *of X is a maximal $\sigma^{\pm}$-chain transitive subshift of X.*

It is not hard to see that every subshift is the union of its $\sigma^{\pm}$-chain components, which are disjoint. SFTs and sofic shifts have a finite number of such components, but in other cases their number may be infinite.

Example 3. Let $X \subset \{0,1,2\}^{\mathbb{Z}}$ be the union of the orbit closures of $^{\infty}02^{\infty}$ and $^{\infty}12^{\infty}$. For each $n \in \mathbb{N}$, we have $0^n 2^n, 1^n 2^n \in \mathcal{L}(X)$, which implies $0^p 2^{n-p} \sim_n 2^n$ and $1^p 2^{n-p} \sim_n 2^n$ for all $0 \leq p \leq n$. Since $\mathcal{L}_n(X)$ consists of exactly these words, X is $\sigma^{\pm}$-chain transitive.

Lemma 4. *Let f be a CA on $A^{\mathbb{Z}}$ such that $\tilde{\omega}(f)$ has a finite number of $\sigma^{\pm 1}$-chain components $X_1, \ldots, X_k$. Then there is a cyclic permutation ρ of $\{1, \ldots, k\}$ such that $f(X_i) = X_{\rho(i)}$ for each $i = 1, \ldots, k$.*

Proof. Since the image of a $\sigma^{\pm 1}$-chain transitive subshift by a cellular automaton is also $\sigma^{\pm 1}$-chain transitive, each X_i is mapped into some other component $X_{\rho(i)}$. This defines a function $\rho : \{1, \ldots, k\} \to \{1, \ldots, k\}$. By Lemma 1, ρ is surjective, hence a permutation, and f maps each X_i surjectively to $X_{\rho(i)}$. Corollary 4.13 in [5] implies that ρ must be a cyclic permutation. $\square$

Proposition 6. *If a subshift $X \subset A^{\mathbb{Z}}$ has a finite number of $\sigma^{\pm 1}$-chain components and a finite factor that does not consist of fixed points, then it is not the generic limit set of any CA.*

Proof. Suppose that f is a CA with $\tilde{\omega}(f) = X$, and let $\pi : (X, \sigma) \to (Y, g)$ be the morphism onto a nontrivial finite factor. Let $X_1, \ldots, X_k$ be the $\sigma^{\pm 1}$-chain components of X. By Lemma 4 we may assume $f(X_i) = X_{i+1 \bmod k}$ for all i. If $Y_p \subset Y$ is the subsystem of p-periodic points, then $\pi^{-1}(Y_p) \subset X$ is an f-invariant subshift consisting of $\sigma^{\pm 1}$-chain components, so it is nonempty for exactly one p, and $p > 1$ by the assumption that Y does not consist of fixed points. By taking a factor map from Y onto $\mathbb{Z}_p$ if necessary, we may assume $(Y, g) = (\mathbb{Z}_p, +1)$ where the addition is modulo p. Define $q : X \to \mathbb{Z}_p$ by $q(x) = \pi(x) - \pi(f(x))$. Then q is continuous and shift-invariant, and is constant in each component X_i. Let r be a common radius for f and right radius for π and q, meaning that $\pi(x)$ and $q(x)$ are determined by $x_{[0,r)}$. The right radii exist since π has some two-sided radius s by continuity and satisfies $\pi(x) = \pi(\sigma^s(x)) - s$, which is determined by $x_{[0,2s]}$, and similarly for q. For $w \in \mathcal{L}_{2r+1}(X)$, denote $\pi(w) = \pi(x)$ and $q(w) = q(x)$ for any $x \in [w]_{-r}$.

Let $u \in \mathcal{L}_{3r}(X_1)$ be arbitrary, let $[v]_i$ be a cylinder that enables it given by Lemma 2, and let $[w]_j \subset [v]_i$ be an X-forcing cylinder given by Lemma 3, so that $f^t([w]_j) \subset [\mathcal{L}_{3r}(X)]$ for all $t \geq T$. We may assume that $f^T([w]_j) \subset [u]$ by extending w if necessary. Let $m \in \mathbb{N}$ be such that $[w]_j \cap [w]_{j+pm+1}$ is nonempty, which holds for all large enough m. Finally, let $[v']_\ell \subset [w]_j \cap [w]_{j+pm+1}$ be an X-forcing cylinder with $f^t([v']_\ell) \subset [\mathcal{L}_{3r+pm+1}(X)]$ for all large enough t.

Let $x \in [v']_\ell$ be arbitrary. Then we have $f^T(x) \in [u] \cap [u]_{pm+1}$ and $f^t(x) \in [\mathcal{L}_{3r}(X)] \cap [\mathcal{L}_{3r}(X)]_{pm+1}$ for all $t \geq T$. This implies $\pi(f^{t+1}(x)_{[r,2r)}) = \pi(f^t(x)_{[r,2r)}) + q(f^t(x)_{[r,2r)})$ and $\pi(f^{t+1}(x)_{pm+1+[r,2r)}) = \pi(f^t(x)_{pm+1+[r,2r)}) + q(f^t(x)_{pm+1+[r,2r)})$ for each $t \geq T$. Since $u \in \mathcal{L}_{3r}(X_1)$, f permutes the components X_i and q is constant in each component, we have $\pi(f^t(x)_{[r,2r)}) = \pi(f^t(x)_{pm+1+[r,2r)})$ for $t \geq T$. For large enough t, this is a contradiction with the fact that $w^{(t)} = f^t(x)_{[0,pm+3r]} \in \mathcal{L}(X)$ satisfies $\pi(w^{(t)}_{[i,i+r)}) = \pi(w^{(t)}_{[0,r)}) + i$ for all $i \in [0, pm+2r]$.

As a corollary, a transitive but nonmixing SFT cannot be the generic limit set of a CA, since it admits a factor map to some $\mathbb{Z}_p$ with $p > 1$.

6 Future Work

In this article we presented a construction for a generic limit set with a maximally complex language. We also showed that structural and dynamical properties may constrain this complexity, but did not prove the strictness of these bounds. Furthermore, we showed that in some cases a global period is an obstruction for being a generic limit set, but did not prove whether this always holds. Using a construction technique presented in [3] to study μ-limit sets, we believe we can answer these and other questions.

A cellular automaton f is nilpotent, meaning that $f^t(A^{\mathbb{Z}})$ is a singleton set for some $t \in \mathbb{N}$, if and only if its limit set is a singleton [4]. As a variant of nilpotency, one may define f to be *generically nilpotent* if $\tilde{\omega}(f)$ is a singleton, as in Example 1. We believe the techniques of [3] can also be used to characterize the complexity of deciding generic nilpotency.

References

1. Ballier, A., Guillon, P., Kari, J.: Limit sets of stable and unstable cellular automata. Fund. Inform. **110**(1–4), 45–57 (2011)
2. Borello, A., Cervelle, J., Vanier, P.: Turing degrees of limit sets of cellular automata. In: Esparza, J., Fraigniaud, P., Husfeldt, T., Koutsoupias, E. (eds.) ICALP 2014. LNCS, vol. 8573, pp. 74–85. Springer, Heidelberg (2014). https://doi.org/10.1007/978-3-662-43951-7_7
3. Boyer, L., Delacourt, M., Poupet, V., Sablik, M., Theyssier, G.: μ-limit sets of cellular automata from a computational complexity perspective. J. Comput. Syst. Sci. **81**(8), 1623–1647 (2015). https://doi.org/10.1016/j.jcss.2015.05.004
4. Culik II, K., Pachl, J., Yu, S.: On the limit sets of cellular automata. SIAM J. Comput. **18**(4), 831–842 (1989). https://doi.org/10.1137/0218057
5. Djenaoui, S., Guillon, P.: The generic limit set of cellular automata. J. Cellular Automata **14**(5–6), 435–477 (2019). https://www.oldcitypublishing.com/journals/jca-home/jca-issue-contents/jca-volume-14-number-5-6-2019/jca-14-5-6-p-435-477/

6. Kari, J.: The nilpotency problem of one-dimensional cellular automata. SIAM J. Comput. **21**(3), 571–586 (1992). https://doi.org/10.1137/0221036
7. Kůrka, P.: Languages, equicontinuity and attractors in cellular automata. Ergodic Theory Dynam. Syst. **17**(2), 417–433 (1997). https://doi.org/10.1017/S014338579706985X
8. Maass, A.: On the sofic limit sets of cellular automata. Ergodic Theory Dynam. Syst. **15**(4), 663–684 (1995). https://doi.org/10.1017/S0143385700008609
9. Milnor, J.: On the concept of attractor. Commun. Math. Phys. **99**(2), 177–195 (1985). http://projecteuclid.org/euclid.cmp/1103942677
10. Olli, J.: Endomorphisms of Sturmian systems and the discrete chair substitution tiling system. Discrete Contin. Dyn. Syst. **33**(9), 4173–4186 (2013). https://doi.org/10.3934/dcds.2013.33.4173

Latin Hypercubes and Cellular Automata

Maximilien Gadouleau[1] and Luca Mariot[2($\boxtimes$)]

[1] Department of Computer Science, Durham University,
South Road, Durham DH1 3LE, UK
m.r.gadouleau@durham.ac.uk
[2] Cyber Security Research Group, Delft University of Technology, Mekelweg 2,
Delft, The Netherlands
l.mariot@tudelft.nl

Abstract. Latin squares and hypercubes are combinatorial designs with several applications in statistics, cryptography and coding theory. In this paper, we generalize a construction of Latin squares based on bipermutive cellular automata (CA) to the case of Latin hypercubes of dimension $k > 2$. In particular, we prove that linear bipermutive CA (LBCA) yielding Latin hypercubes of dimension $k > 2$ are defined by sequences of invertible Toeplitz matrices with partially overlapping coefficients, which can be described by a specific kind of regular de Bruijn graph induced by the support of the determinant function. Further, we derive the number of k-dimensional Latin hypercubes generated by LBCA by counting the number of paths of length $k - 3$ on this de Bruijn graph.

Keywords: Latin squares · Latin hypercubes · Cellular automata · Bipermutivity · Toeplitz matrices · De bruijn graphs

1 Introduction

Several cryptographic protocols with information-theoretic security guarantees can be defined in terms of *Combinatorial Designs*. One such example are (k, n) threshold *Secret Sharing Schemes* (SSS), where a *dealer* wants to share a secret information S among a set of n *players* by giving to each of them a *share* B, so that at least k players are required to recover S by combining their shares. On the other hand, any subset of $k - 1$ or less players do not gain any information on the secret by pooling the respective shares. Such a protocol corresponds to a set of n *Mutually Orthogonal Latin Squares* (MOLS) when $k = 2$ players are required to reconstruct the secret, while it is equivalent to a set of n *Mutually Orthogonal Latin Hypercubes* of dimension k (MOLH) when $k > 2$ [10]. Indeed, the schemes proposed by Shamir [9] and Blakley's [1] can be thought as particular instances of (k, n) threshold SSS, where polynomials and hyperplanes over finite fields are respectively used to represent an underlying set of MOLH in a compact way.

A recent research thread considers the design of secret sharing schemes by means of *Cellular Automata* (CA) [6], the goal being twofold. First, a CA-based

© IFIP International Federation for Information Processing 2020
Published by Springer Nature Switzerland AG 2020. All Rights Reserved
H. Zenil (Ed.): AUTOMATA 2020, LNCS 12286, pp. 139–151, 2020.
https://doi.org/10.1007/978-3-030-61588-8_11

architecture could be useful for efficient hardware-oriented implementations of threshold SSS, by leveraging the massive parallelism of the CA models. This approach already turned out to be interesting in another cryptographic application, namely the design of *S-boxes* based on CA [8]. Second, the locality of the CA model can be used to define access structures that are more constrained than the classic (k, n) threshold, such as the *consecutive access structure* of the CA-based scheme proposed in [6], which finds application in certain distributed cryptographic protocols, as discussed by the authors of [4]. These access structures eventually become *cyclic*, and the maximum number of players allowed is related to the period of spatially periodic preimages in surjective CA [7].

Given the equivalence between (k, n) threshold SSS and families of MOLH, a possible way to tackle these goals is to study how to construct the latter using cellular automata. Recently, the authors of [5] showed a construction of MOLS based on *linear bipermutive* CA (LBCA), thereby addressing the case of $(2, n)$ threshold SSS based on CA. Generalizing this construction to a higher threshold k entails two steps: first, one needs to characterize which CA generate Latin hypercubes, since contrarily to the Latin squares case not all LBCA define Latin hypercubes of dimension $k > 2$. The next step is to define subsets of such CA whose Latin hypercubes are k-wise orthogonal, thus obtaining sets of $MOLH$.

The aim of this paper is to address the first step of this generalization, namely the characterization and enumeration of Latin hypercubes based on LBCA. In particular, we first prove that LBCA which generate *Latin cubes* are defined by local rules whose central coefficients compose the border of an invertible *Toeplitz matrix*. This allows us to determine the number of Latin cubes generated by LBCA by counting the number of invertible Toeplitz matrices. Next, we generalize this result to dimension $k > 3$, remarking that in this case the local rule of an LBCA can be defined by a *sequence* of $k-2$ invertible Toeplitz matrices, where adjacent matrices share the coefficients respectively of the upper and lower triangulars. We finally show that this overlapping relation can be described by a regular de Bruijn graph, and that paths of length $k-2$ on this graph corresponds to LBCA generating k-dimensional Latin hypercubes.

The rest of this paper is organized as follows. Section 2 covers the necessary background on Latin hypercubes and cellular automata used in the paper, and recalls the basic results about Latin squares generated by CA. Section 3 presents the characterization of Latin cubes and hypercubes generated by LBCA defined by invertible Toeplitz matrices. Section 4 proves the regularity of the de Bruijn graph associated to invertible Toeplitz matrices and derives the number of k-dimensional Latin hypercubes generated by LBCA. Section 5 recaps the main contributions of the paper and discusses some directions for future research.

2   Preliminary Definitions and Results

The main combinatorial objects of interest of this paper are *Latin hypercubes*, which we define as follows:

Definition 1. *Let X be a finite set of $N \in \mathbb{N}$ elements. A* Latin hypercube *of dimension $k \in \mathbb{N}$ and order N over X is a k-dimensional array with entries from X such that, by fixing any subset $i_1, \cdots, i_{k-1}$ of $k-1$ coordinates, the remaining coordinate i_k yields a permutation over X, that is, each element in X appears exactly once on the i_k coordinate.*

Remark that when $k = 2$ one obtains the definition of *Latin square* of order N, i.e. a square matrix where each row and each column is a permutation of X. Usually, Latin squares and hypercubes are defined over the set $X = [N] = \{1, \cdots, N\}$ of the first N positive integers. In this work, we consider the case where X is the vector space $\mathbb{F}_q^b$, with $\mathbb{F}_q$ being the finite field of q elements. Hence, the order N of the hypercube will be q^b, i.e. the number of all q-ary vectors of length b.

Next, we define the model of *cellular automaton* used in the rest of this paper:

Definition 2. *Let $d, n \in \mathbb{N}$, with $d \leq n$, and let $f : \mathbb{F}_q^d \to \mathbb{F}_q$ be a function of d variables over the finite field $\mathbb{F}_q$, with q being a power of a prime. The* Cellular Automaton *(CA in the following) of length n and local rule f over the alphabet $\mathbb{F}_q$ is the vectorial function $F : \mathbb{F}_q^n \to \mathbb{F}_q^{n-d+1}$ defined for all vectors $x = (x_1, \cdots, x_n) \in \mathbb{F}_q^n$ as:*

$$F(x_1, \cdots, x_n) = (f(x_1, \cdots, x_d), \cdots, f(x_{n-d+1}, \cdots, x_n)) \ . \tag{1}$$

In other words, each coordinate function $f_i : \mathbb{F}_q^n \to \mathbb{F}_q$ for $i \in [n-d+1]$ of a CA F corresponds to its local rule f applied to the neighborhood $\{x_i, \cdots, x_{i+d-1}\}$. For our examples, in the following we will mainly consider the case $q = 2$, where a CA boils down to a particular type of *vectorial Boolean function* $F : \mathbb{F}_2^n \to \mathbb{F}_2^{n-d+1}$. This corresponds to the definition of *no-boundary cellular automaton* (NBCA) studied in [8] as a model for cryptographic S-boxes.

The last preliminary definition we need is that of hypercube associated to a CA. In what follows, we assume that the vectors in $\mathbb{F}_q^b$ are totally ordered, and that there is a monotone and one-to-one mapping $\Psi : [N] \to \mathbb{F}_q^b$, in order to associate sets of integer coordinates to sets of q-ary vectors.

Definition 3. *Let $b, k \in \mathbb{N}$, with $d = b(k-1) + 1$. Moreover, let $F : \mathbb{F}_q^{bk} \to \mathbb{F}_q^b$ be the CA of length bk defined by a local rule $f : \mathbb{F}_q^d \to \mathbb{F}_q$. Then, the hypercube associated to F of order $N = q^b$ is the k-dimensional array $\mathcal{H}_F$ where for all vectors of coordinates $(i_1, \cdots, i_k) \in [N]^k$ the corresponding entry is defined as:*

$$\mathcal{H}_F(i_1, \cdots, i_k) = \Psi^{-1}(F(\Psi(i_1)||\Psi(i_2)|| \cdots ||\Psi(i_k)) \ , \tag{2}$$

where the input $\Psi(i_1)||\Psi(i_2)|| \cdots ||\Psi(i_k)$ denotes the concatenation *of the binary vectors $\Psi(i_1), \cdots, \Psi(i_k) \in \mathbb{F}_q^b$.*

Thus, by Definition 3 the hypercube associated to a CA F of length bk and local rule f of $b(k-1) + 1$ is constructed by splitting the input vector of F in k blocks of size b, which are used to index the coordinates of the hypercube, while the output vector represents the entry to be put at those coordinates. Figure 1 depicts an example of 3-dimensional hypercube $\mathcal{H}_F$ of block size $b = 2$ over $\mathbb{F}_2$ (thus, of order $2^2 = 4$) associated to the CA $F : \mathbb{F}_2^6 \to \mathbb{F}_2^2$ which is defined by the local rule $f(x_1, \cdots, x_5) = x_1 \oplus x_3 \oplus x_5$. In this case one can see that $\mathcal{H}_F$ is indeed a Latin *cube*, i.e. a Latin hypercube of dimension 3.

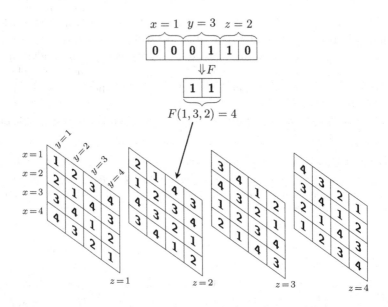

Fig. 1. Latin cube of order 4 generated by a CA $F : \mathbb{F}_2^6 \to \mathbb{F}_2^2$ defined by local rule $f(x_1, \cdots, x_5) = x_1 \oplus x_3 \oplus x_5$. The encoding used is $00 \mapsto 1$, $10 \mapsto 2$, $01 \mapsto 3$, $11 \mapsto 4$.

We now give the formal statement of the problem investigated in this paper, namely the construction and enumeration of Latin hypercubes with CA:

Problem 1. Let $F : \mathbb{F}_q^{bk} \to \mathbb{F}_q^b$ be a CA equipped with a local rule $f : \mathbb{F}_2^d \to \mathbb{F}_2$ where $d = b(k-1) + 1$. When is the hypercube $\mathcal{H}_F$ associated to F a Latin hypercube? How many local rules $f : \mathbb{F}_q^{b(k-1)+1} \to \mathbb{F}_q$ induce a CA such that the resulting $\mathcal{H}_F$ is a Latin hypercube?

Problem 1 requires studying under which conditions the local rule f induces a permutation between any of the k blocks of b consecutive cells used to index the coordinates of $\mathcal{H}_F$ and the output CA configuration, when all remaining blocks are fixed. We first start by addressing the extremal cases of the leftmost and rightmost blocks in CA defined by *bipermutive* local rules.

A function $f : \mathbb{F}_q^n \to \mathbb{F}_q$ of $n \geq 2$ variables is *bipermutive* if there exists a function $g : \mathbb{F}_q^{n-2} \to \mathbb{F}_q$ such that

$$f(x_1, \cdots, x_n) = x_1 \oplus g(x_2, \cdots, x_{n-1}) \oplus x_n \tag{3}$$

for all $x = (x_1, \cdots, x_n) \in \mathbb{F}_q^n$, where $\oplus$ corresponds to the sum operation over $\mathbb{F}_q$. When $q = 2$, Eq. (3) basically amounts to the XOR of the leftmost and rightmost input variables with the result of function g computed on the central $n - 2$ variables. A proof of the following result can be found in [5]:

Lemma 1. *Let $F : \mathbb{F}_q^{bk} \to \mathbb{F}_q^b$ be a CA with bipermutive rule $f : \mathbb{F}_q^d \to \mathbb{F}_q$, where $d = b(k - 1) + 1$. Then, the restriction $F|_{\tilde{x}} : \mathbb{F}_q^b \to \mathbb{F}_q^b$ obtained by fixing either the rightmost or leftmost $b(k - 1)$ variables in the CA input to $\tilde{x} \in \mathbb{F}_q^{b(k-1)}$ is a permutation over $\mathbb{F}_q^b$ for all $\tilde{x} \in \mathbb{F}_q^{b(k-1)}$.*

Thus, by Lemma 1 bipermutivity of the local rule f is a sufficient condition for verifying the Latin hypercube property on the leftmost and rightmost coordinate of the hypercube $\mathcal{H}_F$. This also means, in turn, that for dimension $k = 2$ (that is, when there are no blocks in the middle between the leftmost and the rightmost one) bipermutivity is a sufficient condition to ensure that $\mathcal{H}_F$ is a Latin square:

Corollary 1. *Let $F : \mathbb{F}_q^{2b} \to \mathbb{F}_q^b$ be a CA with bipermutive rule $f : \mathbb{F}_q^d \to \mathbb{F}_q$ of diameter $d = b + 1$. Then, the hypercube $\mathcal{H}_F$ associated to F is a Latin square of order q^b.*

From Corollary 1, one also gets the following straightforward counting result:

Corollary 2. *Let $b \in \mathbb{N}$. Then, the number of Latin squares of order q^b generated by bipermutive CA corresponds to the number of bipermutive local rules of $b + 1$ variables over $\mathbb{F}_q$, which is $q^{q^{b-1}}$.*

Hence, Corollaries 1 and 2 solve Problem 1 for dimension $k = 2$, in the particular case of bipermutive CA. In what follows, we shall solve Problem 1 in Theorems 2 and 5 for any dimension $k > 2$.

3   CA-Based Latin Hypercubes from Toeplitz Matrices

3.1   Latin Cubes

Remark that for dimension $k > 2$ bipermutivity is not enough. As a matter of fact, Lemma 1 requires the $b(k - 1)$ variables to be adjacent. To verify the Latin hypercube property for a middle coordinate $1 < i < k$ one needs to fix all variables on the left and on the right except for the "hole" represented by the block of b bits associated to coordinate i. As a consequence, it is necessary to characterize a proper subset of bipermutive local rules that generate Latin hypercubes when used as local rules of CA.

We begin by addressing the case of *Latin cubes*, that is with dimension $k = 3$. Referring to Problem 1, we have a CA $F : \mathbb{F}_q^{3b} \to \mathbb{F}_q^b$ that maps configurations of $3b$ cells in vectors of b cells, defined by a bipermutive local rule $f : \mathbb{F}_q^d \to \mathbb{F}_q$ of diameter $d = 2b+1$. Since the permutation between the output CA configuration and the blocks $x_{[1,b]}$ and $x_{[2b+1,3b]}$ is already granted by Lemma 1, we only need to consider the middle block $x_{[b+1,2b]}$.

In what follows, we will also make the additional assumption that, beside being bipermutive, the local rule is *linear*: In other words, there exist a binary vector $a = (a_1, a_2, \cdots, a_{d-1}, a_d) \in \mathbb{F}_q^d$ such that

$$f(x_1, x_2, \cdots, x_{d-1}, x_d) = a_1 x_1 \oplus a_2 x_2 \oplus \cdots \oplus a_{d-1} x_{d-1} \oplus a_d x_d \ , \qquad (4)$$

where sum and product are considered over $\mathbb{F}_q$. Notice that a linear rule defined as in (4) is bipermutive if and only if both a_1 and a_d are not null. In particular, from now on we will assume that $a_1 = a_d = 1$, and we will define a linear bipermutive rule by means of the vector $(a_2, \cdots, a_{d-1}) \in \mathbb{F}_q^{d-2}$ defining the $d-2$ central coefficients. Additionally, we will refer to a CA defined by such a rule as a LBCA (Linear Bipermutive CA).

For all $x \in \mathbb{F}_q^{3b}$, let $y = F(x) \in \mathbb{F}_q^b$ be the result of the CA applied to vector x. Since the local rule f is linear, one can express y as a system of b linear equations and $3b$ variables:

$$\begin{cases} y_1 &= x_1 \oplus a_2 x_2 \oplus \cdots \oplus a_{2b} x_{2b} \oplus x_{2b+1} \\ y_2 &= x_2 \oplus a_2 x_3 \oplus \cdots \oplus a_{2b} x_{2b+1} \oplus x_{2b+2} \\ &\vdots \\ y_b &= x_b \oplus a_2 x_{b+1} \oplus \cdots \oplus a_{2b} x_{3b-1} \oplus x_{3b} \end{cases} \qquad (5)$$

Suppose now that we fix the $2b$ variables $x_1, \cdots, x_b$ and $x_{2b+1}, \cdots, x_{3b}$ respectively to the values $\tilde{x}_1, \cdots, \tilde{x}_b$ and $\tilde{x}_{2b+1}, \cdots, \tilde{x}_{3b}$. This actually amounts to fixing the leftmost and the rightmost coordinates in the cube $\mathcal{H}_F$ associated to F. Moreover, the system (5) becomes a system of b linear equations and b variables corresponding to the block $x_{[b+1,2b]}$, since the remaining $2b$ variables have been set to constant values. In order to ensure that there is a permutation between $x_{[b+1,2b]}$ and y, it means that the matrix of coefficients a_i multiplying the vector $x_{[b+1,2b]}$ in (5) must be invertible:

$$M_F = \begin{pmatrix} a_{b+1} & a_{b+2} & \cdots & a_{2b} \\ a_b & a_{b+1} & \cdots & a_{2b-1} \\ \vdots & \vdots & \ddots & \vdots \\ a_2 & a_3 & \cdots & a_{b+1} \end{pmatrix} \qquad (6)$$

Remark that the matrix in Eq. (6) is a *Toeplitz matrix*, where the first row of coefficients $a_{b+1}, \cdots, a_{2b}$ is shifted to the right while the coefficients $a_b, \cdots, a_2$ progressively enter from the left. In particular, the matrix is completely characterized by the shifts of the central coefficients $a_2, \cdots, a_b, \cdots, a_{2b}$ of the CA local rule f. To summarize, we obtained the following result:

Lemma 2. *Let $F : \mathbb{F}_q^{3b} \to \mathbb{F}_q^b$ be a LBCA with rule $f : \mathbb{F}_q^{2b+1} \to \mathbb{F}_q$ defined for all $x \in \mathbb{F}_q^{2b+1}$ as*

$$f(x_1, \cdots, x_{2b+1}) = x_1 \oplus a_2 x_2 \oplus \cdots \oplus a_{2b} x_{2b} \oplus x_{2b+1} \ .$$

Then, the hypercube $\mathcal{H}_F$ associated to F is a Latin cube of order q^b if and only if the Toeplitz matrix M_F defined by the coefficients $a_2, \cdots, a_{2b} \in \mathbb{F}_q$ is invertible.

The authors of [3] showed that the number of nonsingular $n \times n$ Toeplitz matrices is $q^{2(n-1)}(q-1)$. Hence, we have the following counting result for Latin cubes:

Theorem 1. *Let $b \in \mathbb{N}$. Then, the number of LBCA $F : \mathbb{F}_q^{3b} \to \mathbb{F}_q^b$ whose associated hypercube $\mathcal{H}_F$ is a Latin cube is $q^{2(b-1)}(q-1)$.*

3.2   Latin Hypercubes of Dimension $k > 3$

We now generalize the investigation to Latin hypercubes of any dimension $k > 3$. In this case, the LBCA $F : \mathbb{F}_q^{bk} \to \mathbb{F}_q^b$ is defined by a rule $f : \mathbb{F}_q^{b(k-1)+1} \to \mathbb{F}_q$ of the form:

$$f(x_1, \cdots, x_{b(k-1)+1}) = x_1 \oplus a_2 x_2 \oplus \cdots \oplus a_{b(k-1)} x_{b(k-1)} \oplus x_{b(k-1)+1} . \qquad (7)$$

Hence, the values of the output vector $y = F(x) \in \mathbb{F}_q^b$ will be determined by a system analogous to (5):

$$
\begin{cases}
y_1 &= x_1 \oplus a_2 x_2 \oplus \cdots \oplus a_{b(k-1)} x_{b(k-1)} \oplus x_{b(k-1)+1} \\
y_2 &= x_2 \oplus a_2 x_3 \oplus \cdots \oplus a_{b(k-1)} x_{b(k-1)+1} \oplus x_{b(k-1)+2} \\
&\vdots \\
y_b &= x_b \oplus a_2 x_{b+1} \oplus \cdots \oplus a_{b(k-1)} x_{bk-1} \oplus x_{bk}
\end{cases}
\qquad (8)
$$

The k-dimensional hypercube $\mathcal{H}_F$ associated to F will be a Latin hypercube only if there is a permutation between any of the central $k-2$ blocks of b cells when all the others are fixed to a constant value and y (the leftmost and rightmost cases already being granted by bipermutivity). Similarly to the three-dimensional case where we had only one central block, this means that all of the following Toeplitz matrices must be invertible for all $i \in [k-2] = \{1, \cdots, k-2\}$:

$$
M_{F,i} = \begin{pmatrix}
a_{bi+1} & a_{bi+2} & \cdots & a_{b(i+1)-1} \\
a_{bi} & a_{bi+1} & \cdots & a_{b(i+1)-2} \\
\vdots & \vdots & \ddots & \vdots \\
a_{b(i-1)+2} & a_{b(i-1)+3} & \cdots & a_{bi+1}
\end{pmatrix}
\qquad (9)
$$

where $M_{F,1}$ is associated to the permutation on the second block, $M_{F,2}$ to the permutation on the third, and so on until $M_{F,k-2}$, which is associated to the permutation on the $(k-1)$-th block. We thus get the following characterization of LBCA that generate k-dimensional Latin hypercubes:

Theorem 2. *Let $F : \mathbb{F}_2^{bk} \to \mathbb{F}_2^b$ be a CA with local rule $f : \mathbb{F}_2^{b(k-1)+1} \to \mathbb{F}_2$ defined as in Eq. (7). Then, the k-dimensional hypercube $\mathcal{H}_F$ of order q^b associated to F is a Latin hypercube if and only if the Toeplitz matrix $M_{F,i}$ in (9) is invertible for all $i \in [k-2]$.*

Since we settled the first part of Problem 1 in the context of LBCA, we now focus on the counting question, i.e. what is the number $L_{b,k}$ of LBCA

$F : \mathbb{F}_q^{bk} \to \mathbb{F}_q^b$ that generate k-dimensional Latin hypercubes of order q^b. In other words, we want to count in how many ways the coefficients $a_2, \cdots, a_{b(k-1)} \in \mathbb{F}_2$ of the local rule f in (7) can be chosen so that the resulting hypercube $\mathcal{H}_F$ is a Latin hypercube.

Remark 1. For dimensions $k = 2$ and $k = 3$, we settled the counting question of Problem 1 respectively in Corollaries 2 and 1. For dimension $k > 3$, remark that one cannot choose independently the coefficients defining the $k - 2$ invertible Toeplitz matrices. Indeed, consider the two adjacent matrices $M_{F,i}$ and $M_{F,i+1}$:

$$\begin{pmatrix} a_{bi+1} & a_{bi+2} & \cdots & a_{b(i+1)} \\ a_{bi} & a_{bi+1} & \cdots & a_{b(i+1)-1} \\ \vdots & \vdots & \ddots & \vdots \\ a_{b(i-1)+2} & a_{b(i-1)+3} & \cdots & a_{bi+1} \end{pmatrix} \begin{pmatrix} a_{b(i+1)+1} & a_{b(i+1)+2} & \cdots & a_{b(i+2)} \\ a_{b(i+1)} & a_{b(i+1)+1} & \cdots & a_{b(i+2)-1} \\ \vdots & \vdots & \ddots & \vdots \\ a_{bi+2} & a_{bi+3} & \cdots & a_{b(i+1)+1} \end{pmatrix}$$

One can notice that the coefficients $a_{bi+2}, \cdots, a_{b(i+1)}$ *overlap* between the two matrices: in particular, they occur respectively *above* the main diagonal of $M_{F,i}$ and *below* the main diagonal of $M_{F,i+1}$. As a consequence $L_{b,k,q}$ for $k > 3$ is lower than $\left[(q-1)q^{2(b-1)}\right]^{k-2}$, which is the number of ways one can choose a set of $k - 2$ invertible Toeplitz matrices of size $b \times b$ over $\mathbb{F}_q$ with repetitions.

We now model the problem of determining $L_{b,k,q}$ in terms of *determinant* functions. Let M_a be the Toeplitz matrix defined by the vector of $2b - 1$ binary coefficients $a = (a_2, \cdots, a_{2b}) \in \mathbb{F}_q^{2b-1}$, and let us define $det : \mathbb{F}_q^{2b-1} \to \mathbb{F}_q$ as the function of $2b - 1$ variables that associates to each vector $a \in \mathbb{F}_q^{2b-1}$ the determinant of the matrix M_a. Thus, we have that the support set $supp(det) = \{a \in \mathbb{F}_q^{2b-1} : det(a) \neq 0\}$ contains the vectors a that define all $b \times b$ non-singular Toeplitz matrices. By Theorem 1 it follows that the cardinality of the support is $|supp(det)| = q^{2(b-1)}(q - 1)$.

Recall that by Remark 1 the elements of two adjacent invertible Toeplitz matrices overlap respectively on the upper and lower triangular parts. Hence, in order to construct a Latin hypercube of dimension k, one can choose from the support of the determinant function det a *sequence* of $k - 2$ vectors so that each each pair of adjacent vectors overlap respectively on the last and the first $b - 1$ coordinates. We now formalize this reasoning in terms of *de Bruijn graphs*. Let $s \in \mathbb{N}$ and A be a finite alphabet, with A^* denoting the free monoid of words over A. Given $u, v \in A^*$ such that $|u| \geq s$ and $|v| \geq s$, we define the s-*fusion operator* $\odot$ as in [11], that is $u \odot v = z$ if and only if there exists $x \in A^s$ and $u_0, v_0 \in A^*$ such that $u = u_0 x$, $v = x v_0$, and $z = u_0 x v_0$. In other words z is obtained by *overlapping* the right part of u and the left part of v of length s. Setting $A = \mathbb{F}_q$ and $s = b - 1$, we obtain the s-fusion operator for our case of overlapping vectors $u, v \in supp(det)$ of length $2b - 1$. The set of overlapping relations can be conveniently described using the de Bruijn graph associated to the determinant function, which we formally define below:

Definition 4. *Let* $det : \mathbb{F}_q^{2b-1} \to \mathbb{F}_q$ *be the determinant function for $b \times b$ Toeplitz matrices over* $\mathbb{F}_q$*. The* de Bruijn graph *associated to* det *is the directed graph*

$G_{det} = (V, E)$ *where the set of vertices is* $V = supp(det)$, *while an ordered pair of vertices* (v_1, v_2) *belongs to the set of edges* E *if and only if there exists* $z \in \mathbb{F}_2^{3b-1}$ *such that* $z = v_1 \odot v_2$, *where* $\odot$ *denotes the s-fusion operator with* $s = b - 1$.

Example 1. Let $b = 2$, $k = 5$ and $q = 2$. In this case, the local rule $f : \mathbb{F}_2^9 \to \mathbb{F}_2$ has coefficients a_1 and a_9 set to 1, while the central coefficients $(a_{2i}, a_{2i+1}, a_{2i+2})$ define the following Toeplitz matrix for $i \in \{1, 2, 3\}$:

$$M_F, i = \begin{pmatrix} a_{2i+1} & a_{2i+2} \\ a_{2i} & a_{2i+1} \end{pmatrix} \tag{10}$$

In particular $M_{F,1}$, $M_{F,2}$ and $M_{F,3}$ will be the matrices respectively associated to the second, third and fourth block. It is easily seen that the determinant of $M_{F,i}$ is $a_{2i+1} \oplus a_{2i} a_{2i+2}$. Figure 2 reports the truth table and the de Bruijn graph of the determinant function $det : \mathbb{F}_2^3 \to \mathbb{F}_2$. Rows in bold in the table correspond to the vectors of the support of det, which in turn are the vertices of the de Bruijn graph. Following Fig. 2, one can construct the local rule f by choosing a

a_{2i}	a_{2i+1}	a_{2i+2}	$a_{2i+1} \oplus a_{2i} a_{2i+2}$
0	0	0	0
1	0	0	0
0	**1**	**0**	**1**
1	**1**	**0**	**1**
0	0	1	0
1	**0**	**1**	**1**
0	**1**	**1**	**1**
1	1	1	0

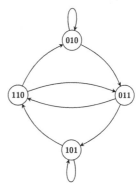

Fig. 2. Truth table (left) and de Bruijn graph (right) of $a_{2i+1} \oplus a_{2i} a_{2i+2}$.

sequence of $k - 2 = 3$ vectors from the support of $det(a_2, a_3, a_4)$ such that both the first and the second and the second and the third overlap respectively on the last and the first bit. This actually amounts to finding a path of length 2 on the de Bruijn graph. An example could be the sequence $(0, 1, 0) - (0, 1, 1) - (1, 0, 1)$. In particular, $(0, 1, 0) = (a_2, a_3, a_4)$ is the vector defining the Toeplitz matrix of the second block. Similarly, the vector $(0, 1, 1) = (a_4, a_5, a_6)$ defines the Toeplitz matrix of the third block while $(1, 0, 1) = (a_6, a_7, a_8)$ defines the Toeplitz matrix of the fourth block. Consequently, the local rule $f : \mathbb{F}_2^9 \to \mathbb{F}_2$ is defined as $f(x_1, \cdots, x_9) = x_1 \oplus x_3 \oplus x_5 \oplus x_6 \oplus x_8 \oplus x_9$, and by Theorem 2 the corresponding LBCA $F : \mathbb{F}_2^{10} \to \mathbb{F}_2^2$ generates a 5-dimensional Latin hypercube of order 4.

4   Counting Sequences of Invertible Matrices

As we said above, the de Bruijn graph of the determinant function summarizes all the overlap relations between vectors of its support, which represent invertible Toeplitz matrices. Thus, we derived that Latin hypercubes of dimension k generated by LBCA correspond to *paths of length $k - 3$* over this graph:

Theorem 3. *Let $b, k \in \mathbb{N}$. Then, $L_{b,k}$ equals the number of paths of length $k - 3$ over the de Bruijn graph G_{det} of the determinant function $det : \mathbb{F}_q^{2b-1} \to \mathbb{F}_q$.*

Hence, in order to count the number of k-dimensional Latin hypercubes generated by LBCA, we need to look more closely at the properties of the de Bruijn graph G_{det} associated to the determinant of Toeplitz matrices. In particular, counting the number of paths of length $k - 3$ over G_{det} requires characterizing the indegrees and outdegrees of its vertices. Looking at Fig. 2 one can see that each vertex has two ingoing and two outgoing edges, hence the resulting de Bruijn graph G_{det} for $b = 2$ and $q = 2$ is 2-*regular*. In the remainder of this section we will show that a regularity property holds in general for every $b \geq 2$ and q power of a prime. We first need the following result:

Theorem 4. *Denote by $T(n)$ the set of $n \times n$ Toeplitz matrices over $\mathbb{F}_q$. Let $A \in T(n)$ be strictly lower triangular, then there are exactly $(q - 1)q^{n-1}$ upper triangular matrices $B \in T(n)$ such that $A + B$ is nonsingular.*

Proof. *The result is clear if A is the all-zero matrix, therefore we assume henceforth that A is nonzero. We shall use the results by Daykin [2] on persymmetric (Hankel) matrices. Clearly, results on persymmetric matrices can be restated in terms of Toeplitz matrices, since the former are the transpose of the latter. Let $H(b)$ be the set of $n \times n$ persymmetric matrices. For any $A \in H(b)$ with $a_{i,j} = 0$ if $i + j \geq b + 1$, denote the number of matrices $B \in H(b)$ with $b_{i,j} = 0$ if $i + j \leq n$ such that $A + B$ is nonsingular as $N(A)$. We thus show that $N(A) = (q-1)q^{n-1}$.*

For any $M \in H(n)$ and any $m \leq n$, we denote the matrix in $H(m)$ consisting of the first m rows and m columns of M as $M[m]$. Let $P \in H(m)$ be a nonzero matrix. Let $R(P)$ be the number of nonsingular matrices $Q \in H(2m)$ such that $P = Q[m]$, and for all m and $i \leq m$, let $T(m : i) = (q-1)^2 q^{2m-i-2}$ if $i < m$ and $T(m : i) = (q-1)q^{m-1}$ if $i = m$. Theorem 3 in [2] gives the following formulas for $R(P)$ and $R'(P)$:

$$R(P) = \begin{cases} \frac{T(2m-v:m-v)}{(q-1)q^{m-v-1}} & \text{if } v < m \\ q \sum_{i=1}^m T(m : i) & \text{otherwise} \end{cases} \quad , \quad R'(P) = \begin{cases} \frac{T(2m-v:m-v)}{(q-1)q^{m-v-1}} & \text{if } v < m \\ q \sum_{i=1}^m T(m : i) & \text{otherwise} \end{cases}$$

We now show that for all nonzero $P \in H(m)$, $R(P) = (q - 1)q^{2m-1}$. We prove the claim for $R(P)$. If $v < m$, we have

$$R(P) = \frac{T(2m - v : m - v)}{(q - 1)q^{m-v-1}} = \frac{(q - 1)^2 q^{2(2m-v)-(m-v)-2}}{(q - 1)q^{m-v-1}} = (q - 1)q^{2m-1} \ .$$

If $v = m$ we have

$$R(P) = q \sum_{i=1}^{m} T(m:i) = q(q-1) \left\{ (q-1)q^{m-1} \sum_{i=1}^{m-1} q^{m-1-i} + q^{m-1} \right\}$$

$$= q^m(q-1)\{(q^{m-1}-1)+1\} = (q-1)q^{2m-1} \ .$$

With a similar argument, one can also show that $R'(P) = (q-1)q^{2m-1}$. Now, let $m = \lceil n/2 \rceil$ and $P = A[m]$. If $n = 2m$ is even, then $N(A) = R(P) = (q-1)q^{n-1}$. If $n = 2m - 1$ is odd then $P_{m,m} = 0$, thus consider the matrices P^a, obtained by setting the value $P^a_{m,m} = a$, for all $a \in \mathbb{F}_q$. Then $N(A) = \sum_{a \in \mathbb{F}_q} R(P^a) = (q-1)q^{n-1}$. □

Theorem 4 thus states that by fixing the leftmost $b - 1$ entries of the vector $(a_2, \cdots, a_{2b})$ that defines a Toeplitz matrix A, one can complete the remaining b ones in $(q-1)q^{b-1}$ different ways so that the resulting Toeplitz matrix is invertible. This brings us to the following corollary:

Corollary 3. *Let $det : \mathbb{F}_q^{2b-1} \to \mathbb{F}_q$ be the determinant function associated to the set $T(b)$. Then, for any vector $\tilde{a} \in \mathbb{F}_q^{b-1}$, the restriction $det|_{\tilde{a}} : \mathbb{F}_q^b \to \mathbb{F}_q$ obtained by fixing either the leftmost or the rightmost $b - 1$ coordinates to $\tilde{a}$ is balanced, that is $|supp(det|_{\tilde{a}})| = (q-1)q^{b-1}$.*

We now show that this corollary implies the regularity of G_{det}.

Lemma 3. *For any $b \geq 2$ the de Bruijn graph G_{det} of the determinant function det is $(q-1)q^{b-1}$-regular.*

Proof. As a preliminary remark, observe that by Theorem 1 the number of vertices in G_{det} is $|V| = (q-1)q^{2(b-1)}$. We prove only that the outdegree of each vertex is $(q-1)q^{b-1}$, the indegree case following from a symmetrical reasoning. Let us fix the first $b-1$ coordinates $a_2, \cdots, a_b$ of det to a vector $\tilde{a} \in \mathbb{F}_2^{b-1}$. Since the restriction $det|_{\tilde{a}}$ of b variables induced by $\tilde{a}$ is balanced, it means that there is a set $_{\tilde{a}}V = \{v \in V : (v_1, \cdots, v_{b-1}) = \tilde{a}\}$ of $(q-1)q^{b-1}$ vertices in G_{det} that begins by $\tilde{a}$. Each vertex in G_{det} that ends by $\tilde{a}$ has an outgoing degree of $q(q-1)^{b-1}$, since it overlaps with all vertices in $_{\tilde{a}}V$. Let $V_{\tilde{a}} = \{v \in V : (v_{b+1}, \cdots, v_{2b-1}) = \tilde{a}\}$ be the set of all such vertices. By Corollary 3 the restriction $det|_{\tilde{a}}$ obtained by fixing the last $b-1$ coordinates to $\tilde{a}$ is also balanced. Thus, the cardinality of $V_{\tilde{a}}$ is also $(q-1)q^{b-1}$, meaning that there are $(q-1)q^{b-1}$ vertices ending by $\tilde{a}$ that have outdegree $(q-1)q^{b-1}$. Since this property holds for any vector $\tilde{a} \in \mathbb{F}_q^{b-1}$, it follows that there are $q^{b-1} \cdot (q-1)q^{b-1} = (q-1)q^{2(b-1)} = |V|$ distinct vertices with outdegree $(q-1)q^{b-1}$. □

Using Lemma 3, we can now determine what is the number of k-dimensional Latin hypercubes of order q^b generated by LBCA:

Theorem 5. *Let $b, k \in \mathbb{N}$, with $k \geq 3$. Then, the number of k-dimensional Latin hypercubes of order q^b generated by LBCA $F : \mathbb{F}_q^{bk} \to \mathbb{F}_q^b$ with local rules $f : \mathbb{F}_q^{b(k-1)+1} \to \mathbb{F}_q$ is $L_{b,k,q} = (q-1)^{k-2}q^{(k-1)(b-1)}$.*

Proof. By *Theorem 3* $L_{b,k,q}$ *equals the number of paths of length* $k - 3$ *over the de Bruijn graph* G_{det}. *We shall prove the result by induction on* k.

For $k = 3$, the number of paths of length 0 over G_{det} obviously coincides with the number of vertices, which is $(q - 1)q^{2(b-1)}$ by *Corollary 1*.

Assume now that $k > 3$, and let us consider $L_{b,k+1,q}$. Clearly, the paths of length $k+1$ are constructed by adding a new edge to all paths of length k, which by induction hypothesis are $(q-1)^{k-2}q^{(k-1)(b-1)}$. Since G_{det} is $(q-1)q^{b-1}$-regular, we thus have

$$L_{b,k+1,q} = (q - 1)^{k-2}q^{(k-1)(b-1)} \cdot (q - 1)q^{(b-1)} = (q - 1)^{k-1}q^{k(b-1)} \ .$$

$\square$

5   Conclusions

In this paper, we addressed the construction of Latin hypercubes generated by LBCA over the finite field $\mathbb{F}_q$, thereby taking a first step towards the generalization of the results in [5] about CA-based mutually orthogonal Latin squares. More precisely, we generalized the block construction of [5] to dimension $k > 2$, showing that the permutation property between any of the central $k - 2$ blocks of the CA and the final configuration is related to the invertibility of the Toeplitz matrices defined by the central coefficients of the local rule. Moreover, we observed that the Toeplitz matrices associated to adjacent blocks share the coefficients respectively on the upper and lower triangulars, a property that can be described by the de Bruijn graph of the determinant function. We finally derived the number $L_{b,k,q}$ of LBCA generating k-dimensional Latin hypercubes of order q^b by counting the number of paths of length $k - 3$ over this de Bruijn graph, which we proved to be $(q - 1)q^{b-1}$-regular. The resulting formula shows that $L_{b,k,q}$ is exponential both in the dimension and the block size of the hypercube, indicating that the family of Latin hypercubes generated by LBCA is quite large. We plan to study this rich structure of Latin hypercubes in future research, in particular by characterizing its mutually orthogonal subsets. Also, another interesting direction for future investigation is to assess whether Latin hypercubes can be generated by other types of CA, besides the bipermutive ones considered here.

Acknowledgments. This work has been partially supported by COST Action IC1405, "Reversible Computation – Extending the Horizons of Computing".

References

1. Blakley, G.R.: Safeguarding cryptographic keys. In: Managing Requirements Knowledge, International Workshop on, pp. 313–317 (1979)
2. Daykin, D.: Distribution of bordered persymmetric matrices in a finite field. J. Reine Angew. Math. (Crelle's J.) **203**, 47–54 (1960)

3. García-Armas, M., Ghorpade, S.R., Ram, S.: Relatively prime polynomials and nonsingular Hankel matrices over finite fields. J. Comb. Theory Ser. A **118**(3), 819–828 (2011)
4. Herranz, J., Sáez, G.: Secret sharing schemes for (k, n)-consecutive access structures. In: Camenisch, J., Papadimitratos, P. (eds.) CANS 2018. LNCS, vol. 11124, pp. 463–480. Springer, Cham (2018). https://doi.org/10.1007/978-3-030-00434-7_23
5. Mariot, L., Gadouleau, M., Formenti, E., Leporati, A.: Mutually orthogonal Latin squares based on cellular automata. Des. Codes Cryptogr. **88**(2), 391–411 (2019). https://doi.org/10.1007/s10623-019-00689-8
6. Mariot, L., Leporati, A.: Sharing secrets by computing preimages of bipermutive cellular automata. In: Wąs, J., Sirakoulis, G.C., Bandini, S. (eds.) ACRI 2014. LNCS, vol. 8751, pp. 417–426. Springer, Cham (2014). https://doi.org/10.1007/978-3-319-11520-7_43
7. Mariot, L., Leporati, A., Dennunzio, A., Formenti, E.: Computing the periods of preimages in surjective cellular automata. Nat. Comput. **16**(3), 367–381 (2016). https://doi.org/10.1007/s11047-016-9586-x
8. Mariot, L., Picek, S., Leporati, A., Jakobovic, D.: Cellular automata based s-boxes. Cryptogr. Commun. **11**(1), 41–62 (2019)
9. Shamir, A.: How to share a secret. Commun. ACM **22**(11), 612–613 (1979)
10. Stinson, D.R.: Combinatorial Designs - Constructions and Analysis. Springer, New York (2004). https://doi.org/10.1007/b97564
11. Sutner, K.: De Bruijn graphs and linear cellular automata. Complex Syst. **5**(1), 19–30 (1991)

Correction to: A Characterization of Amenable Groups by Besicovitch Pseudodistances

Silvio Capobianco and Pierre Guillon

Correction to:
Chapter "A Characterization of Amenable Groups
by Besicovitch Pseudodistances" in: H. Zenil (Ed.): *Cellular*
Automata and Discrete Complex Systems, **LNCS 12286,**
https://doi.org/10.1007/978-3-030-61588-8_8

The authors have made a correction to the authorship of this conference paper [1]. The third author listed as Camille Noûs is fictitious (http://www.cogitamus.fr/camilleen. html) and as such does not fulfill Springer Nature's requirements for authorship. The correct authorship list is: Silvio Capobianco and Pierre Guillon.

[1] Capobianco, S., Guillon, P.: A Characterization of Amenable Groups by Besicovitch Pseudodistances. In: Zenil, H. (ed.) AUTOMATA 2020. LNCS, vol. 12286, pp. 99-110. Springer, Cham (2020). doi: https://doi.org/10.1007/978-3-030-61588-8_8

The updated version of this chapter can be found at
https://doi.org/10.1007/978-3-030-61588-8_8

© IFIP International Federation for Information Processing 2021
Published by Springer Nature Switzerland AG 2021. All Rights Reserved
H. Zenil (Ed.): AUTOMATA 2020, LNCS 12286, p. C1, 2021.
https://doi.org/10.1007/978-3-030-61588-8_12

Author Index

Printed in the United States
By Bookmasters